THE AUTHOR

David Downes was educated at Oxford
and gained his Ph.D. (Criminology) at
the London School of Economics. He is
now Lecturer in Social Administration
at the London School of Economics.

THE DELINQUENT SOLUTION

INTERNATIONAL LIBRARY OF SOCIOLOGY
AND SOCIAL RECONSTRUCTION

Founded by Karl Mannheim

Editor: W. J. H. Sprott

A catalogue of the books available in the INTERNATIONAL LIBRARY OF SOCIOLOGY AND SOCIAL RECONSTRUCTION, and new books in preparation for the Library, will be found at the end of this volume.

THE DELINQUENT SOLUTION

A Study in Subcultural Theory

by
DAVID M. DOWNES

LONDON
ROUTLEDGE & KEGAN PAUL

First published 1966
by Routledge & Kegan Paul Ltd
Broadway House, 68-74 Carter Lane
London, E.C.4
Second impression 1969
Printed in Great Britain
by Eyre and Spottiswoode Ltd
at Grosvenor Press Portsmouth
© *David M. Downes 1966*
No part of this book may be reproduced
in any form without permission from
the publisher, except for the quotation
of brief passages in criticism
SBN 7100 3459 8

for Lester

CONTENTS

Contents

TABLES

Tables

PREFACE

Delinquency is a field in which the scenery changes too rapidly for any writer to be 'up to date'. Both events and other publications crowd in too quickly for any claims to be made to all-inclusiveness. One set of events in particular intervened between the main bulk of the writing, and eventually going to press: the 'Mods and Rockers' cult and the seaside 'riots' of this year and last. No mention is made of these occurrences in what follows, largely because—in the absence of evidence to the contrary—I take them to corroborate, rather than negate, the main sociological argument of the book.

In the field of publications, one important work came too late to be incorporated into discussion of 'subcultural' theorisation: David Matza's *'Delinquency and Drift'* (John Wiley and Sons, Inc., New York, 1964). All that can be said here is that Matza, in his attack on the notion of 'oppositional' values in delinquent subcultures, and in his re-definition of a 'subculture of delinquency', states one of the main themes of this book more forcibly and concisely than I could manage. His book contains a wealth of original and critical theorisation as to how and why boys *'drift'* into delinquency.

Finally, one technical omission must be pointed out in advance. In Chapters 3 and 4, where authors are referred to parenthetically and without footnotes, in practically all cases their work is referred to in full by the main authors under discussion.

D. M. D.

September, 1965

ACKNOWLEDGEMENTS

However belatedly, I would like to thank the following people for help and advice given at various stages of the research on which this book is based. Alex Jacobs, Ralph Samuel and Edith Ramsey each contributed their own view on the nature of the problems of the East End. In New Scotland Yard, Mr. Ronald Orr-Ewing, formerly of S2 Dept., gave very valuable advice on the use of records, and many other insights besides. At the London School of Economics, Dr. Hermann Mannheim and Mr. Eryl Hall Williams were of great help at the outset of the project. Peter Willmott, of the Institute of Community Studies, and Peter Stone, have both made very useful criticisms of the final draft. Naturally, the opinions and views of the above are not necessarily those expressed in this book.

Both supervising the work, and giving invaluable advice at every stage and on all aspects, Dr. Terence Morris contributed far more to the research than any graduate student or colleague has the right to expect.

Finally, while the research was initially aided by the award of a State Studentship, its continuation depended on a generous grant of $2,500 from the Ford Foundation, made possible by Jackson Toby, formerly Consultant for the Foundation's Youth Development Program.

1

THE CONCEPT OF THE DELINQUENT SUBCULTURE

Since 1955, when Albert Cohen first employed the concept of the subculture in relation to certain forms of juvenile delinquency, the term 'delinquent subculture' has become embedded in criminological vocabulary. To Cohen,[1] the concept applied to a 'way of life that has somehow become traditional among . . . the boys' gangs that flourish most conspicuously in the "delinquency neighbourhoods" of our larger American cities'. This way of life can be called a subculture, and can therefore be analysed as such, because it possesses 'knowledge, beliefs, values, codes, tastes and prejudices' which are peculiarly its own. Subcultures are 'cultures within cultures', for the concept of culture should not be reserved for 'the distinctive ways of life of . . . large-scale national and tribal societies'. Moreover, there are 'subcultures within subcultures'; for example, the subculture of a neighbourhood and of a family, clique or gang within the neighbourhood. 'All these subcultures have this in common: they are acquired only by interaction with those who already share and embody, in their belief and action, the culture (i.e. the subculture) pattern'.

Cohen's outline of what constitutes a subculture is more suggestive than definitive, since he regarded the task of 'culture' and 'subculture' definition as given and focussed his attention on the process by which a subculture emerges. He is avowedly more concerned with the process by which a subculture is created than with the mechanisms by which it is maintained. Yet the novelty

---

[1] A. K. Cohen, *Delinquent Boys: The Culture of the Gang* (1955), p. 13.

I

of applying 'subculture' to certain forms of delinquency obscured the difficulties in the way of using the concept at all. That these difficulties are inherent in the concept of the 'subculture', rather than in the substance of Cohen's theory about a particular 'delinquent subculture', is a point missed by many critics of his theory. To avoid the same pitfall, some indication of the difficulties inherent in the definition of 'culture' and 'subculture' seems in order. Before the value of the subcultural approach to an understanding of juvenile delinquency can be conveyed, difficulties of definition must be disentangled from those of substantive theory.

The concept of culture has largely been the preserve of the anthropologist. The central position of the concept in social anthropology largely derived from Malinowski,[2] whose classic definition of 'culture' as comprising 'inherited artefacts, goods, technical processes, ideas, habits and values' generated a concern to re-define and amplify the uses of the concept as a descriptive and explanatory tool. Sociologists have generally been cursory in their use of the concept, rarely attempting any definition more stringent than the 'way of life' criterion. Significantly, in their imaginary interdisciplinary conversation on the concept of culture, Kluckhohn and Kelley[3] include anthropologists, a lawyer, psychologist, biologist and businessman, but not a sociologist. While sociologists usually give a working definition of 'culture' to serve specific purposes, they have contributed little to the ongoing debate about the basic questions 'What is culture?' and 'How do culture and subculture intersect?' To place Cohen's particular application in perspective, and to clarify some important limitations on the whole field of delinquent subcultural theorisation, these questions must at least be touched upon.

Both 'society' and 'culture' are conceptual constructs or models: culture cannot be 'seen', but refers to the distinctive regularities—the 'ways'—which are abstracted from actually seeing and observing human behaviour in a given collectivity. Firth[4]

---

[2] B. Malinowski, 'Culture' in *Encyclopaedia of the Social Sciences* (1933).
[3] C. Kluckhohn and W. H. Kelley, 'The Concept of Culture,' reprinted in C. Kluckhohn, *Culture and Behavior* (1962), pp. 19–73, on which much of the following discussion is based.
[4] R. Firth, *Elements of Social Organisation* (1951), p. 27.

clearly distinguished between culture and social structure, defining '. . . society, culture and community . . .' as:

> different facets or components in basic human situations. If, for example, society is taken to be an organised set of individuals with a given way of life, culture is that way of life. If society is taken to be an aggregate of social relations, then culture is the content of those relations. From the behavioural aspect, culture is all learned behaviour which has been socially acquired.

Culture is essentially that part of learned behaviour which is shared with others. In Ruth Benedict's words, 'culture is what binds men together'. This definition is fundamentally that of Malinowski, who viewed culture in functional terms, as the cement which makes a given collectivity cohere.

Yet culture also sets men apart. C. S. Ford[5] viewed culture as consisting of 'traditional ways of solving problems' or 'of learned problem solutions'. While stable cultures pass on answers to specific problems, the tendency is for cultures to create new problems in solving the old. Culture is both fulfilling and frustrating: hence the inadequacy of the purely functional approach. Culture is not simply 'social heredity', a term which connotes a dead, static weight. Men are not only carriers, they are also creators of culture. Moreover, culture displays organisation as well as content: mere enumeration of culture traits is a distortion of the reality, since the parts vary by arrangement, emphasis and intensity; values may be dominant or secondary, and so on. Part of the confusion springs from the two main uses to which the concept of culture is put: explanation and description. These uses overlap, but are quite distinct analytically.

No human being, even if only a few months old, reacts completely freshly to any stimulus situation. As an 'explanatory' concept, 'culture' is of use both in analysing the actions of people, whether individually or in groups, and in elucidating the geographical distribution of artefacts, forms of behaviour and historical sequences of behaviour. In this context, it might be defined as 'those historically created selective processes that channel men's reactions both to internal and to external stimuli'. 'Internal' refers to man's basic biological drives—hunger, procreation etc.;

---

[5] C. S. Ford, 'Culture and Human Behavior,' *Scientif. Monthly*, vol. 55, 1942, pp. 546–557; quoted in Kluckhohn and Kelley, op. cit

3

'external' to whatever stimulus situations confront him. 'Selective' connotes man's preference for one solution as opposed to a variety of other solutions available; 'channel' indicates that culture *influences*, rather than *determines*, an outcome: other interactive factors are always present. The extent to which even 'innate' endowments are culturally modifiable testifies to the great plasticity of 'human nature'. The very way we look at the world depends to a large extent on our cultural preconceptions as to what we will see there. As an explanatory concept, 'culture' is most usefully defined as '. . . among other things . . . a set of ready-made definitions of the situation that each individual only slightly re-tailors in his own idiomatic way. . . . The human mind can know "reality" only as sieved through an a priori net.' Related concepts, such as 'culture diffusion', 'culture conflict', 'culture lag', 'acculturation', are best understood in this context.

Selectivity is the process most basic to 'culture', for 'culture' is possible only where two or more functionally equivalent *choices* are available for the attainment of an end: hence, to state that men catch fish is not a statement about culture if those men depend on the catch for their lives: only a description of their mode of catching and eating the fish would be a statement about culture. As a descriptive concept, Kluckhohn and Kelley define 'culture' as 'all those historically created designs for living, explicit and implicit, rational, irrational and nonrational, that exist at any given time as potential guides for the behaviour of men' or 'that tend to be shared by all or specially designated members of a group'. 'Designs for living' subsumes both 'real' and 'ideal' facets; 'at any given time' insists that 'culture' is never static; 'tends to be shared' implies that no-one, even in primitive societies, can know 'all' of a culture: such knowledge is limited and differentiated by age, sex, prestige, and role differentials. Similarly, no culture can be regarded as a completely integrated system. Most cultures, like personalities, can be regarded as permeated by apparent contradictions.

The concept of the 'subculture' embodies one such contradiction. What constitutes the 'culture' of a complex society: all its subcultures, their uniformities only, or the dominant subculture? Where, to put it crudely, does culture end and subculture begin? Does subculture merely refract or totally displace

4

culture? Any vagueness over the boundaries of the overall culture will automatically extend to subcultures. Hoijer[6] asserts the importance of language: 'To the extent that a culture as a whole is made up of common understandings, its linguistic aspect is its most vital and necessary part.' Yet the main importance of language lies in its implicit assumptions: every language is a device for categorising experience, as well as for communication, emotion-rousing, etc., as the study of comparative linguistics has stressed. When major obstacles to inter-class communication in language appear—as demonstrated, for example, by Bernstein's discussion of the general limitation of the working-class child to a 'public' language—are we to assume totally disparate cultures? Levi-Strauss has related the culture-subculture question of definition to the scale of research planned: 'significant discontinuities' between culture(s) and subculture(s) can be assessed only within a given frame of reference. Any other approach is bedevilled by the all-embracing nature of the concept; 'Western' culture subsumes American, British, French, etc. cultures; which subsume numerous regional cultures, and so on, to the 'subculture with a subculture' of a factory or a neighbourhood. The broad criteria of mutual intelligibility and self-sufficiency perhaps help to divide distinct 'cultures' but are of little use in hiving off subcultures from the larger culture. Such statements as: 'When people from two groups, despite perceptible variation in the details of their lifeways, nevertheless share enough basic assumptions for reasonably comfortable communication, then their cultures are only variants of a single culture,'[8] are provocative, but barely scientific. Again, their three questions to distinguish between cultures: 'truth' and 'falsity' criteria; attributes of a 'good' person; and what is desirable in experience and in what rank order, are more pertinent to civilisation than to subculture differentiation. They conclude that: 'The dividing line between "a culture" and "subculture" or "cultural variant" has not yet been firmly staked out.'[9]

[6] H. Hoijer, 'The Relation of Language to Culture,' p. 556, in A. L. Kroeber (ed.), *Anthropology Today* (1953), pp. 554–573.

[7] B. Bernstein, 'Social Class and Linguistic Patterns,' Ch. 24 in Floud, Halsey and Anderson, *Education, Economy and Society* (1961).

[8] Kluckhohn and Kelley, op. cit., p. 65. (paraphrase).

[9] Op. cit., p. 67.

What, then, is particularly to be gained by using the subculture concept?[10] It is not very illuminating to label as 'subcultures' well-known differences between the ways of life of different sectors of complex societies. The answer is that certain kinds of questions can most usefully be posed within the subcultural frame of reference. If the resulting answers make sense, can be nullified or verified scientifically, or—better—are simply of use, then the weaknesses inherent in the conceptual source are not crucially relevant.

In outlining a 'general theory of subcultures', Cohen's[11] basic premise was that what people do depends upon the problems they contend with, echoing Ford's definition of culture (and, by extension, subculture) as consisting of 'learned problem solutions'. Whatever factors and circumstances combine to produce a problem derive from either the individual's 'frame of reference'—the way he looks at the world—or the 'situation' he confronts—the world he lives in and where he is located in the world. All problems arise and are solved via changes in one or both of these classes of determinants. The 'situation' limits the things we can do or have, and the conditions under which they are possible. But the situation and the problem it implies are always relative to the 'actor'. 'The facts' never simply stare us in the face: so much is already evident from the discussion of 'culture'. 'Opportunity', 'barrier', 'ambition': these concepts are never 'fixed', but depend upon our goals and aspirations. The 'same' world, the 'same' situation, strikes terror in one person, but to another can appear a calm and peaceful haven.

A good solution creates no new problems: it leaves no residue of anxiety, tension or despair. The really hard problems are those to which no ready-made solution has been provided by a 'culture': the 'situation' remains inflexible. Any satisfactory solution to these problems entails, therefore, some change in the frame of reference itself. For example, giving up a long-cherished goal is an *effective* solution only if that goal is deemed irrelevant or of little importance: otherwise, its hold over us persists, nags and worries. In short, our values must change to accommodate this

---

[10] More than one critic has raised this point, but see especially Barbara Wootton, *Social Science and Social Pathology* (1959), p. 67.

[11] A. K. Cohen, 'A General Theory of Subcultures;' Ch. 3 in *Delinquent Boys*, pp. 49–72.

solution: 'projection' and 'rationalisation' are well-known psychological mechanisms to this end.

Human problems are manifestly not distributed randomly among the 'roles' that make up a social system. 'Frames of reference' vary by age, sex, ethnic group, occupational, class and prestige-group categories. The 'same' problems affect people differently according to the sectors they occupy: 'growing old' involves vastly different problems for the manual worker, whose job places a high premium on physical vigour, and for the white collar worker. The patterned distribution of problems accounts for the creation and selection of similarly distributed solutions. This explanation is inadequate, however, if there exist good alternative responses to the specific problems involved.

To say that the best solutions create no new problems implies, above all, that they must not impair our standing with those whose friendship and esteem we value most. It is not only that the assent of our reference groups matters, and enhances our solutions: more than any other single factor, such assent *validates* our solutions. So strong is the need for reference-group support for our solutions, that if they prove unacceptable to the group's standards, we are very likely to look for a group that will assent: the continual realignment of groups, the constant search for foci for new loyalties, is a common form of social process.

The migration of an individual from one group to another does not, however, constitute subcultural innovation: this can emerge only where there exist, 'in effective interaction with one another, a number of actors with similar problems of adjustment', for whom no effective solution as yet exists for a common, shared problem. Only on this basis is the *joint* elaboration of a new solution possible: and it emerges on a group basis, via a process of mutual conversion to a new point of view.[12] That the group basis is a necessary catalyst is illustrated in extreme form by the behaviour of 'crowds' or 'mobs'. These kinds of 'collective behaviour' embody quickly worked-out collective solutions to common problems: the moral frame of reference is not so much obliterated as rapidly transformed. This emergence of new 'group standards' is synonymous with that of a new subculture: it is simply that, in the case of 'collective behaviour', the subculture so hastily created is short-lived. For, once generated, a

[12] The success of 'group therapy' is in part explained by this process.

7

subculture will generally persist only as long as the problems to which it provides a solution persist (although, if it comes to serve different needs equivalently, it will outlast the problem which generated it).

One particular category of problems are those that derive from our need for 'status', which might be defined as our need to achieve and maintain the respect of our fellows (our reference group). They accord us their respect on the basis of certain criteria, which form one aspect of their 'cultural frame of reference'. The more severely we are found lacking by these criteria, the more we are faced with a 'problem of adjustment'. Those sharing such a problem could respond to it by gravitating towards one another and establishing new criteria of status, based on attributes they *do* possess: these new criteria may be different from or even antithetical to those of the former group. The more the former group rejects the new, the more the new is strengthened in its emergent norms. The new group's value-system is further reinforced if its members devalue the esteem of the former group. The former group becomes the 'out-group', toward which hostility is felt, and whose members are repudiated as 'outsiders'.

Not all problems are amenable to subcultural solutions. Some problems are shared by people who lack the opportunity for 'interaction': some problems arise simply *because* there is no basis for interaction, e.g. the 'suburban neurosis' of 'lonely' wives. Other problems may be laden with associations which prohibit interaction: for example, those problems to do with sexual inadequacy. 'Solutions' to these problems generally take personal, private or neurotic forms. Perhaps this in part explains the phenomenon of the 'solitary' delinquent, who is not allowed to interact with those similarly circumstanced, or who is not acceptable to 'the boys', for whatever reason. Where the nature of the problem does not inhibit interaction, however, the basis for the emergence of a subculture is present. It is Cohen's thesis that, in American society, certain problems of adjustment occur most typically in those 'role sectors' where the delinquent subculture is most endemic.

One source of confusion in Cohen's 'general theory of sub-cultures' is his failure to classify 'subcultures' into two main kinds:

8

(*a*) those which precede, or which are formed *outside* the context of the 'dominant culture': for example, the 'culture' of immigrant groups which become 'subcultures' in the context of the host culture; also, regional subcultures which precede, but come to co-exist, merge with or differentially respond to the enveloping 'dominant culture'.

(*b*) those which originate *within* the context of the dominant culture: these fall into two sub-categories:

(i) those which emerge in *positive* response to the demands of the social and cultural structures; for example, occupational subcultures, age-group subcultures, and

(ii) those emerging in *negative* response to the social and cultural structures' demands; e.g. delinquent subcultures; religious-messianic-revivalist subcultures; political-extremist subcultures.

Patently, Cohen's analysis applies primarily to sub-category (ii) of the second kind of subculture. This question of definition underlies much of the confusion that has arisen over the exact difference between the 'delinquent subculture' and 'working-class culture'.[13] In similar vein, Yinger distinguished three clearly different meanings for 'subculture' in his review of over 100 sources, and located the sources of confusion in the vague definition of 'subculture' as meaning simply 'cultures within cultures'.[14] Subculture has evidently been used as an 'ad hoc' concept whenever the writer wished to stress the normative aspects of any behaviour that differed from some general standard.

Of the three usages analysed by Yinger, one—the anthropological reference to 'certain universal tendencies that seem to occur in all societies'—is practically obsolete. The two other usages are both currently in vogue, and contain some ambiguities even when separated. The concept of 'subculture' is applied both to the normative systems of sub-societies (e.g. the working-class subculture) and the emergent norms that appear in conflict situations (e.g. the delinquent subculture). The first usage accommodates both vague regional enclaves (e.g. the subculture of the South) and transient occupational groups (e.g. the 'subcultures among the faculty' cited by Riesman, or Cohen's 'the subculture of a factory and of a shop within the factory'). The

[13] See especially references to the work of W. B. Miller in Chs. 3 and 4.

[14] J. Milton Yinger, 'Contraculture and Subculture,' *Amer. Sociol. Rev.* Vol. 25, No. 5, Oct. 1960, pp. 625–635.

second usage arises 'when the reference is to norms that arise specifically from a frustrating situation or from conflict between a group and the larger society'. To Yinger, the second usage implies a social-psychological as well as a cultural dimension, and stresses one particular kind of linkage between norms and personality: that is, 'the creation of a series of inverse or counter values (opposed to those of the surrounding society) in face of serious frustration or conflict.' The model for such a 'contra-culture'—as Yinger proposes they should be termed—is Cohen's construct of the delinquent subculture. But the 'Beats' or the 'Black Moslems'—any group which creates and carries a set of counter-norms—would be equally valid examples.

Yinger suggests three factors make adoption of the distinction between contraculture and subculture essential: (a) while the values of most subcultures probably conflict in some measure with the larger culture, in a contraculture the conflict element is (held to be) central: many of the values are (held to be) specific contradictions of those of the dominant culture; (b) study of the nature of the relationship with the larger culture is not essential for an appreciation of subcultural norms, but it is vital for an understanding of contracultural norms; (c) while reliance on the concept of subculture is often merely a substitute for the analysis of role differentiation, contraculture emphatically *connotes* role strain or ambiguity (although in the case of the delinquent subculture, this is to pre-judge the issue somewhat).

Yinger claims that his distinction has particular relevance in the study of delinquency and criminality. 'Perhaps in no other field were there more substantial gains in understanding made possible by the introduction of a sociological viewpoint to supplement and correct individualistic and moralistic interpretations'. This mixture of terms, however, is not peculiar to the field of delinquency. Yinger shows how both sub- and contra-cultural meanings have been confused in writings on social class and occupations. Also, concepts other than 'subculture' have been plagued by dual meanings. 'Anomie' is used both as a social structural fact and as a personality trait. 'Role' is coupled with both prescribed rights and duties and individual performance. In this confusion, Yinger suggests that the term 'contraculture' be adopted to refer to the emergent norms of a group in a conflict-laden situation, retaining 'subculture' to describe traditional sub-society norms. However, the validity of employing the contra-culture concept in the delinquent gang field has yet to be *proved*: its adoption at this stage would serve to pre-judge the issue which Yinger himself has been at such pains to clarify. An alternative solution is to retain the term 'delinquent subculture', as it has been defined by Cohen and other subcultural theorists in the delinquency field, to accommodate what Yinger would prefer to term 'contraculture'; as a corollary, it is vital to eliminate the usage of 'subculture' as a synonym for the norms of traditional sub-societies. For example, Walter Miller's usage of 'lower class culture' seems adequate descriptively. The concept of 'contraculture' will, however, be introduced to clarify argument where appropriate.

2

DELINQUENT GANGS

COHEN implicitly equates gang-life with the 'delinquent sub-culture'. What he implied in his title—*The Culture of the Gang*—Cloward and Ohlin take as their dependent variable:[1] 'We would not necessarily describe as delinquent a group that tolerated or practiced these behaviours unless they were the central activities around which the group was organised . . . A delinquent subculture is one in which certain forms of delinquent activity are essential requirements for the performance of the dominant roles supported by the subculture.' While Cohen[2] in exposition broadens the subculture 'carriers' to take in the 'group or gang, the vehicle of the delinquent subculture and one of its statistically most manageable earmarks', he places such heavy emphasis on the delinquent subculture as an alternative status system and vehicle for the collective approval of socially stigmatised activities that the delinquent gang appears to be the model form sustaining this burden. But to Cloward and Ohlin more than Cohen, delinquent subcultures not only sanction delinquency, or even demand its occasional use: delinquency is their 'raison d'être', their most characteristic mode of activity rather than behaviour they indulge in only 'in extremis'. In a review of Cloward and Ohlin's work, Toby,[3] while praising their lucid restriction of the dependent variable, estimated that gang delinquency by their definition could hardly amount to more than 10 per cent of the cases handled by American juvenile courts. If the same analysis is applied to Cohen's delinquent subculture, it is clear that the most

[1] In their *Delinquency and Opportunity: A Theory of Delinquent Gangs* (1961), p. 7.
[2] Cohen, op. cit., p. 46.
[3] J. Toby, 'Delinquency and Opportunity,' *Brit. J. of Sociol.*, Vol. 12, No. 3, Sept. 1961, pp. 282–289.

serious limitation of subcultural theorisation on delinquency is its generic reliance on gang delinquency. If this limitation holds good, are we wise to lavish so much attention on so limited a sector of delinquent behaviour? Or can subcultural theorisation logically be extended to forms other than gang delinquency?

The delinquent subculture is only *one* way of looking at, and attempting to explain, juvenile gang delinquency. Other investigators simply treat the gang as a datum, and attempt to explain delinquency independently of the gang context. Bloch and Niederhoffer, for example, see the gang as a group form which has existed in all cultures at all times, irrespective of all variables except two—age and sex. The juvenile male adolescent gang becomes delinquent only when certain pressures begin to operate —to Bloch and Niederhoffer,[4] the most salient pressure is that exerted when adolescence is artificially prolonged and, in a society lacking clear-cut 'rites of passage' to adult status, the adolescent is condemned to an amorphous 'teenage' role. A second view of the delinquent gang is that of Cohen, and of Cloward and Ohlin, which sees it as emerging in response to certain problems of adjustment, to which its members adopt a variety of subcultural solutions. As has been stated already, Cloward and Ohlin define the delinquent subculture strictly in terms of the delinquent gang. They write[5] of: '. . . delinquent gangs, or subcultures, as they are typically found among adolescent males in lower-class areas of large urban centres.' A third view, which is a modification of the latter, is that the delinquent gang is only one species of carrier of the various delinquent subcultures. In other words, does the delinquent subcultural process necessarily culminate in *gang* delinquency, or can the values it upholds function via looser, more diffused collectivities?

A great deal of documentation exists on juvenile delinquent gangs in American cities, in particular for New York, but also for Chicago (Short) and Boston (Miller).[6] But considerable differences exist about the form the gangs take, apart from the more complicated questions of the functions they perform for their members, the reasons for their origin and maintenance,

[4] H. Bloch and A. Niederhoffer, *The Gang: A Study in Adolescent Behaviour* (1958).
[5] R. A. Cloward and L. E. Ohlin, *Delinquency and Opportunity: A Theory of Delinquent Gangs* (1961).
[6] See Ch. 4.

etc. The following description of a delinquent gang can be taken as typical, if somewhat dramatised:

> The Cobras are an active 'bopping' club with its base in one of the older Brooklyn projects. 'Minding our turf' is their main pre-occupation. . . . Theirs is a subculture, a sub-society with its own mores, codes, ceremonies, language and interests. The Cobras neither know nor care what goes on in the other world. . . . Here is the street-gang in its most vicious flowering. . . . The Cobras are a structured gang, mainly Negro—they possess a President, a Vice-President, a War Counsellor, an Armourer. . . . They have two categories: the Big People (aged 16–19) and the Little People (aged 9/10–15). . . . The Cobra knows his turf blindfold. As in war, each gang has its own territory, its no man's land, and all else is hostile. Security and nicknames go together, and possess prowess value—e.g. Snake, Killer, Geronimo, Diablo, Johnny the Bop, and Saint. Cobra gang-size is 40–50 in all: twothirds are in irregular attendance at school; of the remainder, half have jobs, half do not. . . . They while away their days, after a late rise, in drink and boredom, building up for an evening of tension and warfare . . . If the fundamental concept of the Cobra is demesne, his basic mystique is 'heart'. Heart is what passes for bravery on the streets; it can lead to a recklessness approaching lunacy: the opposite of heart is 'punking out'. . . . Seven Up is a member of the Cobras. Seven Up has not the slightest importance to anyone except the Cobras. The school is happier for his absence. The aunt he lives with is past caring. No-one cares. Seven Up often injects the phrase 'If I live' or 'If I don't die' into his conversation. He is famous for one thing—heart. This one quality he uses to defy society and gain the warmth of his fellows. It is hard to think what society has done for Seven Up which would warrant his feeling towards it any respect, duty or obligation. . . .[7]

This description of a 'fighting gang' aligns exactly with Cloward and Ohlin's theorisation on the 'conflict' subculture. In their subcultural analysis, they break down the gang code into norms, values and beliefs. The structured gang encases these norms, values and beliefs, and members articulate them with a high degree of consensus. This consensus extends also to leadership, membership and territory, but other observations on gang life differ in kind from this delineation of gang structure and activity,

---

[7] Paraphrase from: Harrison E. Salisbury, *The Shook-Up Generation* (1958).

and have led some investigators to reject the subcultural approach *in toto*.

Yablonsky[8] sees the gang-as-subculture hypothesis as a sociological artefact. He states that too much sociological theory on gangs is based on the false assumption that gangs are defined sociological groups, an assumption culled from the popular, traditional image of gangs as held by the public and as reported by the various media with vested interests in sensationalism and romanticisation. Yablonsky is primarily concerned with breaking down the traditional picture of the structured gang and replacing it with his 'near-group' construct. To illustrate the disparity between popular reports of gang war behaviour and their organisation as revealed by more systematic study, Yablonsky cites case material from 'depth' interviews with 40 participants in what was reported in 1955 to be the 'biggest' gang war in New York's history. While the 'rumble' was reported 'in the defined version of groups meeting in battle over territory', Yablonsky found in his interviews a tremendous variation in perceptions of the event. For example, estimates of the number involved ranged from 80 to 5,000; reasons given for fighting varied from 'Didn't have anything to do' to '"They" always picked on us' to 'I always like a fight; it keeps my "rep."' Yablonsky reconstructs the event as '. . . not a social situation of two structured teen-aged armies meeting on a battlefield to act out a defined situation; it was a case of two near-groups in action.' The importance of this observation is that it stresses that the function of conflict is to generate the cohesion and identity of the group. The near-group achieves its solidarity only under conditions of extreme pressure, produced in ideal form in the highly institutionalised situations of gang warfare. Yablonsky asserts elsewhere—see *The Violent Gang* Chapter II—that the gang which killed Michael Farmer was drawn from a very dispersed area. This contradicts most traditional assumptions about gang recruitment patterns.

Yablonsky located the 'near-group' mid-way on the group-mob continuum. As a collectivity, it is characterised by: (1) diffuse role definition, (2) limited cohesion, (3) impermanence, (4) minimal consensus of norms, (5) shifting membership, (6) disturbed leadership, and (7) limited definition of membership

[8] Lewis Yablonsky, 'The Delinquent Gang as a Near-Group,' *Soc. Problems*, Vol. 7, No. 2, Fall 1959, pp. 108–117. Also, *The Violent Gang*, 1962.

expectations. While Yablonsky nowhere clarifies the exact distinction between (2), (3) and (5), and between (1) and (7) and (4) and (7), he states that 'these factors characterise the near-group's "normal" structure.' He also states that while the 'true' group may at times appear to be a 'near-group', at these times it is generally moving away from or towards its normative, permanent structure, but the 'near-group' never fully becomes a *group* or a *mob*. In his conclusion, Yablonsky speculates as to whether his near-group concept might apply to social problems other than that of the juvenile delinquent gang, to—for example—the structure of the so-called crime syndicates, such as the Mafia. But his exposition of his concept, with reference to the delinquent gang only, reveals the 'near-group' to be a mere neologism for what is more familiarly termed the unstructured gang. Yablonsky nowhere explores the implications of his approach to gang delinquency in group-mob terms, and adopts psychologistic principles to account for 'near-group' violence under 'disturbed' leadership. Yet his correction of the over-emphasis on the 'structured 'gang is valid, as are his strictures on the detached worker, police and press habit of projecting group conceptions on to near-group activity, which leads to a group-fulfilling prophecy.

While Yablonsky failed to extend his analysis of delinquent gangs beyond his advocacy of the near-group concept, Pfautz[9] developed his findings in the direction of collective behaviour theory. Pfautz acknowledged the validity of Yablonsky's findings about gang structure, but regarded the introduction of 'near-group' and the invidious 'true-group' as an unnecessary complication of the theoretical issue. Pfautz claimed that Yablonsky's evidence was extremely favourable to an analysis of violent gang behaviour as an 'expressive' social movement. Although Yablonsky was superficially correct in locating his near-groups mid-way along the group-mob continuum, his theoretical rationale was defective: '. . . the mid-point on the collective behaviour-social organisation continuum is occupied by 'social movements' as a type of human grouping. . . . Social movements exhibit continuity beyond the concrete interacting situation because they develop a 'culture' in the sense of a set of ideas, theories, doctrines, values,

[9] H. W. Pfautz, 'Near-Group Theory and Collective Behavior,' *Soc. Problems*, Vol. 9, No. 2, Fall 1961, pp. 167–174.

and strategic and tactical principles, but lack . . . a fully developed and functionally effective social structure. . . .' Pfautz goes on to claim that the violent adolescent gang is not a delinquent sub-cultural pattern (despite his own claim that they develop a 'culture') but should be regarded as an expressive social move-ment, whose incidental mobilisation of collective behaviour into the gang war is *functionally more important* than the social structure of the core group and the culture of the movement. What is disturbing about the orientation of Yablonsky and Pfautz is not the validity or falsity of bringing collective behaviour theory to bear on the violent gang, but their assumption that subcultural theorisation is *automatically invalidated* as soon as a doubt arises as to the universality of the structured gang.

A parallel to the relationship which is thus assumed to exist between subcultural theorisation and gang structure is the disen-chantment with subcultural theorisation springing from certain examinations of street-corner group behaviour. As part of the Roxbury Project in Boston, Miller[10] and others examined syste-matically the day-to-day behaviour of one adolescent street-corner group, the Junior Outlaws, for a one-year period. While Miller gives no clue as to the effect on that behaviour of the continued presence of a detached worker and other observers, he hoped to assess the importance of aggression as a component in delinquent behaviour. But the main focus was on the broad area of aggression, irrespective of whether or not it involved delin-quency. Miller's data, an exhaustive record of 1,490 'aggressive acts'—both verbal and physical—, showed clearly that the behaviour, functions and culture of his adolescent street-corner group differed in kind from those of Yablonsky's violent gang.

The Junior Outlaws' core group were 18 white Catholic boys aged 14–16; the Juniors were the second youngest group of a four-tiered aggregate street-corner group called the Outlaws. Miller describes their behaviour as midway between extreme and negligible delinquency, and 7 of the 18 became officially involved as delinquents during the study year: 4 for auto theft and/or lewdness, truancy and creating a public disturbance; 3 on sus-picion who were released without sentence. By report and/or

---

[10] W. B. Miller. H. Geertz and H. S. G. Cutter, 'Aggression in a Boy Street-Corner Group,' *Psychiatry: Journal for the Study of Interpersonal Processes*, Vol. 24, No. 4, Nov. 1961, pp. 283–298.

observation, group members committed 30 arrestable acts in addition to these: 5 auto theft, 6 petty theft, 9 assaults, 7 alcohol violations, 1 trespass, 2 public disturbance. In studying the broader area of aggression, every instance of an overtly aggressive act or sequence of acts was recorded and coded for actor, form, intensity, target, and social context. 'One of the most striking and clearcut findings . . . was that . . . 70% of the aggressive actions of all types, from good-natured ribbing to outright physical attack, was directed at fellow group members.' Aggressive acts against teachers, clergy and police amounted to only 2·4%; the targets of the remainder were chiefly other local adolescents (11·8%); neighbourhood adults in frequent contact with the Juniors, in particular recreation workers (6·9%); and the corner-group social worker (5%). Even though the remarkably high proportion of acts directed against group members is, to some degree, a function of interaction, the analysis shows that 'adults as a whole were objects of very little expressed aggression—direct or indirect—contrary to a highly prevalent conception of such gangs as seething with hostility against the adult world.'

In analysing the form, intensity and content of aggressive behaviour, Miller found that a picture emerged '. . . of a type of group in which aggression assumed a very narrow range of expression: narrow in choice of targets, in form, and also limited in intensity . . .', whose content served to enforce '. . . group-condoned norms that had a community-based source of legitimacy.' As simple physical assault on persons or property was rare, amounting to only 7% of the 1,490 aggressive acts, Miller concentrated on analysing the nature and functions of verbal aggression. (In all the physically aggressive acts, no weapon was used; and in only 7 was an emotional intensity higher than 'mild anger' registered.) Of the verbally aggressive acts, only 2% rated 'genuine anger' and none involved 'uncontrollable fury'. The bulk of verbal aggression was either derogatory ('He's just a punk!') or in the form of a directly hostile statement ('You stink!')—these two categories accounted for 65·4% of the verbal aggression: irony and sarcasm had the lowest rating (0·8%). The content of verbal aggression was mainly adverse commentary on personal qualities and behaviour which, by inversion, revealed the qualities and behaviour which the group thought desirable. The 'corner-boy ideal' is:

... skilled and competent in a range of physical and athletic accomplishments; he does not disrupt group enterprises by disorderly behaviour; he is a faithful participant in group activities and dependable in fulfilling group obligations. Despite his skill, ... he is properly modest ... refrains from boasting ... and behaving as a star in collective events. He is smart in the sense of being knowledgeable as to what is current in the world of the corner and its concerns, informed as to game rules and able to hold his own in group repartee. He is scrupulously honest in his dealings with fellow group members, especially in money matters, and is sensitive to ... fair play in contests ... He is physically strong, but careful not to take unfair advantage of this strength in dealings with fellow members. He is 'smooth' with the girls and sexually potent. He drinks, swears and gambles but recognises ... appropriate ... circumstances for these activities.

This 'ideal' coincides closely with Cohen's analysis of the 'stable corner-boy response':

The corner boy's life is organised around what we have called working-class values ... The corner-boy way of life, although it yields satisfactions of its own, notably, those that derive from full and intimate participation in a close-knit primary group, militates against vertical mobility. *The corner-boy culture is not specifically delinquent.* Where it leads to behaviour which may be defined as delinquent, ... it does so not because non-conformity to middle-class norms *defines* conformity to corner-boy norms but because conformity to middle-class norms *interferes with* conformity to corner-boy norms ... In short, the corner-boy culture temporises with middle-class morality; the full-fledged delinquent subculture does not.[11]

Miller's achievement is to have presented the fullest, most relevant account of the 'corner-boy culture' to date, a more salient account than that of Whyte's classic description of Doc and the Nortons.[12] As Short has pointed out: 'It is almost necessary to protest that these (Whyte's) corner boys were not delinquents, they were older (mid-20's), and they were much more stable than are adolescent delinquent gangs.'[13] Miller points out that many patterns emerging from the study, such as

[11] A. K. Cohen, *Delinquent Boys: The Culture of the Gang* (1956), pp. 104, 128–130.
[12] W. F. Whyte, *Street Corner Society* (1943).
[13] J. F. Short, Jr., and F. L. Strodtbeck, 'The Response of Gang Leaders to Status Threats', *Amer. J. Sociol.*, Vol. 68, No. 5, pp. 571–579.

a high ratio of in-group to out-group aggression, low incidence of behind-the-back aggression, and the virtual absence of abstract or impersonal targets, would not necessarily hold true for other corner boy groups manifesting a different combination of age, sex, class and ethnic characteristics. But the distinction between corner boy use of aggression, and that of Yablonsky's violent gang and Cloward and Ohlin's 'conflict' subculture, is clear: the one is a means to group cohesion; the other is a means to status within the core-group or subculture. For the Junior Outlaws, the group is *itself* the arena in which aggression is played out, 'its force dissipated in a continuing, persistent, low-level flow, directed at members of the group itself,' that is, if the group did not exist, we should have to invent it.

While Miller's is the first detailed empirical study of an adolescent corner group, it contain three limitations of some significance. (*a*) For a study which in part seeks to evaluate the working class adolescent's aggression towards middle-class controlled property and institutions, it takes into account only out-of-school behaviour. (*b*) Miller uses data on a corner group as a disproof of subcultural theorisation rather than as evidence in favour of Cohen's delineation of the corner boy response as an alternative to the delinquent subculture. (*c*) The hallmark of the delinquent subculture is the wholesale repudiation of middle-class *norms* and the substitution of counter-norms. To imply that the *target* of the delinquent subculture must necessarily be middle-class persons, property or institutions, is to confuse the source with the outcome of deviance.

The work of Yablonsky and Miller illustrates two non-sequiturs on the relationship between the delinquent gang and subcultural theorisation:

(1) that structured delinquent gangs are necessary vehicles for delinquent subcultures.
(2) that subcultural theorisation takes no account of, and is in some ways refuted by, the existence of adolescent corner groups for whom delinquency is not a central requirement, and whose aggression is not directed primarily against the middle-class world.

In conclusion, and in contrast to the above, the structured delinquent gang is a sufficient, but not a necessary, indication of the validity of the subcultural process; and subcultural theorisation not only takes account of, but depends on, the existence of alternative patterns of delinquent behaviour to that of the delinquent subculture.

The equation of the delinquent subculture with gang structure sprang principally from Cohen's 'collective solution' hypothesis: that the subcultural response can emerge only if a number of like-minded actors are in 'effective interaction' with each other. This pre-requisite, combined with the need for patterned group support to uphold the legitimacy of anti-social norms, implied the gang framework, an implication made explicit by the Cloward-Ohlin definition. But if the counter-values bear some relation to those of the surrounding culture, and even coincide with certain values held discreetly by the larger culture, they may emerge without the enclosing framework of a tightly-knit, structured group, as long as there exists a minimum of peer support. Also, in a society with somewhat different priorities, without such overt or covert stress on achieved mobility, for example, Cohen's X (common problems of adjustment) may be of a significantly different nature; or, if equivalent, need not necessarily cause his Y (the culture of the *gang*) owing to the operation of intervening variables different to those located by Cloward and Ohlin. For example, the absence of syndicated crime; full juvenile employment; and more institutional support for working class criteria of status than exists in the U.S.A. These issues will be followed up in Chapters 5–7.

3

AMERICAN THEORISATION ON DELINQUENT SUBCULTURES

ONE OF the principal contributions of Cloward and Ohlin to the study of delinquent subcultures was their elucidation of five classes of question, 'all of which must be answered by a comprehensive theory':[1]

1. What are we studying? What is the exact nature of the delinquent adaptation to be explained?
2. How is it located structurally?
3. To what problem(s) of adjustment might it be a response?
4. Why is a particular adaptation selected? What alternative responses are available?
5. What forces make for the differential persistence and stability of these responses?

Employing this framework in criticism, Cloward and Ohlin questioned the validity of Parsons' 'female-centred' theory,[2] Bloch and Niederhoffer's 'adolescent-crisis' theory, and Miller's lower-class culture theory. They found these approaches both

---

[1] Op. cit., pp. 31-32.
[2] Contained in T. Parsons, *Essays in Sociological Theory* (Rev. ed., 1954). His theory is broadly that in our society the adult male role is job-centred, the female role home-centred. In his formative years, the male child tends, therefore, to identify with his mother. After the 'latency period,' however, he encounters the culture's demands to adopt the 'masculine' role, and in response reacts exceptionally strongly against the display of all traits associated with 'femininity'. His adoption of aggressive toughness spills over into delinquency on occasions. Obviously no such problem arises for the female adolescent. While Cohen has drawn upon this thesis to explain middle-class delinquency, Parsons advanced the theory to apply to delinquency in general.

22

incomplete—in that they concentrated on stage 1–3 and over-looked the relevance of 4 and 5—and misleading—in that they assumed that insights into one class of question, especially 3, amounted to a total theory. It is doubtful whether these investi-gators, especially Parsons, were trying to do what Cloward and Ohlin chastise them for not doing, that is, proposing a theory on delinquent *subcultures*, as opposed to suggesting new aspects of the delinquency problem in general; but Cloward and Ohlin's framework amounts to a test of validation for all sociological theorisation on crime and delinquency, and could well be extended to other areas of deviant behaviour study.

What follows is an exposition of how these questions have been answered in the most central American work on delinquent sub-cultures: that of Cohen and Short, and Cloward and Ohlin. Cohen's *Delinquent Boys* and Cloward and Ohlin's *Delinquency and Opportunity* have many similarities, and Cohen—in collaboration with Short—refined his theory to the point where it resembled the later work on subcultural differentiation of Cloward and Ohlin. But substantial differences still exist between the two works in the answers they give to all but one of the above classes of question, the exception being question 2. The crucial differences and the key areas of agreement can be set out below; each set of differences can then be more fully explored in terms of Cloward and Ohlin's own critical framework:

(1) *Cohen* takes a 'way of life'—which he generalises to 'delin-quent gangs or groups'—and analyses it from a sub-cultural point of view. *Cloward and Ohlin* take three types of juvenile gang which, by definition, are subcultures.
   Both share the commitment-to-delinquency criterion.

(2) *Both* assert the working-class, male, urban adolescent hegemony of delinquent subcultures.

(3) *Cohen* asserts that the strain induced by middle-/working-class differences crystallises as problems of status.
   Cloward and Ohlin see the problem in terms of anomie, and concentrate on economic discrepancies, which crystallise as problems of differential opportunity.

(4) *Cohen* talks of 'the' delinquent subculture, or—with Short—of the 'parent' and variant sub-subcultures.
   Cloward and Ohlin talk of three distinct subcultures, with

etiologies all their own, which share only the subcultural process and their source in common problems of adjustment. *Both* agree on the perceived alternatives: the 'stable corner-boy' and the 'college-boy' adaptations.

(5) *Cohen* relies heavily on the 'reaction-formation' concept to explain the delinquent's continuing ambivalence towards the dominant culture pattern.

Cloward and Ohlin invoke instead the concept of alienation, and the distinction between the legitimacy and the moral validity of the dominant culture pattern, reinforced by the disparity between 'formal' and 'operative' criteria in a democracy.

(6) *Cohen* blends—to some extent—sociological and 'psychogenic' approaches to juvenile delinquency, but at the expense of rejecting several well-established sociological theories.

Cloward and Ohlin are wholly sociological in approach, and fuse several divergent strands of criminological thought into a single coherent theory.

(7) *Cohen* nowhere mentions the concept of anomie, although he paraphrases and dismisses a variant 'illicit means' theory, despite its structural relevance to his thesis.[3]

Cloward and Ohlin rely wholly upon Merton's elaboration of the concept of anomie in their analysis of the sources of deviant behaviour.

(8) *Cohen* deals at length with middle-class delinquency, and feels the need for an all-inclusive theory of delinquent subcultures.

Cloward and Ohlin concentrate on the differential persistence and stability of working-class delinquent subcultures, and invoke the concept of illegitimate means and the adult crime situation as intervening variables affecting the subcultural outcome.

These theoretical differences seem sharp enough to require further exploration. While this process will not lead to any easy reconciliation between basic differences, a point-by-point contrast may clarify where the essential divergence lies.[4]

[3] Op. cit., pp. 35–36.
[4] If the use of direct quotation in this chapter seems excessive, it springs in part from a desire to avoid some of the basic misinterpretations which have occurred in critiques of subcultural theorisation (See Ch. 4).

I THE FOCUS OF ATTENTION

Writing of *Delinquent Boys* in 1958, Cohen and Short stated: 'It proceeded from the premise that much delinquency—probably the great bulk of it—represents participation in a delinquent subculture.'[5] Whether or not this is an over-estimate, Cohen had asserted in his book that 'There seems to be no question . . . but that there is a delinquent subculture, and that it is a normal, integral and deeply-rooted feature of the social life of the modern American city.' This subculture consists of a 'way of life' that has 'somehow become traditional among . . . the boys' gangs that flourish most conspicuously in the "delinquency neighbourhoods" of our larger American cities.' This subculture had been described in detail by exponents of what Cohen terms the 'cultural-transmission' theory of juvenile delinquency, in particular the 'Chicago' school dominated by Shaw and McKay.* This theory attributed the persistence of juvenile delinquency in 'delinquency areas' to the existence of a delinquent tradition or culture, which persisted irrespective of demographic change. The differential-association theory of Sutherland was also in essence a cultural-transmission theory. Yet these investigators treated the delinquent subculture 'as a datum': certain 'social guidelines', i.e. subcultural norms, preceded the child and demanded his acquiescence, and the concern of Shaw and McKay, and of Sutherland, was 'to explain how that subculture is taken over by the child'. Cohen describes the failure to account for the *origin* of the delinquent subculture as 'a curious gap in delinquency theory.' It was to this unsolved problem that he applied himself, and initially he himself treats the subculture 'as a datum', drawing on an extensive literature to describe its traits.

Cohen presents an 'ideal-typical' or 'full-blown' picture of the delinquent subculture: variants will abound, but its essential nature remains consistent. Its nature is 'non-utilitarian, malicious and negativistic': it displays a fondness for apparently pointless stealing, allegedly 'for fun', a disregard for the object stolen combined with a preference for an object stolen to the same object lawfully obtained; it relishes vandalism, property destruc-

---

[5] 'Research in Delinquent Subcultures,' *J. Soc. Issues*, Vol. 14, No. 3, 1958, pp. 20–37. * See, for example, C. R. Shaw and H. D. McKay, *Social Factors in Juvenile Delinquency*, U.S. National Commission on Law Enforcement and Observance (1931).

tion, defiance of conventional taboos, the flouting of rules, gratuitous hostility towards non-gang peers as well as adults; its 'downright "orneriness"' seemed not only 'different from or indifferent to or even in conflict with "respectable" norms' but appeared to be dictated by its 'negative polarity' to those norms: 'The delinquent's conduct is right by the standards of his subculture precisely *because* it is wrong by the norms of the larger culture.'

The delinquent subculture is also 'versatile', and this trait emphatically excludes females, whose delinquency is largely restricted to theft and sexual waywardness: by contrast, the delinquent subculture indulges in a 'a generalised, diversified, protean "orneriness"', in which stealing looms largest but goes hand in hand with vandalism, rowdiness, trespass and truancy. There is little of the specialisation characteristic of adult gangs and 'solitary' delinquents, and even the stealing of the delinquent subculture is capable of great diversity. Another feature of the delinquent subculture is its commitment to 'short-run hedonism', 'hanging around', the dedication to the impulse of the moment: while this trait is not peculiar to the delinquent gang, belonging rather to the working-class in general, it flourishes more markedly in the delinquent subculture than elsewhere. The same applies to the insistence on 'group autonomy', or the intolerance of restraint except from informal pressures within the group. Yet 'it is not the individual delinquent but the gang that is autonomous'; it imposes its claims on members harshly enough for the breakdown of family controls to be 'as much a casualty as a cause of gang membership'.

With Short, Cohen extended analysis to include variants of 'the' delinquent subculture, which itself was re-named the 'parent male subculture', which was viewed as the progenitor of these variants rather than as *primus inter pares* among a distinct variety of subcultures. The carriers of the 'parent' subculture were held to be the small gangs and cliques of school-age adolescents diffused throughout the working class. Of three working-class variant subcultures, Cohen and Short find the 'conflict-oriented' subculture bears most resemblance to the parent subculture. Specialising in street-gang warfare, it was characterised by large membership, elaborate organisation, internal division into subgangs and external involvement in gang alliances. Significantly, they propose that more common than the 'full-blown' 'conflict' gang will be a 'form intermediate between the conflict gang and the parent subculture: a loosely organised . . . coalition of cliques with only a vague sense of corporate identity, coalescing sporadically and frequently for displays of open violence', a form which coincides exactly with Yablonsky's description of the 'near-group'. Markedly distinct is the 'drug-addict subculture', which avoids violence and prefers income-producing forms of delinquency, utilitarian insofar as is necessary for the maintenance of the addict way of life. While many were delinquent prior to addiction, and cling to the periphery of large gangs, drug-use is accompanied by a loss of status. Also, more mature, post-adolescent addict subcultures exist, with a higher degree of autonomy, to which the adolescent addict can aspire. The central pre-occupations of these 'cats'—the 'kick' and the 'hustle'— 'are in direct antithesis to the central values of the dominant culture'.[6]

Cohen and Short also distinguish a third variant subculture, that of 'semi-professional theft', which emerges in mid-adolescence when the 'parent' subculture tapers off, and a minority harden into the pursuit of theft on a less unsystematic basis: for example, stolen goods are sold as opposed to used oneself, given or thrown away, or returned. In conclusion, Cohen and Short pose the theoretical issue as follows: Are 'the patterns . . . variants of a common subculture or subcultures, *with qualitatively distinct etiologies*, or *quantitative extremes* of the common subculture, with the same variables accounting for their existence and their extremity . . . We have chosen to describe these patterns as *variants*.' The issue is still clouded, however, by the implication that involvement in the 'parent' subculture is a necessary 'breaking in' phase without which later involvement in the 'variant' subcultures is highly unlikely.

Cohen and Short's 'variants' have direct counterparts in Cloward and Ohlin's 'criminal', 'conflict' and 'retreatist' subcultures: these are viewed by Cloward and Ohlin as 'three more or less distinctive kinds of delinquent subculture' and are not seen as variants of any common subcultures. They define the delinquent subculture as a 'special category of deviant subculture' whose behaviour, if officially known, 'would be likely to be defined as

[6] H. Finestone, 'Cats, Kicks and Color', *Soc. Problems*, Vol. 5, 1957, pp. 3-13.

(delinquent) by agents of criminal justice', as opposed to the labels of conceivable delinquency frequently applied by school, church, social agencies or family groups. More crucially, 'a delinquent subculture is one in which certain forms of delinquent activity are essential requirements for the performance of the dominant roles supported by the subculture.' They exclude accordingly the study of acts of delinquency which are 'by-products of essentially lawful role-performance', e.g. student pranks getting out of hand; the often serious delinquencies of neurotic and psychotic adolescents which lack involvement in a delinquent subculture; and 'acts of delinquency by isolated individuals, *or by members of groups in which delinquent acts are not prescribed.*' There is a distinction here between the commitment-to-delinquency criterion of Cloward and Ohlin, and the commit-ment-to-counter-norms of Cohen. The one necessitates law-violation with a high degree of frequency and seriousness; the other implies delinquency of this kind in extreme cases, but accommodates deviant (as opposed to delinquent) behaviour as long as that behaviour involves diametrical opposition to the middle-class normative system. This in no sense means that the targets of Cohen's subculture must be middle-class: it is enough that the behaviour, against whatever target it is directed, is eloquent of affinities with the delinquent subculture and contrary to the dominant culture pattern.

In an attempt to sort out the normative apparatus of the delinquent subculture—in which connection terms such as 'norm', 'standard', 'value' and 'belief' are used interchangeably— Cloward and Ohlin distinguish *between* subcultures by distin-guishing between norms, values and beliefs *within* subcultures. The beliefs and values of delinquent subcultures 'are ... mobilised to support its prescriptions, which become elaborated as a set of norms for directing and controlling the behaviour of their members.' Thus the *'criminal'* subcultures *prescribe* disciplined and utilitarian forms of theft, fraud and extortion, *believe* that the world is populated by 'smart guys' and 'suckers', and *value* stealth, dexterity, wit, 'front' and the capacity to evade detection; the *'conflict'* subcultures prescribe the instrumental use of violence, see their 'turf' as surrounded by enemies, and value 'heart'; the *'retreatist'* subcultures prescribe the illicit use of drugs as a means to 'consummatory' experience, regard the world about them as populated by 'squares' and place a premium on esoteric 'kicks'. 'The integration of beliefs and values provides stability for the essential activities of the subculture'. Cloward and Ohlin emphasise that their naming of the subcultures denotes 'the principal orientation of each form of adaptation from the perspective of the dominant social order', and not necessarily the self-conceptions of members. For example, the 'cat' would reject the idea of himself as being in retreat and define himself as among the elect.

The 'Criminal' pattern allocates prestige 'to those who achieve material gain and power via avenues defined as illegitimate by the larger society.' The successful 'haul', the 'big score', is the delinquent criminal's as well as the adult criminal's image of quick success. The criminal subculture represents an apprenticeship period during which the delinquent learns his trade, comes to respect older criminals and adopt the 'right guy' as his role-model. He regards conventional-world members as 'suckers' and sees success in that world as legalised graft, corruption and 'pull', an attitude-set which neutralises the controlling effect of conventional norms. He cultivates appropriate 'connections', acquires the 'know-how' to contact 'fences' and those intermediaries such as sharp-practice lawyers, crooked policemen and shady businessmen who—by their occupation of 'half-legitimate, half-illegitimate roles'—'encourage and protect the young delinquent in a criminal way of life by giving him a jaundiced perspective on the private morality of many functionaries of conventional society.' Ultimately, if he makes the grade, the adolescent delinquent criminal becomes upwardly mobile and finds a niche in the syndicates, the 'rackets' or the more dubious unions.

'The 'Conflict' pattern is distinguished by the role-model of the 'bopper' whose key qualities are those of the successful warrior. The ideal in the fighting-gang world 'is to acquire a reputation ('rep') for toughness and destructive violence, both against other gangs and by unpredicted assaults on conventional adult world persons and property'. Great stress is laid on defence of the group and the maintenance of honour. The relationships between fighting-gang members and the adult world are 'severely attenuated, or—as the "bopper" would phrase it—"weak".' 'He views himself as isolated, and the adult world as indifferent.' Yet, the 'turf' inspired gang-warfare has led to the attachment to the worst gangs of street-gang workers as a mark of deference from a previously hostile adult world, a 'gesture of attention' which the gangs have converted into a symbol of prestige.

The 'Retreatist' pattern is not synonomous with the 'hipster' cult—which is deviant but not necessarily delinquent—but refers more stringently to those forms of adolescent drug-use that are 'supported by a subculture'. The dominant feature of the 'cat's' subculture is the theology of the 'kick', the ultimate ecstatic experience, an 'out-of-this-world' awareness of 'it', in pursuit of which drug-use is typically merged with alcohol, sex and jazz. The successful 'cat'—the role-model for the lower-class retreatist adolescent—has a lucrative 'hustle', which contrasts sharply with conventional workaday occupations; drug-peddling or pimping are both prestigeful 'hustles', the latter flavoured by an exploitative attitude towards women ('chicks'). But the hustle is secondary to the 'organising, scheduling and experiencing of the kick'. The 'cat' is at pains to differentiate himself from the world of 'squares' as sharply as possible: he is 'cool', sophisticated in clothes and unruffled in demeanour. He does not seek to impose his values on the world: rather, he seeks to detach himself from it to concentrate on achieving the success-goals of the retreatist world.

II STRUCTURAL LOCATION

In advancing any theory on crime and juvenile delinquency, the sociologist sooner or later finds himself at the mercy of the official statistics. Theorisation on delinquent subcultures is no exception, despite the fact that 'these statistics do not differentiate delinquency which represents participation in the delinquent subculture ... from delinquency which does not.'[7] Yet in locating that segment of the social system which chiefly 'carries' the delinquent subculture, 'the answer must come largely from statistics compiled by police, courts and social agencies ... (which) describe ... *samples* of the total delinquent population, not that population itself, and the samples may sometimes be grossly unrepresentative.' Yet Cohen's conclusion, 'by no means novel or startling', is that juvenile delinquency in general 'and the delinquent subculture in particular are overwhelmingly concentrated in the male, working-class sector of the juvenile population'.

[7] Cohen, op. cit., p. 37.

This proposition is perhaps the most fundamental plank of Cohen's theorisation.

Some investigators have challenged the validity of this correlation between juvenile delinquency and social class as a 'statistical artifact produced by the biases of the police and the courts'. Cohen cites Warner and Lunt, Thrasher, Wattenberg and Porterfield[8] as investigators who have all emphasised the existence of delinquency among 'over-privileged' as well as 'under-privileged' communities. Salisbury has drawn a vivid portrait of the vicious forms taken by some middle-class delinquency. Yet do these assertions demand a reversal of the essential conclusions of most research? To say that the non-delinquent is a rarity is not to say that 'the relative frequency of delinquency per child' does nor vary by social class. Other investigators (Kravaceus; Schwarz) have concluded that—if anything—analyses of court cases exaggerate the proportion of delinquents from the upper social levels. Of the 114 'under-privileged' boys in the Cambridge-Somerville Youth Study, 101 were persistent juvenile offenders, but only 40 had official records; it was conservatively estimated that the entire group committed 6,416 infractions of the law during the 5 year study period, yet only 95 of these acts became the matter for official complaint. Conceivably, the 'iceberg' or 'dark number' of undetected law-violations is proportionately higher for working-class than for middle-class boys.

Can these conclusions on the social class distribution of juvenile delinquency *in general* be applied with equal conviction to that of the delinquent subculture? While the statistics themselves do not make the distinction, many studies have separated group or gang delinquency from delinquency of other kinds. The studies of Shaw and McKay, Thrasher, Hewitt and Jenkins, Wattenberg and Balistrieri have all established that integrative—as distinct from isolative—patterns of delinquency are more frequent in lower than in upper social levels, and that this tendency becomes more pronounced the lower the socio-economic scale is descended. Popular impression, and both socio-cultural and statistical studies, combine to indicate that gang delinquency is a working-class phenomenon.

The delinquent subculture is also predominately a *male* pheno-

[8] Cohen, op. cit., pp. 37–38.

31

menon. All sources agree that male delinquency in general is at least four times as common as female delinquency. Female delinquency is also much less versatile than male delinquency: girls are chiefly limited to specialised forms of theft such as shop-lifting, sexual offences, 'ungovernability' and 'bad habits'. 'Again, the group or gang, the vehicle of the delinquent subculture and one of its statistically most manageable earmarks, is a boys' gang'. In the most massive research into gangs ever undertaken, Thrasher found that of 1,313 gangs in Chicago, only 5 or 6 were girls', and only 1 of these was organised around delinquency.[9]

In their more speculative paper on the variants of the 'parent' subculture, Cohen and Short attempt to delineate those types of working-class neighbourhood within which the 'conflict-oriented' and the 'drug-addict' subcultures are most prevalent. The 'semi-professional theft' subculture is viewed as structurally equivalent to the 'parent' subculture; that is, diffused throughout the working-class, but emerging only in late adolescence. By contrast, the 'conflict' gangs are concentrated in 'highly mobile, impoverished' working-class areas, 'characterised by a wide variety of indices of social disorganisation'. The 'addict' gangs share these milieux but, in addition, they flourish among the 'most-discriminated-against' minority groups, particularly the Negroes.[10] All three variants are seen as emerging in mid- to late-adolescence: the 'parent' subculture is logically the preserve of early- to mid-adolescence, gaining its impetus—by implication —from the school milieu, and reaching a climax about the stage of school-leaving to taper off into either variant or conformist adaptations.

For Cloward and Ohlin, delinquent gangs 'are *typically* found among adolescent males in lower-class areas of large urban centres.' They do not feel the need to prove anew that delinquent subcultures are concentrated in this social area. Their concern is to show that 'various types of delinquent subcultures can be expected to arise at different locations in the (lower-class) social structure'. Because official statistics mask the

[9] F. M. Thrasher, *The Gang* (1936).
[10] Other 'contracultural' patterns also flourish in these groups; e.g. the 'millennial' cult; the 'Black Moslems,' etc.

subcultural contexts of delinquency, by breaking down each offence into an individual law-violation unit, the evidence for this is fragmentary only. It appears from street-worker programme reports and impressionistic evidence that the various racial and ethnic groups, each at various stages of assimilation and neighbourhood organisation, differ in the kinds of subculture they support and in the degree to which they support it. For example, in New York, criminal subcultures oriented towards the 'rackets' of vice, gambling and narcotics, are most prevalent in Italian neighbourhoods, while those which are oriented towards burglary, robbery and theft predominate in areas of mixed nationality. Conflict and retreatist groups chiefly emerge in the Negro and Puerto Rican neighbourhoods.

'In the absence of contradictory information', Cloward and Ohlin see no reason to abandon the assumption that urban, lower-class, male adolescents enjoy a virtual hegemony of delinquent subcultures. 'As yet there appear to be only slight tendencies for the delinquent subcultures to diffuse outward from the inner metropolitan areas to suburban communities or smaller urban centres'. The conflict pattern displays the strongest tendencies for spreading as its relative autonomy and independence of adult connections lend it most readily to imitation. Available data suggest that, while 'delinquent subcultures sometimes arise in middle-class areas as well', the three prototype delinquent subcultures display more distinctive and highly integrated forms of organisation in the lower-class. They reiterate the rarity of girls' gangs, which—where they exist—are invariably affiliated subordinates of boys' gangs, as with the fighting gang's 'Debs'. Pre-adolescent and early-teenage gangs are usually closely related to older delinquents' gangs, to whose ranks they aspire.

Cloward and Ohlin also present a powerful argument against the notion that the greater judicial attention paid to lower-class delinquents is a mere reflection of 'class bias' and 'differential arrest rates'. Rather, it amounts to a recognition that 'delinquent subcultures represent the most costly and difficult problem for delinquency prevention and control': firstly, subcultural support implies a high degree of stability and resistance to control or change; secondly, acts of delinquency stemming from 'carriers' of delinquent subcultures are likely to recur with great frequency and seriousness; thirdly, involvement in both criminal and retreatist subcultures often presages successful adult criminal careers. The concepts of differential arrest and sentencing are— more realistically—a reflex of 'the judgment that lower-class delinquency involves greater long-run social costs—at least partly because lower-class offenders are more likely to be enmeshed in a delinquent subculture.' The isolated and the middle class offenders' delinquency is likely to be less stable, as peer supports are weak or absent: they are thus more amenable to the reformative pressures of family, community and social agencies.

III THE PROBLEMS OF ADJUSTMENT

Having described and located the delinquent subculture, Cohen seeks to account for its emergence by demonstrating that 'certain problems of adjustment tend, in consequence of the structure of American society, to occur most typically in those role sectors where the delinquent subculture is endemic.' While the existence of certain common problems of adjustment does not necessitate the emergence of the delinquent subculture, a causative linkage is highly probable if the *kinds* of problems and their *context* can be shown to adequately motivate the delinquent subculture.

Cohen sees each adolescent male as occupying a certain position in the status hierarchy. In part, he is absolutely powerless to affect that position: his 'life-chances' have created it for him. His status position is 'ascribed' insofar as it is dependent upon the status of the family into which he was born. 'To some degree . . . the position of the family in the social structure, particularly its status *vis-à-vis* other families, determines the experience and problems which *all* members of the family will encounter in the larger world.' A high degree of consensus exists on social class rankings and, although communities differ in the significance they attach to it, the husband's occupation is the most important single criterion of status. By the pre-adolescent age of 11 or 12, 'the child is learning to make the distinctions the adults about him make'. He is starting to place others, and himself, in the status hierarchy and, if he is a working-class child, he is starting life with an initial handicap.

In a democracy, however, status evaluations take place on the basis of 'achieved' as well as 'ascribed' criteria. The child's 'status universe' extends to the whole society, not—as in a caste or feudal system—simply to his own stratum or order. Apart from the evaluations the child personally makes, he is himself judged democratically 'against all comers' in terms of the same criteria, and regardless of family background. Yet to say that these criteria are uniformly applied is not to imply that the ability to *achieve* them is uniformly distributed throughout the social class system.

In effect, these criteria are derived from those norms that

> are most clearly exemplified and applied by what we shall loosely call 'middle-class' in contrast to 'working-class' people, that is, by middle-class parents, teachers, social workers, ministers and church workers . . . and, to a considerable extent, by middle-class children. Whether these norms are applied by working-class children or not, *these children cannot be indifferent to them*. They are the norms of the people who *run things* in politics, business, religion and education.

The pursuit of these norms is by no means confined to middle-class people. 'Class lines drawn in economic and occupational terms will not be homogeneous with reference to cultural beliefs and values.' 'Though we refer to them . . . as "middle-class" norms, they are really manifestations of the dominant American value system and even working-class children must come to terms with them.'

These norms are described by Cohen as a 'tempered version of the Protestant Ethic' which 'prescribed an obligation to strive, by dint of rational, ascetic, self-disciplined and independent activity, to achieve in worldly affairs. A common corollary is . . . that "success" is itself a sign of the exercise of these moral qualities.' The burden of this ethic falls overwhelmingly on the male, for whom upward mobility is geared to independent occupational achievement, while for the female it is geared to marriage with an occupationally successful male. The ethic crystallises into nine criteria; the possession of ambition; the recognition of individual responsibility; the cultivation and possession of skills; worldly asceticism; rationality; the accentuation of manners, courtesy and personality; the control of physical and verbal aggression; the pursuit of 'wholesome' recreation; and the respect for property.

If he attempts to meet these criteria, the working-class child is at a double disadvantage: firstly, his parents are—'in a gross statistical sense'—less likely than middle-class parents to embody and exemplify the standards of behaviour they imply; secondly, they are less likely than middle-class parents to train their child in the acquisition and evaluation of these qualities. Working-class parents, by middle-class standards, are not ambitious either for the job or the income which would render them 'respectable' in middle-class eyes. Their aspirations are typically to better working-class jobs: even a foremanship is rarely coveted. Also, against the middle-class 'ethic of individual responsibility' the working-class parent prefers the 'ethic of reciprocity': 'The working-class person is more dependent on and 'at home' with primary groups and avoids secondary, segmental and formal relationships more than the middle-class person.' These and other differences mean that the working-class boy who *does* aspire beyond his class generally does so *despite* his parents. The central tendency, however, is for middle-class and working-class children to be 'younger versions' of their parents. While most working-class children assimilate these norms *to some degree*, only a minority—the 'college' as distinct from the 'corner' boys—internalise them strongly enough to feel impelled to pursue the goal of middle-class membership.[11] This 'intra-class variability' means there can be no 'one-to-one correspondence between social class and value systems', but this should not obscure the definite central tendency for middle- and working-class children alike to grow up in their parents' image.

This being the case, why should the working-class child assimilate these norms *at all*? If he does so, he is likely to experience not only shame at the low social status of his family, but also mixed feelings of inferiority and resentment at the middle-class child, who enjoys the privileges of special 'connections' and of superior power and property attendant upon membership of a middle-class family. Despite the operation of the democratic ethic—which insists that all children share the awareness of choice—indifference to middle-class norms would seem to be the appropriate attitude-set for the working-class child. Yet it is difficult for the working-class child to remain indifferent to these criteria in face of the concerted pressures of the school and other

[11] W. F. Whyte, *Street Corner Society* (1957).

middle-class dominated institutions through which he is coercively socialised. The school is the principal arena where middle-class and working-class children compete for status in terms of the *same* middle-class criteria. 'The school exists to "promote", "encourage", "motivate", "stimulate", in brief, *reward* middle-class ambition and conformity to middle-class expectations.' Despite the formal accent on individualisation, the teacher cannot encourage conformity and at the same time 'refrain from condemning the non-conformist', and all the pressures on the teacher militate for the dissemination and encouragement of the dominant culture pattern: firstly, the teacher is hired, by middle-class agencies, to foster middle-class personalities, skills, character and manners; secondly, he is likely himself to be a middle-class person; thirdly, the rigours of examination syllabi impose on the teacher the need to favour the well-behaved, studious minority in his working-class classroom. However much individualisation is urged upon the teacher, examination successes are the criterion of his own worth, as well as of that of the pupil. Working-class children are most likely—due to their upbringing —to be classroom 'problems', with respect to both 'conduct' and achievement. 'Evaluated against the total range of the ability distribution' (Troyer), classroom failures—drawn disproportionately from the lower social class levels, undergo loss of self-respect, insecurity and loss of the ability to learn. It is this vicious spiral, this 'failure to achieve status in middle-class *contexts* . . . which creates the problems of adjustment to which the "parent" subculture and its variants appear to be an attempted solution.'[12]

Low achieved status is demonstrably more unpleasant than low ascribed status: it is a more direct reflection of *personal* inadequacy. Yet 'the working-class boy, particularly if his training and values be those . . . defined as working-class, is more likely than his middle-class peers to find himself at the bottom of the status hierarchy whenever he moves in a middle-class world, whether it be of adults or of children. To the degree to which he values middle-class status, either because he values the good opinion of middle-class persons, or because he has to some degree inter-

---

[12] Short (with Cohen), 'Street-Corner Groups and Patterns of Delinquency' (1961, *unpubl.*).

nalised middle-class values himself, he faces a problem of adjustment and is in the market for a "solution".'

Cloward and Ohlin make, at the outset, a distinction between the problem of adjustment and the conditions making for the emergence of delinquent norms. 'It is our view that pressures towards the formation of delinquent subcultures originate in marked discrepancies between culturally induced aspirations among lower-class youth and the possibilities of achieving them.' In order to explain these pressures towards deviance, they invoke the concept of 'anomie', or normlessness, as it was originally conceived by Durkheim. According to Durkheim, anomie resulted from a breakdown in the regulation of goals such that men's aspirations became unlimited. Durkheim's theorisation had great point for the industrial society, which 'must organise itself in such a way that it can allocate people to roles more or less on the basis of merit and endowment rather than . . . social origins, and it must provide—outside the family— the formal learning experiences that are pre-requisite to occupational achievement.' Each individual must, therefore, be motivated to find his 'natural level' in society: competition, incentives, and ambition are the means and drives by which the selective process is carried through. 'It is not enough for a few to make the race: all must be motivated to strive.' One of the principal ways of solving the incentives problem is to define success-goals as potentially available to all, regardless of race, creed and socio-economic position. Hence the upward striving of industrial 'democratic' societies, the pursuit of higher status: 'the industrial society emphasises *common* success-goals as a way of ensuring its survival'. Yet the solving of this problem creates others: unlimited aspirations, fostered to ensure cohesion, also exert intense pressures for disorder: symptomatic is the acute dissatisfaction of the members of delinquent subcultures with the prospects that life holds for them.

Merton set himself the same task as Durkheim—to account for the emergence of deviant behaviour—but revised Durkheim's formulation by asserting that 'anomie develops not because of a breakdown in the regulation of goals alone but, rather, because of a breakdown in the relationship between goals and legitimate avenues of access to them.' Merton's concept of anomie allows:

(*a*) the inclusion of the results of striving for *limited* goals when the possibilities of achieving even these is restricted. Aspirations are rarely *un*-limited: people typically aspire towards the next 'rung', the 25 per cent increase rather than a trebling of income.

(*b*) the explanation of pressures towards deviance in *normal* circumstances, not—as with Durkheim—only under critical conditions, such as economic crisis. Deviant behaviour can now be seen as stemming from *everyday* pressures, for although such crises as slump and boom do connect with rates of deviant behaviour, their effect is to exacerbate or ameliorate existing tendencies rather than to create them.

(*c*) the distinguishing between the severity of pressures towards deviance as they originate *at different points in the social structure*, for example, why lower-class rather than middle-class youth is liable to engage in extremes of law-violating behaviour. 'There is every reason to believe that persons variously located in the social structure have rather different chances of reaching success-goals, despite the prevailing ideology of equal opportunity.'

Where the desire for conventional goals has been fully internalised and where—at the same time—socially structured 'life-chances' present the slimmest opportunity of achieving them, there—most conceivably—will exist the most powerful pressures towards deviant behaviour. Logically, the social area most vulnerable to these pressures will be the lower levels of society.

To support this hypothesis, an examination of lower-class aspirations is essential. In *absolute* terms, the aspirations of upper- and middle-class people—measured *irrespective* of their present position—have been found to be consistently higher than those of the lower-class. (Hyman; Empey). Even in absolute terms, a 'significant proportion' of lower-class people exhibit a high level of aspiration. When aspirations are measured *in relation to* present position, however, it is found that the poor desire a proportionately larger increase in income than persons in higher strata. Relatively, therefore, the economic aspirations of the poor point to greater proportionate discontent in the lower-class than in the higher strata. 'If . . . lower-class persons experience relatively greater dissatisfaction with their present position and also have fewer legitimate ways of changing their status, then they should experience greater pressures towards deviant behaviour.'[13]

Yet to assert class differences in levels of aspiration does not entail the assumption that class uniformity exists as to goals. Whyte evolved his 'college'/'corner' boy distinction from the former's primary interest in 'social advancement' and the latter's in the 'local community', and this dichotomy by no means exhausts the possibilities of intra-working-class variability. Cloward and Ohlin interpret Cohen's theorisation as leaning on the assumption that many lower-class youth seek to affiliate with the middle-class. They part company with this interpretation that the crucial distinction is between upward mobility into the middle-class or relative contentment with lower-class life. They insist instead that 'many discontented lower-class youths do not wish to adopt a middle-class way of life, or to disrupt their present associations and negotiate passage into middle-class groups. The solution they seek entails the acquisition of higher position in terms of lower-class rather than middle-class criteria.' In this they are in fundamental agreement with Miller's emphasis on aspirations *within* lower-class society. (See Chapter 4).

Cloward and Ohlin believe that the lower-class youth's problems of adjustment crystallise in terms of 'money' and not 'status'—which implies the impulse for a 'change in membership group'. To support this contention, they state that whereas upper-class people rank others in terms of style of life and ancestry, and middle-class people in terms of money and morality, lower-class people rank others in terms of money alone (Warner and Lunt).[14] The aspirations of the lower-class majority towards an improvement in economic position has no necessary connection with a change in membership group. In a typology of lower-class youth by aspiration, Cloward and Ohlin distinguish four types. Types I and II are the 'college' boys, who *do* aspire either to middle-class membership alone, or to middle-class membership *and* an improvement in economic position. Type III aspires to improvement in economic position alone; Type IV aspires to

[13] Op. cit., p. 90.

[14] This is one of the weakest links in Cloward and Ohlin's chain of argument, in that no account is given to the probability that 'money' means quite different things to people at different levels of the social class system. To the middle-class person, 'money' may connote potential for conspicuous consumption; to the working-class poor, 'money' may simply mean 'security'.

neither. In correlating this typology with a typology of delinquent behaviour, Cloward and Ohlin assert that the boys to whom Cohen referred are frustrated Types I and II, whereas Cloward and Ohlin's delinquent subcultures are the preserve of Type III boys, and it is they who

> experience the greatest conflict with middle-class carriers, who not only devalue the lower-class style of life and seek to induce a desire for change in membership group, but also devalue the materialistic success-goals towards which Type III adolescents orient themselves. Type III youth . . . are looked down upon both for what they do *not* want, (i.e. the middle-class style of life) and for what they *do* want (i.e. 'crass materialism').

Type IV youth are similarly criticised not because—like Type III youth—they want the 'wrong' things, but because they are 'unmotivated'.

> Note that our hypothesis challenges the view that the school participates in producing delinquency by imposing middle-class success-goals which lower-class youth cannot achieve. Type III youth are alienated from the school because of a conflict regarding *appropriate* success-goals; this conflict simply reinforces their own definitions of criteria of success. If these youngsters subsequently become delinquent, it is chiefly because they anticipate *that legitimate channels to the goals they seek will be limited or closed.*[15]

Education is the principal avenue for upward mobility in an industrial society (Lipset and Bendix), and barriers to education amount to severe restrictions on opportunity. While education is widely valued in American society, 'it is not *equally* valued among the several social classes.' Hyman has shown the strong tendency for the proportion recommending higher education to increase 'with each upward step in the socioeconomic hierarchy'. This means that a substantial proportion of lower-class youth between the ages of 14 and 20 do *not* orient themselves towards a higher education. This is due only in part to a *cultural* devaluation of education, of the kind that Toby analysed in his comparison of the attitudes towards education of Jewish and Italian immigrants and their children. Equally crucial are simple structural barriers: many lower-class children are compelled, by socioeconomic necessity, to leave school at the minimum age. Cloward and

[15] Op. cit., p. 97.

Ohlin view lower-class attitudes towards education as essentially *adaptive*. Education is not inherently devalued: rather, expectations have been scaled down to accord with 'realistic limitations'.

For whatever reasons, the educational system is effectively blocked as a means to opportunity for most lower-class youths. Alternative routes to success-goals, such as entertainment and sport, are—if anything—even more restricted. For many lower-class youths, therefore, 'there seems no legitimate way out of poverty'. In a society which discourages high aspirations, poverty conceivably acts to immunise the poor against discontent (Durkheim). 'It is only when a system of cultural values extols, virtually above all else, certain *common* success-goals *for the population at large* while the social structure rigorously restricts or completely closes access to approved modes of reaching these goals *for a considerable part of the same population*, that deviant behaviour ensues on a large scale.' (Merton). 'Of those located in the lower reaches of the social structure, the culture makes incompatible demands. . . . The consequence of this structural inconsistency is a high rate of deviant behaviour.' These class differentials in pressures towards deviance are stronger for males than for females, and for adolescents than for younger or older persons. It is the male 'who must go into the market place', it is the adolescent who undergoes the crucial process of occupational decision-making. It is these pressures which make for the desperation and dissatisfaction so characteristic of delinquents, not simply 'inadequate socialisation' or easy acquiescence in lower-class norms. 'Delinquent subcultures represent specialised modes of adaptation to this problem of adjustment . . . The criminal and conflict . . . provide illegal avenues to success-goals. The retreatist subculture consists of . . . persons who have withdrawn from . . . defeat.'

IV THE SUBCULTURAL SOLUTION

Both sets of theorisation are in agreement that the elimination of guilt is necessary prior to full-scale participation in a delinquent subculture; that a variety of conformist responses exist as alternatives to delinquent subcultures; and that a variety of subcultures exist. The theorisation of Cohen and Short on these items is, however, radically different for the most part from that of Cloward and Ohlin.

(a) The Elimination of Guilt

To the problem of adjustment previously outlined by Cohen, the delinquent subculture is one response. Yet, even granted that the working-class boy's disenchantment with the dominant culture pattern is severe enough to provoke this response, to switch his belief in its legitimacy to a belief in that of the delinquent subculture is a costly process. The conversion to the delinquent subculture is gradual, and is likely to involve 'guilt, self-recrimination, anxiety and self-hatred', in consequence of the fact that however much our behaviour appears to conform to one set of norms, 'we often internalise more than one set of norms, each of which would dictate a different course of action in a given life-situation'; whichever course we follow, 'we fall short of the full realisations of our own expectations and must somehow cope with the residual discrepancy between those expectations and our overt behaviour'.[16]

Despite the 'clean break' which the delinquent boy appears to have made with the dominant culture pattern, its influence plausibly lingers on. The over-riding need then becomes to 'cope with' this anxiety, and this the delinquent boy achieves by the psychological mechanism known as 'reaction-formation', or 'over-reaction' against the source of aggression. By it, he seeks to maintain his defences against seduction. 'The delinquent boy . . . after all, has been socialised in a society dominated by a middle-class morality and . . . can never quite escape the blandishments of middle-class society.' 'Reaction-formation, in his case, should take the form of an "irrational", "malicious" . . . hostility towards the enemy within the gates as well as without: the *norms* of the respectable middle-class society.'

Cohen and Short later attempted to extend their use of the concept of 'reaction-formation' to accommodate certain criticisms by Sykes and Matza,[17] who objected to the notion that the delinquent boy forgoes *at any stage* his belief in the legitimacy of the dominant culture pattern. They proposed instead that a set

[16] Op. cit., p. 126.
[17] G. M. Sykes and D. Matza, 'Techniques of Neutralisation', *Amer. Sociol.*, *Rev.*, Vol. 22, 1957, pp. 664–670.

of 'techniques of neutralisation' were at hand for the delinquent boy to justify his delinquency prior to its commitment, and thus render it possible for commitment to the dominant culture pattern to be waived at the delinquent boy's convenience. Cohen and Short stressed that 'reaction-formation' was 'one of the most elementary techniques of neutralisation': moreover, it not only helped the boy to come to terms with his delinquent impulses; 'it helps to account for the nature of the delinquent behaviour itself.' More recently, however, Cohen and Short appear to be relinquishing their belief in the central importance of 'reaction-formation': '. . . This mechanism appears to be unnecessary for the explanation of the behaviour we have observed',[18] that is, lower-class gang behaviour which is not markedly 'malicious' or 'negativistic'. The implications of this retraction will be discussed in Chapter 4.

For Cloward and Ohlin, 'the process by which such persons (Type III youths) become delinquent has less to do with reaction-formation than with the selective withdrawal or qualification of sentiments supporting the legitimacy of institutional norms.' They assert that 'members of a newly emerging delinquent sub-culture must pass through a complex process of change in attitudes towards themselves, other persons and the established social order *before* such a major shift in allegiance can take place.' Among other pre-conditions, they must be freed from commitment to and belief in the legitimacy of certain aspects of the existing 'organisation of means'; they must also be able to ward off guilt and fear.

Cloward and Ohlin maintain that members of delinquent subcultures are 'alienated' from the larger society, that is, they have withdrawn their attributions of legitimacy from established social norms. Whether consciously or not, the delinquent has divined the distinction between the legitimacy and the moral validity of social norms, that is between those norms to which compliance is authoritatively demanded, and those whose pursuit is morally recommended. By this withdrawal of attributions of legitimacy to certain norms of the larger society, the delinquent is permitted to engage in law-violation without the psycho-

---

[18] Short, 'Street Corner Groups and Patterns of Delinquency' (1961, *unpubl.*).

logical 'sleight of hand' of defining such behaviour as morally desirable.

What underlies this denial of legitimacy? A common source of alienation is the failure, whether anticipated or actual, to achieve success-goals by socially approved means: where this occurs, the most significant step towards alienation 'is the attribution of the cause of failure to the social order rather than to oneself, for the way in which a person explains his failure largely determines what he will do about it.' Whereas a person blaming himself will feel pressures to improve *himself* rather than the system, a person blaming the system will be alienated from that system. By implication, self-blame supports the legitimacy of established norms.

Little is known about what conditions determine attributions of causality to internal or external sources. Henry and Short,[19] writing of determinants of the choice between suicide and homicide, postulated social status and the strength of the relational system as two crucial variables. Cloward and Ohlin suggest two other variables as instrumental in generating blame for failure on to the social system: firstly, a sense of unjust deprivation is created by the relative discrepancy between institutionally induced expectations (as distinct from aspirations) and their possibilities of achievement; secondly, the *visibility* of barriers to aspirations. The latter applies with especial force to Negroes and other non-white ethnic groups, who are daily made aware of the gap between democratic ideals and democratic practice. 'When a system is found deficient in terms of its own criteria, one becomes free not only to criticise it but to withdraw sentiments supporting it.' This perception that there are 'rules within the rules' is a recognition that democratic values divide into the 'formal' and the 'operative', and the dichotomy affects lower-class youth in general. It frequently means that the lower-class youth is frustrated in his expectations, as well as in his aspirations, in the things to which he feels *entitled* as well as those he *hopes* to achieve.

> Hard work, perseverance and honesty may lose their force as norms when there are more persons capable of meeting these criteria than there are opportunities. . . . Ultimate success is likely to involve such criteria as race, speech mannerisms, familial ties and 'connections'. Many candidates who are capable of meeting

[19] A. F. Henry and J. F. Short, Jr., *Suicide and Homicide* (1954).

the *formal* criteria cannot meet these supplementary *operative* criteria. . . . For (the emerging delinquent) the process of aliena- tion has its roots in the discrepancy between the formal criteria of evaluation that he feels he can meet, and the operative criteria which allocate limited opportunities to a surplus of eligible candidates. . . . The discrepancy between formal and operative criteria of evaluation *appears to be inherent in the organisation of a democratic society*. . . . It seems inevitable that such ideologically repudiated criteria will be used most frequently at those places in the social structure where rewards and opportunities are most scarce.

It is a commonplace that 'delinquents take especial delight in discovering hypocrisy in the operation of the established social order.' In this content, guilt and fear are still-born, and the 'techniques of neutralisation' presented by Sykes and Matza as devices for their elimination, appear more feasibly to be 'justifi- catory beliefs and values which rationalise the shift in norms as a natural response to a trying situation', although they retain their eliminatory function for delinquents who lack subcultural support.

(b) Delinquent and Alternative Responses

To Cohen, 'the working-class boy whose status is low *in middle- class terms cares* about that status. . . .' It has already been postu- lated that his problems of adjustment are chiefly *status* problems; that in a democracy one measures oneself against 'all comers' of one's own age and sex; that most children are sensitive '*to some degree* about the attitude of *any* persons with whom they are thrown into more than . . . superficial contact'. In addition, most parents want their children to be 'better off' than them, so that 'even in the working-class milieu from which he acquired his incapacity for middle-class achievement, the working-class boy may find himself at a status disadvantage against his more upwardly mobile peers.' Even in his own eyes, the working- class 'corner-boy' feels some degree of ambivalence towards middle-class, 'college-boy' criteria. All this sooner or later con- fronts him with a genuine problem of adjustment: to it partici- pation in the creation and maintenance of the delinquent sub- culture is one response. Other modes of response exist, each entailing costs and yielding gratifications of its own.

Firstly, there is desertion of the 'corner-boy' way of life for the *'college-boy'* response. This involves 'great effort and sacrifice, for the rewards are long-deferred and hard-won'. It is difficult to be a college-boy and 'run with' the corner-boys. 'Nevertheless, a certain proportion of working-class boys accept the challenge of the middle-class status system and play the status game by the middle-class rules.'[20]

Secondly, and most common, is the *'stable corner-boy'* response: an acceptance of the corner-boy way of life. While 'making the best' of the situation does not resolve corner-boy dilemmas in a largely middle-class world, it eschews the 'uncertainties and moral costs' of both college-boy and delinquent responses. Neither does it 'radically rupture good relations' with middle-class 'carriers' or involve the complete renunciation of upward mobility.

Thirdly, the *'delinquent'* response fulfils the·dual needs of those 'corner-boys' unable to revise their aspirations downwards: it removes their status-frustration 'by redefining the criteria of status so that (their) present attributes become status-giving assets' *and* it legitimises aggression against the sources of that frustration, that is, the *norms* of the respectable middle-class society. This aggression is not available for the corner-boy, who is inhibited by his continued avowal of the legitimacy of the rules in terms of which he is stigmatised. While the delinquent response is characterised by its 'explicit and wholesale repudiation of middle-class standards and the adoption of their very antithesis ... *the corner-boy culture is not specifically delinquent.*' Where it leads to delinquent behaviour, 'it does so not because non-conformity to middle-class norms *defines* conformity to corner-boy norms but because conformity to middle-class norms *interferes with* conformity to corner-boy norms.' Whereas 'the corner-boy culture does not so much repudiate the value of many middle-class achievements as it emphasises certain other values which make such achievements improbable', the delinquent subculture erects *counter*-values. 'In short, the corner-boy culture temporises with middle-class morality; the full-fledged delinquent subculture does not.'[21]

[20] For English corroboration on this score, see B. Jackson and D. Marsden, *Education and the Working-Class* (1962).
[21] Op. cit., p. 130.

By this refusal to compromise, 'the delinquent's very non-conformity to middle-class standards sets him above the most exemplary college-boy'. The more people who recognise this status, the more stable and satisfying the delinquent subculture. The delinquent system of values and way of life is most efficient, therefore, as a group solution. 'We do not suggest that joining in the creation and perpetuation of a delinquent subculture is the *only* road to delinquency.' Various motivations can lead to common adaptations: as with any social group, persons are motivated to join for by-products of membership that have nothing to do with the original 'common core' of motivation. Friendship, boredom, self-protection or ethnic loyalties could each motivate membership, yet these factors occur at all social levels, at any age and for both sexes: they are not distributed throughout the social system in a pattern correlative with the delinquent subculture and could not, therefore, be held to account for its emergence, even though they contribute to its maintenance. 'For most delinquents, delinquency would not be available as a response were it not socially legitimised and given a kind of respectability, albeit by a restricted community of fellow-travellers. . . . There is a certain chemistry in the group situation . . . which releases potentialities not otherwise visible.' This is especially true when the source of the subculture lies in status-frustration: 'Status, by definition, is a grant of respect from others', but for the delinquent boy 'status as against other children' is offered 'in the eyes of his fellow delinquents only'. Hence the 'sectarian solidarity' of the gang is strengthened by the delinquent boy's reaction-formation against *all* non-status-conferring groups whose recognition and attention he still—however latently—desires.

While Cloward and Ohlin's views differ from those of Cohen on the pressures which make for the selection of either the delinquent or the alternative responses, they are in fundamental agreement with his delineation of those responses. These differences have already been outlined, but Cloward and Ohlin probe further into the pre-requisites of a collective solution to joint problems of adjustment. Where problems are seen as due to inadequacies of the system rather than the self, Cloward and Ohlin postulate the greater likelihood that a collective, rather than an individual, adaptation will result. Self-blame—'an important index of attitudinal conformity'—pre-disposes actors to 'solitary adaptations': 'It is unlikely that they will join with others . . . for they see their adjustment problem as essentially personal.' For the alienated delinquent, however, collective support provides security, reassurance and 'needed validation for a frame of reference to which the larger society is hostile'. Provided that a subcultural solution is 'ecologically' viable, that is, there exist 'in effective interaction with one another . . . a number of actors with similar problems of adjustment' (Cohen), the delinquent subculture can emerge. Once blame for their troubles is located in the social system, and once the law-abiding adult community take punitive measures against their collective acts of deviance, the delinquents' isolation from the dominant social order is complete: they become, in Thrasher's words, a 'conflict group'.

(c) Subcultural Differentiation

While Cohen and Short described and located a variety of subcultures, they did no more than tentatively speculate about their determinants. The forces governing the emergence of the 'parent' male subculture have already been outlined. On the 'semi-professional theft' subculture, Cohen and Short claim that 'the literature is practically silent'. With respect to the 'conflict-oriented' subculture, they refer to Kobrin's[22] theorisation on differences in the degree of integration between conventional and criminal value-systems, but this line of enquiry is developed more fully by Cloward and Ohlin. In considering the 'drug-addict' subculture, Cohen and Short concentrate on reconciling the approaches of Finestone and others in Chicago and Chein and Rosenfeld[23] in New York. Finestone found 'mature' addicts to be clustered among 'the most depressed sectors of the most disadvantaged minority groups'. 'Except in a servile and unrewarding capacity', young adult males in these sectors are denied access to the dominant social order: their reaction is hypothesised as being to turn their back on the 'sober' and 'serious' activities it enjoins, and to make a virtue of 'play'—of hedonistic, irrespon-

[22] S. Kobrin, 'The Conflict of Values in Delinquency Areas', *Amer. Sociol. Rev.*, Vol. 16, 1951, pp. 653–661.

[23] I. Chein, and E. Rosenfeld, 'Juvenile Narcotics Use', *Law Contemp. Problems*, Vol. 22, 1957.

sible activity which seeks to extract the maximum reward from the 'kick' of the present moment. By contrast, Chein and Rosenfeld see the teenage drug-addicts as 'severely disturbed individuals' who suffer from a 'weak ego, an inadequately functioning superego, and inadequate masculine identification.' At about the age of 16, they shelve adult-role decision-making and take to drugs 'to reduce anxieties resulting from personal incapacity . . .' etc. Cohen and Short suggest the possibility that this kind of character structure 'occurs with exceptionally high frequency in lower-class Negro areas. A family constellation of floating, irresponsible males centring around a hard-working, over-burdened mother, is common in this segment of the Negro population', and might be expected to produce the traits ascribed to the addict's personality.

Cloward and Ohlin give the fullest treatment hitherto as to why different types of subculture develop. For the purpose of analysis, they view each individual as occupying a position on both legitimate and illegitimate opportunity structures.[24] It should not be assumed that, once a person has rejected the legitimate opportunity system, he has a set of illegitimate opportunities ready at hand. Illegitimate means, like legitimate means, are differentially available, and the goals-means discrepancy applies to both with equal validity. This has often been noted empirically without being incorporated into a theory of deviant behaviour. For example, Shaw and McKay stressed the value-systems of different areas, and Sutherland the systems of social relations that help or hinder the acquisition of these values. In his work on the professional thief, Sutherland[25] stated: 'Tutelage is given to only a few persons *selected* from the total population.' Factors other than merit and motivation affect this selection. Both criminal learning and criminal performance structures are differentially available: professional crime as a way of life is most feasible in those areas in which crime 'flourishes as a stable, indigenous institution'.

When we say that the form of delinquency . . . adopted is conditioned by the presence or absence of appropriate illegitimate

[24] R. A. Cloward, 'Illegitimate Means, Anomie and Deviant Behavior', *Amer. Sociol. Rev.*, Vol. 24, April 1959, pp. 164–176.
[25] E. H. Sutherland, *The Professional Thief* (1937).

means, we are . . . referring to crucial differences in the social organisation of various slum areas, for our hypothesis implies that the local milieu affects the delinquent's choice of a solution to his problems of adjustment. One of the principal ways . . . slum areas vary is . . . the extent to which they provide the young with alternative illegitimate routes to higher status.

Of crucial importance is the degree to which the slum milieu integrates different age-levels of offenders and the extent to which it integrates conventional and deviant values: the one indicates the need for successful criminal adult role-models to exist 'in intimate and stable association' with young delinquents before they envisage the adult criminal world as an alternative pathway to success; the other refers to Kobrin's proposition that slum areas differ in the degree to which deviant and conventional value-systems are integrated with each other. Kobrin's theorisation was anticipated in part by Sutherland's concept of 'differential group organisation' and by Whyte's rejection of Shaw and McKay's assertions that the slum was disorganised when—in many cases—it is organised on principles different from those of the conventional world. Whyte showed the integration which existed between the rackets, local politics and 'social' clubs at every level of the community in an Italian-American slum. In Kobrin's analysis, the polar types are the 'integrated' and the 'unintegrated' area. The 'integrated' area exemplifies not only links but inter-dependence between the 'carriers' of conventional and deviant values. It has institutionalised stable adult crime, and accommodates both stable learning structures and opportunity structures for the performance of criminal roles. The 'uninte-grated' area is the disorganised slum whose value-systems are incessantly ruptured by demographic upheavals. Links between the two systems, therefore, lack institutional machinery. While it is probably marked by a high rate of adult crime, this crime is unlikely to be organised and *systematic*, for 'illegal opportunity structures tend to emerge only when there are stable patterns of accommodation between the adult carriers of conventional and deviant values.'

The 'integrated' area, therefore, is the essential environment for the emergence of the 'criminal' subculture. By integrating different age-levels of offenders, it confronts the corner-boy with successful —and highly visible—adult criminal role-models. The successful banker or businessman are far more remote than the criminal from the lower-class youth's local milieu: their expertise and friendship make them more attractive than conventional role-models. Criminal subcultures also frequently incorporate different age-levels: illegitimate learning takes place—especially when support is found in the neighbourhood—even at the 'play-group' stage. The 'integrated' area also accommodates the 'fence' and the various 'middlemen' of crime. Unless the young delinquent learns how to establish relationships with them, 'possession of a stable, protected criminal style of life is effectively precluded'.

'The *content* of the delinquent subculture is (therefore) a more or less direct response to the local milieu in which it emerges. . . . The social milieu affects the nature of the deviant response *whatever the motivation and social position* (i.e., age, sex, socio-economic level) of the participants in the delinquent subculture.'[26] In an 'integrated' area, for example, even malicious- and nega-tivistic-appearing delinquency 'may represent efforts to express solidarity with the norms of the criminal world,' and is a function of 'over-conformity' to valued rules. Hence the social context of delinquency which appears 'non-utilitarian' should be closely examined: the pursuit of theft combined with disregard for the object stolen may be instrumental for learning the techniques of theft and not, as Cohen asserts, expressive of defiance generated by 'status-frustration'. But the presence of the two integrative variables makes for the social control of delinquent behaviour despite its source in illegal, rather than legal, agencies of control. The adult crime structure disciplines the delinquent into con-trolling his aggression, and channels his energies into rational role performance.

The 'unintegrated' slum area, afflicted by the transiency and instability inherent in high rates of vertical and geographical mobility, changing land-use, and massive housing projects which constantly disperse residents and reassemble 'strangers', deprives the young of both legitimate and illegitimate opportunities. 'This is not to say that crime is non-existent in such areas, but what crime there is tends to be individualistic, unorganised, petty, poorly paid and unprotected. This is the haunt of the small-time thief . . . the pimp . . . the unsophisticated "con" man. . . .' Under these conditions, 'delinquencies of juveniles tend to acquire

[26] Op. cit., p 160.

a wild, untrammelled character' (Kobrin). The joint frustrations of blocked ambitions with regard to both the legitimate and the illegitimate opportunity structures, coupled with the weakness of both conventional and deviant social controls, generates and permits the extremities of street-gang warfare. The youths are thrown back upon their own status-creating resources. 'Heart' and 'guts' are all that is needed for 'rep': skill in the manipulation of violence is less important than the simple, basic physical ability to 'take it'. 'Connections' and 'pull' are not needed for what Cloward and Ohlin term 'warrior adjustment'. As long as both opportunity structures are blocked, violence continues unchecked. Hence the diminution of violence attendant on the deference paid to such gangs by the deployment of street-club workers. 'The advent of the street-gang worker symbolises the end of social rejection and the beginning of social accommodation'. This interpretation is borne out by the *increase* in violence among gangs to which workers were *not* attached. The renewal of aggression if a worker terminates his attachment is a constant threat, *unless* members have been assimilated by the conventional opportunity system. The worker has to act as a social, not a moral, catalyst: he must create channels to legitimate opportunities. Where such channels cannot be opened up, the gang will temporise with violence only as long as the worker maintains personal liaison.

Just as the determinants of the criminal and conflict subcultures are differential access to legitimate and illegitimate opportunities, and the differential availability of illegitimate means in integrated and unintegrated areas, so the criminal and conflict subcultures operate on a selective basis themselves: both subcultures are status-conscious systems, and not every young delinquent who is motivated to join them has either the expertise or the wit to qualify for the criminal subculture, or the 'guts' and 'heart' to 'run with' a conflict group. In this situation, the retreatist subculture provides a feasible alternative for the delinquent boy who is a 'double failure'. All investigators agree that the retreatist subculture is loosely-structured, non-violent and essentially non-utilitarian: without the pressing need to defend or acquire a 'position', either by systematising an illicit way of life or by placing himself in jeopardy, the retreatist is freed to pursue the 'kick'.

While retreatism is often conceived as an isolated adaptation, stable drug-use cannot be fully explained by this kind of motivation. Affiliation with others is necessary both to acquire the technique of addiction and to ensure the continued supply of drugs. The lore and opportunities for drug-use must involve some degree of retreatist socialisation. As the 'web of associations' persists, the retreatist becomes increasingly inculcated with the norms, values and beliefs of the subculture. 'Despite these pressures towards subcultural formation . . . ties among addicts are not so solidary as . . . among criminal and conflict subcultures. Addiction is . . . an individualistic adaptation, the 'kick' is a private experience. . . .' Merton identified two factors as making for retreatism: firstly, failure to succeed by legitimate means; secondly, internalised prohibitions against the use of illegitimate means. To Cloward and Ohlin, this explanation fails to account for the fact that the great majority of adolescent drug-users have a pre-addiction history of delinquency, in particular lower-class adolescent drug-users. Cloward and Ohlin assert that 'double failure'—the failure to achieve success-goals by both legitimate and illegitimate means—supplies a motivation functionally equivalent to the possession of internalised prohibitions: failure to make use of illegitimate means amounts to the same blockage as distaste for such use. Once addiction has begun, the retreatist becomes even more isolated *vis-à-vis* the criminal and conflict subcultures than formerly. Similarly, many boys who, in late- or post-adolescence, are deprived of the conflict subculture turn to drug-use to stave off subcultural disintegration. However, while 'double failure' means an increased vulnerability to the retreatist subculture, many adolescents who experience it adopt instead the law-abiding 'corner-boy' adaptation, and revise their aspirations downwards.

V THE STABILITY OF DELINQUENT SUBCULTURES

While Cohen and Short pay scant attention to the differential persistence and stability of their 'parent' and 'variant' subcultures, they make significant assumptions about the effect of age-grading on subcultural participation. With the exception of the 'conflict-oriented' subculture—'Such gangs include a wide age range'[27]—the variant subcultures post-date immersion in the 'parent male' subculture:

> The earlier stage of this sequence (i.e. from petty, assorted delinquency to more frequent and utilitarian crime) describes what we have called the parent subculture. *Most participants in this subculture appear to drop out or to taper off after the age of sixteen or seventeen.* A minority . . . begin to differentiate themselves from their fellows, at about this age, and to move in the direction of more utilitarian, systematic, and pecuniary crime— . . . 'semi-professional theft'.[28]

Similarly, 'addiction characteristically occurs after the age of sixteen. . . .' Therefore, while the 'parent' subculture is most common, its stability is limited and its persistence slackens in mid-adolescence. The conflict-oriented subculture, which might be termed a violent caricature of the 'parent' subculture, possesses a wider age-range but is still limited to adolescence. By contrast, the 'semi-professional theft' and 'drug addict' subcultures both possess more 'mature' young adult counterparts. The greater stability of these subcultures derives principally from the stimulus provided by the role-models of the professional thief and the successful 'cat'.

Cloward and Ohlin surmise that the two most important variables affecting subcultural stability are (i) the integration of different age-levels of offenders, and (ii) integration between subcultures. Both criminal and retreatist subcultures exhibit a wide integration of different age-levels, although the criminal subculture is more integrated *internally*. By contrast, the conflict subculture draws on the narrowest age range. In addition, adults in general have no interest in the maintenance of conflict groups, and powerful pressures towards disintegration operate as adulthood approaches. Again, while the criminal and retreatist subcultures are linked on a distributor-consumer basis, neither associate themselves with the conflict subculture. Neither do conflict norms support addiction, while criminal and retreatist norms mutually stabilise their respective functions. Strongly integrated on both variables, the criminal subculture is *most* resistant to change; the more loosely organised retreatist sub-

[27] Op. cit., p. 25.
[28] Op. cit., p. 27.

culture is moderately resistant to change; the conflict subculture, antipathetic to both variables, is most unstable and most suscep-tible to change. This vulnerability has been borne out by social work experience: conflict gangs have proved amenable to street-worker intervention, while retreatist and criminal gangs have remained impervious.

In analysing patterns of change in delinquent subcultures over time, as well as between areas, Cloward and Ohlin predict that, as access to both legitimate and illegitimate means becomes increasingly restricted, the permanent residual slum population of the vast immigrations of earlier eras will increasingly engage in aggressive and violent delinquency. 'As a society changes, so does its type of crime'.[29] Further restrictions to legitimate opportunities for lower-class youth will follow the dwindling demand for manual labour and the increasing demand for formal academic qualifications as a pre-condition of white-collar employ-ment. Similarly, restrictions of access to illegitimate opportunities are already apparent due to the bureaucratisation of crime that began in the post-Prohibition era and which, by the early 1940's, had affected even the local rackets in Whyte's 'Cornerville'. This trend was accelerated by the disappearance in America of the local urban political machine, formerly a key linkage between conventional and deviant value-systems, as well as an integrative feature of slum life and a channel for social ascent. The relative impersonality of the social services which replaced local political agencies led to a sense of disruption and a loss of neighbourhood identity. Cloward and Ohlin's prognosis, therefore, is that the criminal subculture will be virtually eradicated while the retreatist and conflict subcultures proliferate.

VI CONCLUSIONS

From the foregoing exposition, it is hoped that the previously outlined major points at issue have emerged. While it is difficult to reconcile the crucial differences between the two sets of theorisation, it is equally difficult to see them as mutually exclu-sive. If Cloward and Ohlin's original set of five classes of question is recalled, however, it is apparent that real consensus exists only on question 2—that referring to structural location. In the answers

[29] Daniel Bell, *The End of Ideology.*

they give to questions 4 and 5, Cloward and Ohlin are almost alone in the field, and are vastly superior to Cohen and Short, although they had the advantage of Cohen's pioneering work. Also, in their work on subcultural differentiation, Cohen and Short—however sketchily—anticipated Cloward and Ohlin's major typology of delinquent subcultures. It is unlikely that Cohen and Short would quarrel, moreover, with the substantive work of Cloward and Ohlin on illegitimate means and intervening variables, although their theorisation cries out for further empirical research. The main differences, then, lie in the answers both sets of investigators give to questions 1 and 3, and it is here that Cloward and Ohlin appear—both semantically and structurally—to misinterpret and under-estimate the theorisation of Cohen and Short. These differences primarily centre around the question of 'aspirations' to middle-class 'status' and the concept of the 'parent' subculture.

Cloward and Ohlin, firstly, interpret Cohen's position as follows:

> Cohen . . . assumes that many lower-class youth seek to affiliate with the middle-class: 'It is a plausible assumption . . . that the working-class boy whose status is low in middle-class terms cares about that status, that this status confronts him with a genuine problem of adjustment' (Cohen: p. 129). Indeed, Cohen suggests that delinquency results when access to this goal is limited. . . . Cohen's tendency to equate high levels of aspiration among lower-class youth with an orientation towards the middle class implies that lower-class youth who are dissatisfied with their position (1) internalise middle-class values and (2) *seek to leave their class of origin* and affiliate with the carriers of middle-class values.[30]

By interpreting a desire for 'status' in 'middle-class terms' as a 'desire for a change in membership group', Cloward and Ohlin permit themselves to base their typology of lower-class youth's aspirations on the analytic distinction between 'status' and 'money', a valid distinction, but a misleading one to demolish Cohen with. As Short and Cohen have more recently pointed out:

> Status deprivation . . . by gang boys . . . does not represent deprivation as a result of an orientation towards membership in

[30] Op. cit., pp. 90–92.

the middle class . . . This is a too-limited conception of the status problems of lower-class boys. These problems are not so much associated with failure to achieve membership in the middle-class as they are with failure to achieve status *within the context of adult, middle-class dominated institutions,* such as the school . . . and economic and political institutions. . . .[31]

This point undermines Cloward and Ohlin's own theorisation, to some extent. While flatly rejecting the notion that the lower-class youth commonly aspires to middle-class membership (in which they are on very safe ground), they assert very strongly that many lower-class youths entertain a high level of aspiration. By choosing to refute Cohen in this way, however, they are forced into the position of denying that the school impinges in any way upon the lower-class youth, *whatever his aspirations,* provided those aspirations are not oriented towards membership in the middle class. This contention is demonstrably less viable than that for which they criticise Cohen.

The position taken by Cloward and Ohlin with respect to lower-class 'status-seeking' logically determines their attitude towards the concept of the 'parent' subculture.[30] After a summary which tends to parody the position of Cohen and Short that the 'parent' subculture flourishes in early- to mid-adolescence, is non-specialist and versatile, and is diffused generically throughout the working class, Cloward and Ohlin state:

> We question the validity of this point of view, for it rests upon . . . an unwarranted premise; namely, that the social milieu influences the content of subcultural solutions at some points in the age cycle but not at other points. . . . We assume that the local cultural and social structure impinges upon and modifies deviant responses from the very outset. . . . In other words . . . the content of delinquent subcultures (should be expected) to vary predictably with certain features of the milieu in which these (sub)cultures emerge.

These comments amount to far too summary a dismissal of Cohen's theorisation. One of the glaring differences between the two approaches to the whole problem of adolescent delinquency is that between Cohen's accent on early- to mid-adoles-

[31] J. F. Short, Jr., 'Street Corner Groups and Patterns of Delinquency' (1961, *unpubl.*), pp. 17–18.
[32] Op. cit., pp. 159–160.

cence and Cloward and Ohlin's emphasis—implicit throughout
—on mid- to late-adolescence. Cloward and Ohlin's criticisms
imply that adolescence is one undifferentiated phase through
which the lower-class youth moves in attitudinal stasis. Yet,
just as Cohen avowedly focusses attention on delinquent 'boys',
so Cloward and Ohlin are principally concerned with *late* adolescence. The sources on which Cohen draws for his argument are
mainly concerned with boys aged between 10 and 16, and this
tendency is emphasised by the stress he lays on child socialisation
differences between working and middle classes. One of the chief
sources on which he draws is research by Barker culled from a
questionnaire completed—in school—by 13–16-year-old boys.
The school, moreover, was an Indiana junior high school, and
this points up a conceivable source of confusion. The sources
upon which Cloward and Ohlin draw are mainly studies of late-
adolescent delinquency and late-adolescent problems. For
example, in their section on the class distribution of aspirations,
they draw heavily on a study by Hyman[33] which analysed opinions
about education by a sample of youths aged 14–20. This is not to
say that Barker's and Hyman's work would not apply to higher
or lower age-levels: it is simply to assert a difference of orientation between Cohen and Cloward and Ohlin, and this difference
crystallises around their elimination of the school as a causal
link in the generating of delinquent subcultures.

In this context, Cohen and Cloward and Ohlin appear to be
discussing—to some extent—different aspects of the same
phenomenon. It is conceivable that Cohen's theory has far more
validity than that of Cloward and Ohlin with regard to delinquent
subcultures which emerge among young, school-age adolescents
in stable, metropolitan, working-class communities and in
working-class communities in smaller urban centres; similarly,
it is conceivable that Cloward and Ohlin's theorisation has more
validity with regard to school-leaving-age and late-adolescent
delinquent subcultures in metropolitan slum areas. Perhaps, in
New York, with its huge immigrant ghettoes and grotesque
contrasts between wealth and squalor, the 'disorganised slum'
youth has little time for, and sees little point in, the school. Yet

---

[33] H. H. Hyman, 'The Value-Systems of Different Classes: A Social-Psychological
Contribution to the Analysis of Stratification' in R. Bendix and S. M. Lipset (eds.),
Class, Status and Power (1953).

Cloward and Ohlin's theory has little point for delinquent sub-cultures which emerge outside slum areas (although their theorisation on anomie and alienation has general validity). In Cohen's favour, it might be argued that the school—unlike the slum—is a universal institution: whereas types of school vary widely in the types of skills they seek to impart, they display a high degree of consensus on the value-system they both seek to impose and deploy as criteria. This value-system is that described by Cohen. Again, perhaps—in the slum—the school is an alien institution to be by-passed as quickly as possible: in this situation, the local milieu would exert its maximum influence. But in smaller urban and stable metropolitan working-class areas, the school is more likely to be regarded as a salient means, if not the principal avenue, to occupational success, as Cloward and Ohlin themselves emphasise it to be. In this situation, the school and its criteria would matter to the working-class boy, whether he seeks to 'better himself' in middle-class *or* working-class terms. As Cohen stressed, the criteria employed by the school are those of the 'people who *run things* in politics, business, religion and education', and if the working-class boy is indifferent to politics, religion and education, he is nevertheless likely to be affected by the extent to which he measures up to criteria congenial to those 'carriers' of 'middle-class values' who 'run' jobs and wages.

It is conceivable, therefore, that Cloward and Ohlin over-stated their case in dismissing the age-grading principle adopted by Cohen and Short. As Short himself has complained, Cloward and Ohlin impute to young teenagers a 'rationality' and perception about available economic opportunities more appropriate to that stage in their life-situation at which they are confronted by the harsh need for occupational decision-making. Possibly the slum child is sufficiently detached from the school milieu to achieve a realistic disenchantment with the social structure at an early age. But—until the critical school-leaving stage approaches—it is more plausible that the majority of non-slum, lower-class teenagers are too enmeshed in the school milieu to make realistic appraisals of their chances in the 'marketplace'. And, when they eventually encounter the occupational hazards of the conventional world, they will be assessed—for all but the unskilled manual occupations—by standards strongly influenced by middle-class criteria. They do not have to have middle-class 'goals' to suffer in the middle-class status 'game'.

Whatever their differences, Cohen and Cloward and Ohlin share the basic premise that:

> those values which are the core of the 'American way of life' . . . are among the major determinants of that which we stigmatise as 'pathological'. . . . The problems of adjustment to which the delinquent subculture is a response are determined, in part, by those very values which respectable society holds most sacred. The same value system, impinging upon children differentially equipped to meet it, is instrumental in generating both delinquency and respectability.

Cloward and Ohlin make much the same point:

> Delinquency is not, in the final analysis, a property of individuals or even of subcultures; it is a property of the social systems in which these individuals and groups are enmeshed. The target for preventive action, then, should be defined, not as the individual or group that exhibits the delinquent pattern, but as the social setting that gives rise to delinquency.

4

EXTENSIONS AND CRITIQUES OF SUBCULTURAL THEORISATION

IN 1957, Cohen wrote: 'The existence of delinquent subcultures has been established beyond cavil. The problem of accounting for their existence, their content and their distribution has only begun to be explored.'[1] The vigour of the criticism encountered by his work implies that this conclusion was premature. Experienced investigators, such as Miller and Yablonsky, have denied the applicability of the concept to, on the one hand, the moderately delinquent adolescent street-corner group and, on the other, the violent gang. An attempt has already been made to align these differences by suggesting (Chapter 2) that the 'gang' is neither a sufficient nor a necessary vehicle for the delinquent subculture(s). The hallmark of the delinquent subculture is the existence of a set of *counter*-norms, values and beliefs as the basis for law-violation. This conclusion is implicit in the work of Cloward and Ohlin on the retreatist subculture, which is accommodated by 'loosely structured' groups, 'not as solidary' as those carrying the criminal and conflict models. If, with Miller, we see the delinquent subculture as a simple microcosm of lower-class culture, then the term loses all value, and should be discarded. These definitional problems raise questions of the entire validity of the subcultural approach. If we concede, with Cloward and Ohlin, the centrality to delinquent subcultures of the commitment to delinquency, then we are narrowing our range

---

[1] A. K. Cohen, 'Sociological Research in Delinquent Subcultures', *Amer. J. Orthopsych.*, Vol. 27, No. 4, Oct. 1957, pp. 781–788.

considerably. These questions can best be approached in the context of considering criticisms of—and alternatives to—subcultural theorisation. In addition, recent sociological work on juvenile delinquency will be discussed for its tangential bearing on subcultural theory.

(a) 'Limiting' critiques

This term refers simply to critiques which question certain elements of subcultural theorisation, but accept the fundamental validity of the subcultural approach. Such critiques are few, as both Cohen and Cloward and Ohlin were alert to weaknesses in their chain of argument, and forestalled much criticism by employing it themselves. But Kitsuse and Dietrick, Toby and Bordua have produced criticism substantial enough to check any easy acceptance of certain stages of both sets of theory.

Kitsuse and Dietrick[2] are mainly concerned with demolishing Cohen's use of the concept of 'reaction-formation'. They assert that Cohen himself implies that the working-class boy is not sufficiently motivated to status within the middle-class system to be anything more than 'sensitive' in a minor way to failure in terms of its criteria. Cohen's use of reaction-formation assumes that the working-class boy cares sufficiently about middle-class status to be faced with a 'genuine problem of adjustment'.

> In this description of the working-class boy's perceptions of the middle-class system, the implication is clear that it is *not* that the working-class boy's aspirations are frustrated (i.e. he is motivated but unable to achieve prestigeful status in the middle-class system) but rather that he does not want to strive for status in the system, and he resents the intrusion of 'foreigners' who seek to impose upon him an irrelevant way of life.

That is, he 'opts out' or wishes to. Hence, Cohen cannot employ reaction-formation to explain the non-utilitarian, malicious and negativistic character of the delinquent subculture.

The argument of Kitsuse and Dietrick is very similar to that of Cloward and Ohlin, insofar as they both assert that the main conflict is one of appropriate success-goals, not the failure to achieve middle-class success-goals. To this we can only repeat the earlier argument that, whether the working-class boy sees

[2] J. I. Kitsuse and D. C. Dietrick, 'Delinquent Boys: A Critique', *Amer. Sociol. Rev.*, Vol. 24, No. 2, April 1959.

status in terms of his own or other-class criteria, the school as an institution affects those status-chances to a considerable degree. But Kitsuse and Dietrick further maintain that, to the working-class boy, the school is an 'irrelevant' institution, resented and held in low esteem. If this is his attitude from the outset, it is no bar to Cohen's argument. The school demands the working-class boy's attendance and—to some degree—his attention. He does not have to *believe* in it to care about his situation within it. Resentment against it as a shackling agency is conceivably more likely to spur reaction-formation than either indifference or orientation towards it. This argument, like that of Kitsuse and Dietrick, is an assertion only, but in the absence of contradictory information, it appears that Cohen's argument would be seriously weakened only if the supreme indifference of the working-class child towards the school was established.

Two subsidiary points raised by Kitsuse and Dietrick: firstly, that the 'college' boy is theoretically as ambivalent about the middle-class system as the 'delinquent boy': he should, therefore, be equally prone to a wholehearted repudiation of middle-class morality in the event of frustration. Again, this point is reiterated by Cloward and Ohlin, who assert that the thwarted 'college-boy' is the only serious candidate for Cohen's theory. This argument fails to respect the sequential priorities of Cohen's theory. Becoming a 'college' boy is just as devious and gradual a process as becoming a 'delinquent' boy. It is only when he has thoroughly tested himself against the criteria of the system, and established that he can succeed by them, that the working-class boy commits himself to the 'college-boy' response, and ceases to 'run with' the corner-boys. The decision is too costly to be taken without some inner certainty about the eventual outcome. In the event of failure, the potential 'college-boy' is just as likely to blame himself as the system, in which case he would tend to essay an isolative rather than a collective response. Secondly, Kitsuse and Dietrick assert that the gang poses for the delinquent boy the very problems of adjustment he joined it to solve, granted its hierarchical and status-conscious nature. This point, significantly, implies the concept 'double failure' so crucial to Cloward and Ohlin's conception of the retreatist subculture. It can only be added that the assets needed for status in the gang are precisely those qualities for the possession of which the boy has selected this adaptation. He is, therefore, at least competing for status on his own terms, not those of an alien system, and to the extent to which he feels 'at home' in the gang, he will reconcile himself to relatively low status within it.

Toby[3] is concerned with the limitations of subcultural theorisation rather than with any inherent weaknesses it might display. He is principally concerned with their definition of a delinquent subculture as:

> one in which delinquent behaviour is not only *required* of members but is a *central activity* of the group. A clique of hot-rodders which permitted or even encouraged members to steal accessories for their cars would not qualify as having a delinquent subculture according to the Cloward-Ohlin criteria. . . . Neither would occasional stealing engaged in by a clique of two or three boys when they needed money. Their street-corner associates did not *require* them to steal, although they did not condemn such thefts. They regarded stealing as acceptable for those willing to run the risks. Is the universe of delinquent behaviour which Cloward and Ohlin are addressing too small a portion of all American juvenile delinquency?

While preferring too restrictive a definition of the dependent variable to the usual grab-bag of heterogeneous acts thrown together under the rubric of 'delinquency', Toby suspects that gang delinquency as defined by Cloward and Ohlin amounts to less than ten per cent of the cases handled by American juvenile courts. The major question he then poses is *'whether the etiological process postulated by Cloward and Ohlin is relevant to other types of delinquency as well'*. Suppose, for example, that one crucial variable —that of excessive ecological density—is eliminated. This does not affect the social structure, but it does affect the distinctiveness of lower-class and middle-class cultures, the pressures towards deviance, the process of alienation and the nature of the collective solution that will emerge. The variable of isolation may be the critical one for both source and type of deviance. If the ecological density is reduced, so is the scale of the isolation of the social group from which the delinquent subculture is recruited. The slum in the great city packs the unskilled together; their isolation from social and physical contacts with the middle class is much

[3] Jackson Toby, 'Delinquency and Opportunity: A Critique', *Brit. J. Sociol.*, Vol. 12, No. 3, Sept. 1961.

more intense than it would be in an area of lower density, or of more mixed class composition. This is essentially the idea under-lying 'social status context' research, (see pp. 91–95). In form, an immense diversity has been noted: the structured, semi-structured and unstructured gang; the near-group; the street-corner group; the clique; 'diffuse' groups. Synonymous and overlapping categories abound, but the versatility of the 'collec-tive' response is apparent. In this situation—and whatever limits it imposes—the only feasible solution appears to be that proposed by Yinger and adopted by Cohen, and in part Cloward and Ohlin: to restrict the subcultural variable to those groupings which have created and maintained a 'contraculture' of whatever content.

A further source of concern to Toby is the insistence of Cloward and Ohlin that their explanation automatically invali-dates those offered by other theorists, while maintaining simul-taneously that '. . . the pressures that lead to deviant patterns do not necessarily determine the particular pattern of deviance that results.' Toby objects to this monopolisation of the etiology of gang delinquency: 'Cannot *different* types of motivation drive a youngster towards the *same* delinquent adaptation?' Cohen allowed for the validity of alternative theories by postulating the variety of motivations that could attract a boy to the delinquent subculture once it had emerged. In short, Toby fears 'premature closure of the motivational issue' and is willing to accept opportunity structure analysis without the cost of abandoning the complementary etiological theories. For example, Cloward and Ohlin feel that the 'inadequate socialisation' or 'social disorgani-sation' theories of Shaw and McKay are themselves inadequate due to the need to explain delinquent tendencies positively instead of 'residually' or due to the ineffectiveness of adult controls. 'Perhaps they are right when highly-structured adolescent gangs are considered. Perhaps Shaw and McKay are right when delinquent behaviour is looked at more broadly.' Toby believes that a variety of motivations can underlie even *gang* delinquency: any broader spectrum makes eclecticism essential.

Bordua[4] makes the same point, but stresses in addition the inter-relationships between the various theories, especially the richness of Miller's data for both Cohen and Cloward and Ohlin,

---

[4] D. J. Bordua, 'Sociological Theories and Their Implications for Juvenile Delinquency', *Children's Bureau Conference Report*, Vol. 2, 1960.

despite Miller's own insistence on the 'holistic' nature of 'lower-class culture'. Bordua's main aim, however, is to put recent theorisation on gang delinquency into perspective, and he selects Cloward and Ohlin in particular as proponents of a uni-dimensional analysis of gang-life, which compares badly with the diversity and thoroughness of Thrasher's classic account of the gang over thirty years ago. He regards Thrasher's work on gangs as still the best,[5] and labels his formulations the 'classical view'. In brief, Thrasher saw the gang as a development of the pre-adolescent 'play group'. Slum youngsters—'running wild' and engaging in petty, but often utilitarian delinquencies—were soon forced by the 'teeming' areas in which they lived to coalesce in-to groups in the contest for reputation, facilities, territory and protection. Weak adult and parental control allowed this situation to develop to the point where conventional world agencies were led to intervene. Some gangs acquiesced in this control: those which rejected it soon faced severer sanctions and in defying this hostility became a 'conflict' group or gang proper. Thrasher constantly stressed the 'ordinariness' of most gang behaviour, even where a gang's 'career'—beginning as a spontaneous play group—ended in adult crime. To Bordua, he conveys 'the distinctive flavour of essentially healthy boys satisfying universal needs in a weakly controlled and highly seductive environment. Compared to the deprived and driven boys of more recent formulations with their status problems, blocked opportunities . . . Thrasher describes an age of innocence indeed,' although he stressed that innocence ended when the workaday world made de-mands of the boy that gang-life had hardly equipped him to meet.

In short, Thrasher sees delinquency—in the uninhibited context of the slum—as simply *attractive* to boys; Cohen and Cloward and Ohlin see it as essentially a *reactive* process. Bordua is not entirely happy with this orientation, and criticises Cloward and Ohlin in particular for 'confusing justification and causation and equating the end with the beginning'.[6] Firstly, they insist that it is among those actually fitted for success where the sense of injustice will flourish; secondly, they state that delinquent subcultures are

---

[5] D. J. Bordua, 'A Critique of Sociological Interpretations of Gang Delinquency', in M. E. Wolfgang, L. Savitz and L. Johnston, *The Sociology of Crime and Delinquency* (1962), pp. 289–301.

[6] Op. cit., in Wolfgang *et al.*, pp. 298–301.

formed by boys who do not essentially differ in their capacity to cope with the larger institutions from other boys, and thirdly, they fail to assess the degree to which 'these gang boys are in fact *prepared* to meet the formal criteria for success'. Opportunity blockage is often the *result* of participation in gang delinquency and despisal of *actual* opportunity, as opposed to its cause. Bordua states that Cloward and Ohlin's position is diametrically opposed to that of Cohen, who states that many working-class boys are unable to meet the demands of the school and middle-class dominated institutions. While these are valid points, Bordua makes too much of them. It is fair to infer from his critique an under-estimation of the delinquent's perception of 'social hypocrisy' in the co-existence of 'formal' and 'operative' criteria. As Cloward and Ohlin state, this duality of criteria exists most visibly where there are least opportunities in relation to the number of persons capable of meeting the necessary 'formal' criteria. In this situation, it is reasonable to anticipate failure to achieve even one's expectations, and the alienative sense of injustice results. By the time an actual opportunity occurs, as Bordua insists (n., p. 300) that they do, the delinquent subculture has intervened. Moreover, the Cloward-Ohlin position separates causation and justificatory processes only analytically: in objective reality, the two concepts merge, and justification *amounts* to causation.

Bordua raises two final points: firstly, he concludes that 'there have been profound changes in the way social theorists view the processes of gang formation and persistence. These . . . derive only partially, perhaps even unimportantly, from changes in the facts to be explained.' While this implies that there is little essential difference between the 1920's and the 1960's—an assertion one would expect least of all from an American, especially after Bell's work—he follows it with the powerful secondary conclusion that: 'It seems peculiar that modern analysts have stopped assuming that 'evil' can be fun and see gang delinquency as arising only when boys are driven away from "good".' This theme is crucial to the work of Sykes and Matza, which will be discussed later.

(b) 'Extensive' critiques
This term refers to work on juvenile delinquency which paradoxically combines an explicit repudiation of the very concept of

the delinquent subculture with the supplying of evidence which can be held to support and amplify subcultural theorisation. The anthropological work of Walter Miller and the sociological theorisation of Sykes and Matza fall into this category.

Miller, as Bordua points out, is the direct inheritor of Thrasher's 'classical view'. Miller's theory is simply that lower-class group delinquency, far from representing participation in delinquent 'counter'-cultures, is the direct, intensified expression of the dominant culture pattern of the lower-class community—'a long-established, distinctively patterned tradition with an integrity of its own'.[7] This culture is characterised by a family structure typified by the female-based household, whose main trait is lack of reliance on the occupational performance of an adult male. Lower-class culture crystallises around six 'focal concerns', which Miller presents in chart form, and ranks in order of explicit attention. The 'perceived alternatives' represent polar positions, and to each concern the delinquent orients himself in either overt and/or covert, and positive and/or negative ways:

CHART OF FOCAL CONCERNS OF LOWER-CLASS CULTURE

	Perceived Alternatives	
Area	(state, quality, condition)	
1. *Trouble*: law-abiding behaviour.	law-violating behaviour.	
2. *Toughness*: physical prowess, skill; 'masculinity', fearlessness, etc.	weakness, effeminacy, timidity, ineptitude, cowardice, caution.	
3. *Smartness*: ability to outsmart, making money by 'wits'; shrewdness, adroitness in repartee.	gullibility; making money by hard work, dull-wittedness, verbal maladroitness; slowness.	
4. *Excitement*: thrill, danger; risk; change, activity.	boredom; 'deadness'; safeness; sameness, passivity.	
5. *Fate*: being 'lucky', favoured by 'fortune'.	ill-omened, being 'unlucky'.	
6. *Autonomy*: independence; freedom; external restraint, esp. superordinate authority.	dependency, 'being cared for', presence of external constraint and strong authority.	

[7] W. B. Miller, 'Lower-Class Culture as a Generating Milieu of Gang Delinquency', *J. Soc. Issues*, Vol. 14, No. 3, pp. 5–19.

Miller's set of 'focal concerns' demands full quotation as the most concise statement in the literature with which we are dealing, not so much of the elements which comprise lower-class culture, as of those elements which sociologists are talking about—often vaguely—when they seek to differentiate the 'common core' of lower-class culture from that of the middle-class. To Miller, moreover, engagement in these 'concerns' leads the adolescent into head-on clash with the larger society, whose legal code is underwritten by middle-class values. Miller holds that the lower-class delinquent has internalised lower-class culture *only*: without experiencing any ambivalence whatever towards the middle-class system, he inevitably collides with its power structure. In addition even where law-abiding routes are available, he frequently takes the short-cut illegal route to an objective simply because of the more immediate return and the 'relatively smaller investment of energy'. Miller prefers to see the delinquent gang as a variant or 'sub-type' of the prototype adolescent street-corner group. It emerges where (a) sex-role problems are most severe. Nurturance in the female-based household is a trait especially of the lower lower-class, which has emerged from the generations-old 'shaking-down process' of immigration, internal migration and vertical mobility. The lower-class adolescents' predilection for the one-sex peer group is merely a reflection of the adult disregard for the twin head family unit and corresponding preference for associations with adults of their own sex. For the adolescent, the one-sex peer group is a vehicle for the pursuit of masculine status and reassurance. (b) the degree to which the street group engages in delinquent behaviour, and 'constructs its internal status criteria around the law-violating end of the "trouble" continuum' (Bordua), varies greatly with local circumstances, e.g. presence/absence of police, rackets, youth services, church activity. In the gang proper, 'belonging' and 'status' become two additional 'focal concerns', the latter in particular involving an emphasis on 'adultness' and an aversion to 'kid's stuff'. Miller's most general answer to the question as to why a delinquent gang emerges is the attempt to 'achieve ends, states, or conditions which are valued'. 'Status' often operates as an inter-gang as well as an intra-gang objective, and this gang struggle for 'rep' exemplifies Miller's 'overt'-'covert' dichotomy: when a gang fight is 'cooled' or police intervene to forestall it, the delinquent mingles overt disgust with covert relief. Miller chastises Cohen for interpreting such delinquency as 'malicious' and 'negativistic', and asserts that it is 'positive' from the delinquents' viewpoint, as it achieves those objectives valued within the actor's most significant cultural milieu. This description of the lower-class style of life 'within its own terms' is the main virtue of Miller's position: he tells us what the lower-class culture is for, and avoids delineating its culture either as that of the middle-class manqué or as that of a pathetically inadequate, 'submerged' and fragmented cluster of 'problem' families.

The empirical strength of Miller's approach contrasts with its theoretical weaknesses. Possibly the most signal of these is his tendency to view the lower classes 'holistically' in both cultural *and* structural terms. He sees their way of life as somehow hermetically sealed from the impact of crucial middle-class dominated institutions, apart from the law. This makes his approach a social class variation of Sellin's ethnic 'culture conflict' theory, which attributed high rates of delinquency in densely-packed urban areas to the clash between native and immigrant cultures.[8] Also, while presenting an 'ideal-type' picture of the social structural characteristics and 'focal' concerns of lower-class culture, Miller is hard put to explain what Cloward and Ohlin term 'subcultural differentiation', and his slack ascription of 'variants' to local circumstances does not readily reveal exactly what local circumstances determine these variants. He also seems to over-draw the picture of the female-based household as the typical lower-class family structure. According to Bordua, only the migrant Negroes have a definite history of this form, though it is to be stressed that Miller's 'female-based' household differs from Parson's 'female-centered' household (see n., p. 22) in that one relies heavily on the female, the other on the male, for economic support. In addition, Bordua has pointed to the dangers of tautology in Miller's work: his 'focal concerns' are derived from observation of the behaviour they are designed to explain; a parallel example is that of the 'social disorganisation' theory of Shaw and McKay, the rate of delinquency in an area being the chief criterion for its 'social disorganisation' which in turn was held to account for the delinquency rate. More crucial,

[8] Thorsten, Sellin, *Culture Conflict and Crime* (1938).

Miller overlooks the many areas of similarity between the lower and middle class culture patterns. Cohen in particular emphasised the cultural heterogeneity of social classes demarcated on occupational and economic criteria. 'There is no one-to-one relationship between social class and value systems.' If Miller's view is accepted wholeheartedly, there exists great difficulty in accounting for the emergence of the 'college-boy' response, if the stigmatisation of academic success as 'effeminacy' has reached such proportions at all ages and at all levels in the lower class. In short, Miller relies upon the cultural 'apartness' of the lower class much more heavily than any other theorist. By failing to distinguish adequately between lower class norms in general and delinquent norms in particular, he is forced into the position of implying that the lower-class way of life is intrinsically law-violating. The entire lower-class is seen as a delinquent subculture, if not a delinquent contraculture.

It can hardly be held that Miller's refutation of the subcultural viewpoint is adequate. He has, rather, supplied it with an array of supportive material. The distinctiveness of lower-class and middle-class cultures is crucial to subcultural theorisation, and Miller's description of what exactly constitutes that distinctiveness surpasses in detail that of both Cohen and Cloward and Ohlin. His picture also involves, however, a shift in emphasis away from our pre-occupation with the most seriously delinquent groups to the bulk of moderately delinquent groups. Both Cohen and Cloward and Ohlin play down the delinquent potential of the 'stable corner-boy' response. Cohen implies that truancy is his most typical anti-social activity and states that the 'stable corner-boy' settles for relative contentment with the lower-class style of life. If the lower-class way of life is that described by Miller, then he is 'settling for' a career of law-violation almost as serious as that adopted by participants in delinquent subcultures. The stable corner-boy, in effect, could well be responsible for a great deal of that 90 per cent of court cases which Toby cannot see 'delinquent subcultures' accounting for. In this event, the focus of attention might well be shifted to the 'stable corner-boy' as distinct from the 'delinquent' response, as the most serious class of offenders numerically, if not criminally.

As an antidote to Walter Miller's view of the upward diffusion of lower-lower-class culture to the lower class in general, the work of S. M. Miller and F. Riessman[9] proposes that the picture so often presented by sociologists of a more or less uniform culture pattern shared in by the lower classes in general is artificial. Their view gives a new perspective to the applicability of the theories of Cohen and Cloward and Ohlin. Miller and Riessman emphasise the division of the working classes into 'working'—'regular members of the non-agricultural labour force in manual occupations'—and 'lower'—irregular working people. The working-class subculture (in the sense of sub-society) is itself stratifiable into subcultures, and should not be regarded as a homogeneous category: the irregular worker contrasts with the stable—and frequently highly mobile—fairly high income skilled workers, the semi-skilled factory operatives, the worker in varied service trades and the unskilled worker. They assert that the 'working' class subculture has more in common with that of the 'middle' class than with that of the 'lower' class: moreover, it can be seen as the fulcrum for variations within the working class as a whole.

In brief, they regard the 'stable American worker' as 'traditional, "old-fashioned", somewhat religious and patriarchal'. He insists on obedience from his children more than is the practice with middle-class parents, although middle-class parents demand conformity to certain patterns of behaviour as distinct from obedience in particular commands. 'The worker likes discipline, structure, order, organisation and directive, definite leadership, although he does not see such leadership in opposition to humane, warm, informal, personal qualities.' He is family-centred, that is, his leisure is almost totally within the kin group, and—while desiring a good standard of living—is not attracted towards the middle-class style of life 'with its accompanying concern for status and prestige.' Radical on certain economic issues, he is illiberal and authoritarian politically (Lipset), especially with respect to civil liberties and foreign policy. He is more interested in 'getting by' than 'getting ahead': his outstanding lack is education, which he desires for his children despite a feeling of alienation from teachers, schools and many middle-class dominated institutions: while suspicious of 'college' education, he values 'technical' knowledge with clear-cut goals, e.g. engineering.

[9] S. M. Miller and F. Riessman, 'The Working Class Subculture: A New View', *Soc. Problems*, Vol. 9, No. 1, Summer 1961, pp. 86–97.

Perhaps the most central determinant of his life is the striving for stability and security.

The main difference between 'stable working-class' and 'lower-class' cultures (ignoring the graduations in between) is a function of the latter group's greater proneness to 'excitement' and minimal ability to cope with insecurity. Lower-class culture is found among peoples relatively new to urban industrial life: Negroes, Puerto Ricans, transplanted Southern whites, who are discriminated against in the labour market and socio-culturally. This contradicts Walter Miller's view of the 'shaking-down' process over generations, but affirms his general description and location of lower-class culture. Miller and Riessman suggest that 'the development of the stable working-class style of life among lower-class and working-class youth might be the goal of educational and other socialising and remedial forces rather than instilling the middle-class value structure'. Instead of trying to 'bourgeoisify' delinquent lower and working-class adolescents, the accent should be placed on the best working-class values, e.g. co-operation and mutual aid rather than 'career'. The gulf between lower-class and working-class values is great, but less so than that between lower- and middle-class values.

While Miller and Riessman's 'new view' is not so new after all, either for America (e.g. Lipset) or Britain (e.g. Zweig), it applies a necessary corrective to over-simplified approaches to delinquency and social class. While Cohen specified the intra-variability of working-class culture, he did not go into detail about such differences. While Cloward and Ohlin concentrated on slum milieux, Miller tends to generalise the impact of 'lower-class culture' to '40–60 per cent of Americans'. Subcultural theorisation must come to terms with the considerable stratification that exists within the working class; if the term 'juvenile delinquency' means little, the unqualified use of 'working class' means even less.

The main limitation of the work of Sykes and Matza[10] is, indeed, this vague reliance on the term 'juvenile delinquency'. They reject the idea of the delinquent subculture as 'a system of values that represents an inversion of the values held by respectable, law-abiding society,' and claim that this image of delinquency

[10] G. M. Sykes and D. Matza, 'Techniques of Neutralisation: A Theory of Delinquency', *Amer. Sociol. Rev.*, Vol. 22, No. 6, Dec. 1957, pp. 664–670.

as based on 'competing' or 'countervailing' values has serious defects. They argue that if the delinquent subculture in which the delinquent viewed his behaviour as 'morally correct' in fact existed, he would exhibit no feelings of guilt or shame at detection and confinement. The major reaction would be, rather, that of the conscientious objector, the nuclear disarmer or the outraged religious minority group. Yet a great deal of evidence suggests that delinquents *do* experience a sense of guilt or shame, and that this is not 'put on' to appease authorities. Secondly, 'the juvenile delinquent frequently accords admiration and respect to law-abiding persons', in particular the 'really honest' person. Hence, 'while supposedly thoroughly committed to the deviant system of the delinquent subculture, he would appear to recognise the moral validity of the dominant normative system in many instances'. Thirdly, 'juvenile delinquents often draw a sharp line between those who can be victimised and those who cannot': the selection of targets is often limited by variables of kinship, ethnic group, social class, age, sex, etc. Fourthly, 'it is doubtful if many juvenile delinquents are totally immune from the demands for conformity made by the dominant social order.' Sykes and Matza hold that the greater probability is that the child inter-nalises these demands for conformity, but can *neutralise* these demands when appropriate circumstances arise, and the ways in which he accomplishes this neutralisation form the major part of the content of the delinquent 'learning process' so central to Sutherland's notion of 'differential association'. This is not to say that the delinquent denies the validity of these demands for conformity, and substitutes a new normative system for them. 'Techniques of neutralisation' provide—in advance of deviant behaviour—a psychological 'get-out' whereby the delinquent evades the delinquency issue. 'Somehow, the demands for con-formity must be met and answered: they cannot be ignored as part of an alien system of norms and values.'

In brief, Sykes and Matza doubt the subcultural process. Yet why do delinquents violate the laws to which they conform and in which they believe outside the operation of their own delin-quency? The enabling process is a function of the rarity with which social norms are 'categorical imperatives', appearing instead as 'qualified guides for action', limited in their applicability in terms of time, place, person and social circumstances. Marked by 'flexibility', the rules are not felt to be binding under all conditions. In criminal law, this 'flexibility' appears in the guise of 'mitigating circumstances', by which the offender avoids *moral* condemnation if it can be shown that *criminal* intent was absent. Sykes and Matza argue 'that much delinquency is based on what is essentially an unrecognised extension of defences to crimes in the form of justifications for deviance that are seen as valid by the delinquent but not by the legal system or society at large.' Unlike the mechanisms of rationalisation, which amount to *ex post facto* justification, 'techniques of neutralisation' precede delinquent behaviour and render it possible. Violations are thus seen as 'acceptable' rather than 'right', and the delinquent, far from representing radical opposition to law-abiding society, appears rather as an 'apologetic failure'.

Five major 'techniques' are proposed by Sykes and Matza: (*a*) the denial of responsibility: the delinquent sees himself as more acted upon than acting. He approaches a 'billiard-ball' self-concept, seeing himself as helplessly propelled into delinquency by forces beyond his control. Society is 'stumbled against' rather than 'kicked'. The delinquent also displays an acute awareness of the motivation ascribed to him by social workers, etc., as stemming from a 'poor home', a 'slum background', 'bad companions'. By seeing himself as more 'sinned against than sinning', 'the delinquent prepares the way for deviance from the dominant normative system without the necessity of a frontal assault upon the norms themselves'; (*b*) the denial of injury: the delinquent makes the distinction—again enshrined in the legal code—between acts wrong in themselves and acts which are illegal but not immoral. A great deal depends on the harm inflicted on persons rather than property: e.g. vandalism for 'fun'; auto theft for 'joy-rides'. (*c*) denial of the victim: even if the delinquent both accepts responsibility for, and recognises the consequences of his act, he may frequently assert that 'the injury is not wrong in the light of the circumstances'. In a reversal of roles, the delinquent becomes the avenger, the victim the wrong-doer, e.g. assaults on minority groups, vandalism at school. This indulgence in acts defined as *mala prohibita* as distinct from *mala in se* is enhanced when the victim is abstract and preferably *at a distance from the delinquent*. Diminished awareness of the victim additionally weakens internalised controls. (*d*) condemnation of the condemners: by concentrating attention on the 'corrupt', 'stupid' or 'disciiminatory' practices of police, school or society at large, the delinquent shifts the focus of attention from his own delinquent act to the motives and behaviour of those who condemn his law-violation. (*e*) appeal to higher loyalties: the delinquent sees himself in the dilemma of divided loyalties, and attributes his behaviour to a reluctant sacrifice of the demands of the larger society for those of the smaller social groups to which he belongs. Hence 'deviation from certain norms may occur not because the norms are rejected but because other norms . . . are accorded precedence'. Sykes and Matza see these 'techniques' exemplified in the typically delinquent phrases: 'I didn't mean it'—'I didn't really hurt anybody'—'They had it coming to them'—'Everybody's picking on me'—and 'I didn't do it for myself'. 'These slogans and their variants *prepare* the juvenile for delinquent acts, but they represent tangential . . . blows at the dominant normative system rather than the creation of an opposing ideology', and are extensions of patterns of thought already prevalent rather than radically new departures.

What Sykes and Matza signally fail to achieve in this paper is an explanation of why the *need* for these techniques is so pressing at the lower end of the social structure. They fail to show that the distribution of such need is correlative with the social class distribution of juvenile delinquency. Their techniques are available to all: but who needs them most, and why?

Sykes and Matza[11] feel that the over-riding need is best explained in answering the question: 'What makes delinquency attractive in the first place?' They view former answers to this question as bedevilled by the assumption that the delinquent is a *deviant*, that is, however commonplace the pressures that drive him to deviance, his ultimate stance is one of opposition to the dominant social order, i.e. the world of the middle class. They assert instead that (a) the values behind much juvenile delinquency are far less deviant than is commonly supposed; (b) this faulty picture is due to gross over-simplification of the middle-class value system.

The vast majority of accounts of juvenile delinquency and its underlying values agree in substance, if not in interpretation,

[11] D. Matza and G. M. Sykes, 'Delinquency and Subterranean Values', *Amer. Sociol. Rev.*, Vol. 26, No. 5, pp. 712–719.

that three themes recur with startling regularity: delinquents are deeply immersed in a restless search for excitement, thrills or kicks'; commonly exhibit a disdain for 'getting on' in the realm of work; and equate aggression—whether verbal or physical—with virility and toughness. In courting danger and provoking authority, the delinquent 'is not simply enduring hazards; he is also creating hazards, in a deliberate attempt to *manufacture* excitement.' Neither does his disdain for work entail a disdain for money: on the contrary, the 'big score' is the delinquent's goal, and he sees illegal means as his only way of achieving it. Also, the concept of reaching manhood via an ability to 'take it' and 'hand it out' is a familiar one to delinquents, and does not necessarily involve the extremities of street gang warfare. This cluster of values, far from denoting the delinquent's apartness from the conventional world, connote his adherence to it.

The emphasis on daring; the rejection of the prosaic discipline of work; the emphasis on luxury and conspicuous consumption; the respect paid to manhood demonstrated by force: all find their counterpart in the values of Veblen's leisured elite. Only the *mode* of expression—delinquency—is unfamiliar. 'The values are obscured by their context', e.g. daring, if anti-social, is seen primarily as an act of defiance, not an act of courage.[12] Yet all these values have their counterparts in the dominant social order: the 'stag' party, board-room cynicism, fiercely competitive sports serve as parallels. More specifically, however, 'the values of a leisure class seem to lie behind much delinquent activity'. Sykes and Matza see adolescents in general and delinquents in particular as the 'last leisure class', and assert that 'in our haste to create a standard from which deviance can be measured, we have reduced the value-system of the whole society to that of the middle-class.' They prefer to view class value systems on the model of the 'distribution of frequencies' rather than as 'distinct groupings of specific values unique to the social class in which they are (allegedly) found', that is: 'Most values . . . appear in most social classes; the social classes differ, however, in the frequency with which the values appear'. Moreover, all classes embrace certain 'subterranean' values—values which are in conflict or even contradiction with other deeply held values, but

[12] Cf. Merton's comment on in-group virtues and out-group vices: 'I am daring; you are reckless; he is delinquent.'

which are still recognised and accepted by many: these contradictory values may co-exist with conformist values within a single individual 'and give rise to profound feelings of ambivalence in many areas of life.' They are 'deviant' values only insofar as they represent private as opposed to public morality. These values are generally held in abeyance until appropriate circumstances—sports, holidays, recreation—are present, but 'most societies provide room for . . . a sort of periodic anomie, in which thrill-seeking is allowed to emerge'. Gambling, night-clubbing, the 'kicking over the traces' of the businessman's conventions, all reflect the espousal of subterranean values 'that now often exist side by side with the values of security, routinisation' and workaday stability. In expressing these values, 'it is obvious that something more than the delinquent's sense of appropriateness is required, but . . . in many cases the delinquent suffers from bad timing'. Neither can the dominant society be viewed as unquestioningly committed to the Protestant ethic of 'hard work': Riesman's 'inside-dopester', Whyte's 'organisation man', Mills' 'fixer' are all concepts undermining the Weberian sociologists' affirmation of *the* work values of society. In what Sykes and Matza term the 'compromise between the Protestant Ethic and a Leisure ethic', the delinquent appears 'much more in step with his times'. And if he pushes such an ethic to its logical conclusion in a way that most of society's members might not willingly do, 'he has not necessarily moved into a new realm of values. . . . 'Via books, movies, TV, and magazines, and via aggrandisement of the profit-motive, the dominant society exhibits a widespread taste for violence and legitimises the ruthlessness inherent in fortune-making. Not only do the mass media frequently act as vehicles for the dissemination of criminal techniques: 'there are numerous examples of the acceptance of aggression and violence on the part of the dominant social order', viz. the glorification of armed combat skills, the punitive aspects of much industrial conflict and the actual treatment of delinquents themselves by the police. In brief, 'the delinquent may not stand as an alien in the body of society, but may represent instead a dangerous reflection or caricature'. Far from erecting a set of counter-values, the delinquent shares the subterranean values of society and this very adherence binds him to the dominant social order. Hence the celerity with which he 'reforms' in many cases as adulthood approaches. To the objection that—if this were the case—much juvenile behaviour other than simply delinquent behaviour would be analysed as an extension of the adult world rather than as a product of a distinctly adolescent subculture, Sykes and Matza reply that this is 'precisely their thesis'.

In the weakest part of their argument, Sykes and Matza admit that the attractiveness of delinquency—and the 'techniques of neutralisation' which render it possible as modes of behaviour—applies with equal force to adolescents 'at any class level, for they move in a limbo between earlier parental domination and future integration with the social structure through the bonds of work and marriage'. They therefore postulate that 'insofar as these (subterranean) values do lie behind delinquency . . . delinquent behaviour (prevails) among all adolescents rather than those confined to the lower class'. In support of this classless orientation, they adduce from a minimal amount of data that delinquency occurs frequently at upper- and middle-class levels and assert that the degree to which this is true correspondingly undermines theorisation based upon the structural location of most delinquency in the adolescent, urban male segment of the working classes. They acknowledge the failure of their propositions to account for the social class distribution of delinquent behaviour, and the degrees and types of delinquent behaviour which commonly exist as patterned variations. Neither do they account for sex differentials, and—by their cursory dismissal of the concept of the delinquent subculture—they are forced into the position of focussing their attention on the vague, undifferentiated mass of 'much juvenile delinquency', though they state that 'when such values are coupled with frustrations and resentments (this is more than . . . being deprived in socio-economic terms) . . . leisure values are typically converted into delinquent behaviour.' Here they almost come full circle to the theorisation of Cohen in particular, having added another aspect—leisure values—to his picture of 'the act of conformity as the source of deviance'. In fact, they avoid this similarity principally by denying the overwhelming concentration of delinquency in the lower class, the weakest point of their thesis, and that which they base on *absence* of evidence. As Cohen and Cressey[13] have reiterated,

[13] Cohen, op. cit., pp. 36–44. Cressey, see ref., p. 96.

it has yet to be shown that the official statistics give a distorted picture, as distinct from an incomplete one. Sykes and Matza also fail to develop their own implication that there exist considerable differences in the distribution of leisure among adolescents, and its differential availability will make for variations in impact on their value systems. The adolescents' is a temporary leisure 'by sufferance rather than by virtue of a permanent aristocratic right'. It is also an 'anticipatory' leisure, a period of freedom from the demands of self-support, and the extent to which they are free from demands for self-support must be assessed alongside their involvement in school, commitment to the demands of deferred gratification and 'career-orientated schedules', and the facilities available for leisure as opposed to mere idleness. There are, in fact, 'light-years' between the cultivated gentleman of leisure and the street-corner 'layabout', and Sykes and Matza tend to over-draw the comparison. Yet they rightly stress that 'we stand to learn more about juvenile delinquency by exploring the delinquent's similarity to society rather than his dissimilarity', and their formulation that 'the delinquent's values are the subterranean values of a society which is placing increasing emphasis on leisure' helps to redress the balance between 'attraction' and 'reaction' theories of delinquency which Bordua claimed had been lost since Thrasher.

The attractiveness of delinquency, then, is a missing component in subcultural theorisation, which connotes an almost exclusively harsh 'world-view' on the part of delinquents in general, and members of delinquent subcultures in particular. Amid the concentration of analyses of the aggression and frustration of delinquents, the signal absence of any reference to humour, for example, implies an over-readiness to interpret even genuine 'fun' as 'malice' and even genuine 'wit' as 'front'. Sykes and Matza's theory—although inadequate on many levels—does suggest that the conventional view of delinquency, and especially group delinquency, as springing from 'boredom' is not altogether a perversion of the truth. What they fail to pursue systematically is the differential availability of leisure to adolescents by social class, and the corollary existence of clear-cut leisure goals—as distinct from 'work' goals—to which, again, there is differential access by social class. The leisure-goals of thrill-seeking, violence and romance are connected with but quite distinct from the work-goals crystallising around jobs, income and status. While, as Sykes and Matza have conveyed, these leisure goals—whether pursued discreetly or not—are common to adolescent and adult age-levels, the adolescent is freer to pursue them to the extent to which he is free from adult responsibilities. Also, while adolescents at all class-levels embrace them—hence the fostering of 'youth culture' and the commercialised creation of the 'cult of adolescence'—the upper- and lower-class adolescent is freer than his middle-class and middle-class oriented counterpart to pursue them. The commonplace parallel between the behaviour of the 'playboy' and the 'delinquent' is not entirely satirical. Both are freed from the onus of adult commitments and from the career-mindedness of middle- and working-class 'college-boys'. The celerity with which upper-class adolescents imitate the more expressive modes of behaviour of lower-class adolescents, such as dance and pop-music trends, is eloquent of their joint involvement in the pursuit of leisure goals common to both class-levels on a uni-generational basis. Yet the lower-class adolescent does not share the apparatus with which to utilise leisure possessed by the upper-class adolescent: he lacks the fast car, the *savoir faire*, the surplus 'spending' money with which to indulge his leisure inclinations. In short, the leisure-goals for which the lower-class boy is most available are precisely those to which he most lacks access. The search for avenues to leisure-goals has implications not only for behaviour in which delinquency is the central thrill-seeking element (Sykes and Matza), but also for much behaviour which 'spills over' into delinquency. The lower-class adolescent experiences a double motivation towards delinquency if he is frustrated both in the sphere of work success-goals and in the realm of leisure success-goals. The middle-class dominated youth agency is seen as a barrier to the pursuit of leisure-goals in much the same way as the occupational opportunity structure restricts job-potential. The channels for the expression of 'subterranean' values are not available for the lower-class adolescent as they are for the conventional-world adult. The lower-class delinquent is also likely to view 'excitement' over competitive sports, the family car, gadgets and cultural media as distinctly 'tame'. As Sykes and Matza note, he is pressurised into the 'manufacture' of excitement: he overcomes the constrictions of his milieu by challenging those constrictions. The distinctive content of such behaviour as 'joy-riding', 'doing a ton', fighting and generally 'raising hell' by rowdyism and 'disturbing the peace' is plausibly explained as much by the official proscription of such behaviour as by any inherent magic it may possess. Seeking out means to express 'subterranean' values in the pursuit of leisure-goals implies an element of *dual* frustration to the maintenance of delinquent subcultures, but also applies more generally to 'fringe' delinquency which emerges as a by-product of thrill-seeking adolescent behaviour.

A further source of support for the view that 'generational' and 'social class' pressures combine in the etiology of delinquency in general, and delinquent subcultures in particular, is the work of Bloch and Niederhoffer.[14] They see the gang arising in the attempt to fill the social structural gap in our society between childhood and adulthood. They stress that age-graded position —not class—is crucial, and view the gang as a 'classless' phenomenon whose function is to create and maintain a set of status criteria in response to the inability of adolescents to gain access to the rights and privileges of adults. It is the principal example of a theory which hinges round a single problem of adjustment, and fails to deal with the content, location, varieties and persistence of delinquent gang behaviour. Moreover, Bloch and Niederhoffer fail to draw the distinction between 'manhood' and 'adulthood'. The delinquent's equation of virility, toughness and masculinity is not to be equated with a desire for adult status. The delinquent commonly displays an aversion to adulthood in general, and—more universally—this finds intense expression in the 'teenage' cult. Far from embodying masculinity (or femininity), the adult is far more frequently and typically seen by the adolescent, whether delinquent or non-delinquent, as a person who has been *robbed* of these qualities by the burdens of jobs, family responsibilities and the routinisation of life in general. Far from desiring adulthood, the adolescent frequently seeks to *postpone* its onset. Adults are typically viewed as 'dead', and—with the exception of certain charismatic 'idols'—the adolescent sees the life-enhancing qualities of masculinity and femininity as personified in teenagers themselves. This view of adulthood as incompatible with rather than epitomising 'manhood' gives a peculiarly desperate edge to the lower-class male's frustrations in the realm

[14] *The Gang: A Study in Adolescent Behavior* (1958).

of leisure, for he is at best ambivalent towards the imminent restrictions of a fast-approaching adulthood. He is in no doubt as to the inevitability of adult 'status': he views it with mixed feelings and seeks, rather, to defer its particular set of gratifications as long as possible. He invariably succumbs to the adult role before he is prepared for it ideally, but—from his point of view—the social pressures which impose it upon him are too strong, rather than too weak.

(c) 'Applied' validation

Compared with the wealth of data and speculation supplied by the searching critiques of investigators who are disinclined to accept the very concept of the delinquent subculture, studies which have been applied the concept in research have produced relatively 'thin' supportive material and some data which appear at odds with the concept of the delinquent sub-culture itself. Polsky[15] has described the status ranking *within* a delinquent subculture, although his observations took place in the highly restricted setting of a correctional institution based on the 'cottage' model, and can only doubtfully be generalised to delinquent subcultures at large. The pre-occupation with status within the subculture is, however, remarkable: in 'Cottage 6', the 'top clique' dominated the 'small crowd' and 'the bushboys' with an almost despotic command. Polsky views the authoritarian expectations of all echelons in the subculture as the principal barrier to conventional-world adjustment and the relinquishing of aggression.

In a study of subcultural differentiation, Spergel[16] found it necessary to subdivide the 'criminal' subculture into 'racket' and 'theft' adaptations. He also conceived 'the drug addict pattern of the post-gang adolescent as a sub-type for *each* of the delinquent subcultures.' The 'theft' adaptation appears to be very similar to that envisaged by Cohen and Short as the 'semi-professional theft' subculture, and arises in areas with 'partial legitimate and illegitimate opportunities'. With some overlapping—that is, with the 'polar type' of area a rarity—each area's delinquents generally

---

[15] H. Polsky, 'Changing Delinquent Subcultures: A Social Psychological Approach', *Soc. Work*, Vol. 4, No. 4, Oct. 1959, pp. 3–15.

[16] I. Spergel, 'An Exploratory Research in Delinquent Subcultures', *Soc. Serv. Rev.*, Vol. 35, No. 1, March 1961, pp. 33–47.

and consistently exemplified their deduced characteristics. Delinquents from the 'theft' subculture area had the highest incidence of 'joy-riding', car-theft and burglary; the 'racket' area displayed moderate incidence of car-theft; the 'conflict' area very little. Informal interviews and the administration of a 19–item 'value-norm index' questionnaire revealed that 'racket' area delinquents displayed the most extreme criminal value orientation: 73 per cent of their total response as compared with 46 per cent of 'conflict' and 47 per cent of 'theft' subculture 'carriers' responses indicated 'illegitimate orientations'. Of 'racket' youngsters, 9 out of 10 quoted 'connections' as most needed to 'get ahead' and education as least needed. By contrast, 7 out of 10 youngsters in 'theft' and 'conflict' subcultures placed education first and 'ability' second. Spergel stresses the antithetical qualities of education and 'connections' for 'racket'-oriented youths. 'Theft' and 'conflict' delinquents seemed to share the priority accorded education by the dominant social order, despite the fact that they left school at the minimum age. Delinquents in each area had higher income aspirations than non-delinquents, though the result was reversed when expectations of actual income were considered. Expectation responses correlated closely with actual existing opportunities. Addicts—who were generally post-delinquents—had lower income aspirations than delinquents of all subcultures. Spergel's evidence seems to confirm the theorisation of Cloward and Ohlin on subcultural differentiation, and his sub-division of the 'criminal' subculture seems justified. He is silent, however, on the implications for Cloward and Ohlin's theorisation of the 'conflict' and 'theft' delinquents' predilection for education. The disparity between the delinquents' expectations and aspirations is powerful supportive evidence for their utilisation of the concepts of anomie and alienation, although Spergel is vague about the ages of his respondents.

Kobrin's study[17] of an adolescent street corner group in Chicago (part of the huge Chicago University Youth Studies Programme) concentrates on group structure and chronological 'career' rather than aspirations, attitudes and values. The 'Eagles' were a single 16–member adolescent group in an 'ethnic' working-class

[17] S. Kobrin, 'Sociological Aspects of the Development of a Street Corner Group', *Amer. J. Orthopsych.*, Vol. 31, No. 4, Oct. 1961, pp. 685–702.

neighbourhood. The behaviour of the Eagles was a reflection of neighbourhood street life. Five elements predominated: 'a conscious flouting of adult authority in general, and conventional behaviour in particular'; 'readiness for physical combat'; 'rejection of the discipline of school'; 'a tendency towards sexual aggression'; and 'delinquency itself'. The character of this delinquency was 'moderate', and the higher a group was placed in the status hierarchy, the more moderate its pattern of delinquency became. Kobrin[18] sees the street corner group as the natural vehicle via which the lower-class male adolescent works out one of his principal problems of adolescent development: 'the management of dependency needs', which springs from the lower-class parental habit of granting the preadolescent and early adolescent male the autonomy he demands at that stage; the parallel problem for the middle-class child is 'the establishment of independence', for the middle-class parent is less willing to concede the autonomy demanded by the early adolescent. Kobrin located the five future core members of the Eagles at the age of 9–10 due to their troublesome reputation at school, community and social agency levels alike. Only one of the group gave indications of emotional disturbance or unstable family background: by the age of 12–13, they had merged with a rival group to form the Eagles, with 16 members at this stage. Psychiatric assessment revealed that the two non-delinquent members and the four most persistently delinquent members were 'severely' and 'moderately severely' disturbed emotionally. The core of the group—'transient delinquents'—were mostly emotionally stable. Though Baittle[19] terms the Eagles a delinquent subculture, Kobrin nowhere implies that this group corresponds to this description. The Eagles appear to be the embodiment of the 'stable corner-boy' response. To what extent this adaptation was a function of the presence of a detached worker can be assessed from the fact that 'the Eagles suffered a decline of influence among the more delinquency-prone boys of the neighbourhood. . . . One year after the re-orientation of the Eagles, several boys affiliated with it and withdrew at once, expressing disgust at its moderation and

[18] S. Kobrin, 'The Impact of Cultural Factors on Selected Problems of Adolescent Development in the Middle and Lower Class', *Amer. J. Orthopsych.*, Vol. 32, No. 3, April 1962, pp. 387–390.

[19] B. Baittle, 'Psychiatric Aspects of the Development of a Street Corner Group,' *Amer. J. Orthopsych.*, Vol. 31, No. 4, Oct. 1961, pp. 703–712.

disparaging its leaders' masculinity.' Yet the Eagles, prior to reformation, indulged in such 'moderate' delinquency as shop-lifting, larceny, strong-arm robbery of other teenagers, occasional burglary, and vandalism directed against the school and settle-ment houses, apart from assaults arising from gang conflicts and the sexual delinquency of the 'gang shag' with prostitutes from a nearby 'vice' district (the local girls were protected by rigorous separation of the sexes on the ground of 'ethnic subculture demands'—presumably Italian). The versatility is the hall-mark of Cohen's 'parent male' subculture, and street worker interven-tion at this stage seems to have effected a conformist adaptation. At the age of 16, the Eagles were near disintegration, leaving three 'loners' still delinquency-prone.

In further preliminary reports on the Chicago Youth Studies Programme, Short[20]—and Strodtbeck[21]—are principally concerned with probing the norms and values underlying full-fledged delinquent subcultures, mainly of the 'conflict-oriented' type, and mainly late-adolescent Negro. Their data give good ground for the view that 'the solutions . . . provided by delinquent subcultures are primarily *status* rewarding rather than economi-cally rewarding. . . .' They also assert that 'opportunity structure theory places too great a burden on the rational calculation of future economic opportunities. The formation of gangs begins at the pre-teen level when economic opportunities have little salience or reality for youngsters'. This does not in itself invalidate Cloward and Ohlin's theorisation, but limits its applicability in ways previously suggested. Cloward and Ohlin themselves lay great stress on the fact that 'conflict' delinquents are thrown back 'upon their own status resources'. This was in part a self-contradictory assertion, however, and Short concentrates on detailing the status pre-occupations of gang boys. Their material reaffirms the status potential as distinct from the economic potential of attachment to a gang of detached workers. They also describe the ways in which gang leaders are constantly beset by status problems. Short also emphasises the tremendous variety in structure of the groups which 'carry' delinquent subcultures,

---

[20] Short, op. cit.
[21] J. F. Short, Jr., and F. L. Strodtbeck, 'The Response of Gang Leaders to Status Threats: An Observation on Group Process and Delinquent Behavior,' *Amer. J. Sociol.*, Vol. 68, No. 5. March 1963, pp. 571-579.

and criticises Yablonsky's assumption that absence of rigid hierarchy and strict membership undermines subcultural theorisation. Such variety is, rather, a function of ecological and demographic variability, which operate as 'limiting' factors on the nature of the 'collective' response.[22] Research by Jansyn[23] has shown that gang boys vary their estimates of membership in 'relation to similar conditions and questions' and predictably vary their assessments of group size according to circumstance. But gang membership tends to be 'fluid', and leaders are not 'coercive authoritarians' and do not maintain their leadership by 'aggressive dominance-seeking', a conclusion that suggests Polsky's 'cottage' autocracy was a reflex of institutionalisation.

The functions of the street corner group are Short's primary concern. Jansyn's work in particular has shown that 'delinquent behaviour, on both an individual and a group basis, served to increase the solidarity of the group and that group leadership and membership varied according to specific group goals . . . implemented at a given time.' The idea that the group and delinquency are mutually stabilising forces is further borne out by the changes in attitude revealed by responses of lower-class Negro gang boys to questions designed to elicit their evaluations of 'middle-class images'. Individually, the boys gave positive evaluations for academic success, book-learning and deferred gratification: all were early school 'drop-outs'; similarly, they positively affirmed the virtues of marriage, hard work, thrift, etc., and in a later *group* session disclaimed these attitudes vigorously. It seems likely, however, that this shift in declared values exposes the shortcomings of the individual interview situation rather than the pressures of the group.

Incidentally to these priorities, Short places some emphasis on the 'aleatory' factor in delinquency: this refers to 'behaviour settings which, in particular behaviour episodes, are contributory to delinquent involvement but which, in and of themselves, are independent of delinquency'. These settings are found 'disproportionately in lower class life', e.g. the high incidence of guns, the 'milling' character of street life. This argument appears to be

---

[22] See also Short, 'The Sociocultural Context of Delinquency', *Crime and Delinq.*, Vol. 6, No. 4, Oct. 1960, pp. 365–375.

[23] Jansyn, L., 'Solidarity and Delinquency in a Street-Corner Group' (1960, *unpubl.*).

an elaborate cul-de-sac of the rich-people-tend-to-have-better-funerals-than-poor-people type. At best it is a neologistic way of re-casting certain elements of 'social disorganisation' theory or Miller's 'lower-class culture' approach.

With this exception, Short gives important indications of the directions that the testing of subcultural theorisation will take. He has established that variability of group structure is commensurate with subcultural processes: the task for research is to establish the extent to which groups, of whatever structure and status-giving potential, 'carry' values diametrically opposed to the dominant culture pattern. Two subsequent reports by the Chicago Youth Studies Programme have, in fact, raised doubts as to whether: (*a*) delinquent gangs are differentiated along clear-cut criminal/conflict/retreatist lines at all, and (*b*) justify or derive their behaviour from values at variance with those of the middle and/or non-gang lower classes. Short, Tennyson and Howard[24] reported that simply *finding* a 'criminal' gang was impossible, and a 'retreatist' gang very difficult, though 'conflict' gangs are numerous. If this is the finding for metropolitan Chicago, where great care was taken to locate the most troublesome gangs via police and YMCA agencies, the generality of these phenomena is highly dubious. Their factor-analysis of the 37 behaviour items culled from observation of 598 gang boys is too complex for summary, but clearly little evidence emerged to support the Cloward–Ohlin delineation of fully 'criminal' or 'retreatist' subcultures. While 'conflict' and 'retreatist', but not 'criminal', behaviours emerged as fairly distinct emphases, 'criminal' behaviour appeared to be a thread running through the activities of all the gangs studied. One large white gang did accommodate a 'criminal' clique, who otherwise shared the patterns of behaviour of the larger gang: 'Only in their pattern of theft activities were they a clique.' But more generally the data pointed to the Cohen–Short picture of 'semi-professional' theft as a development from or even within a more generalised and conflict-oriented 'parent delinquent subculture', rather than that of the Cloward-Ohlin fully-developed delinquent subculture. They largely suspend judgment on the delinquent subculture implications of their findings, and 'tentatively' conclude only

[24] J. F. Short, Jr., and R. A. Tennyson and K. I. Howard, 'Behavior Dimensions of Gang Delinquency,' *Amer. Sociol. Rev.*, Vol. 28, No. 3, June 1963, pp. 411–428.

that such phenomena exist, but that they are not as 'pure' as they have been pictured, and 'they become articulated in ways much more complex than existing theories specify'. However, these modifications of Cloward and Ohlin's hypotheses about sub-cultural differentiation were in part originally forestalled by their presentation as 'ideal types'. More serious for subcultural theo-risation's basic tenets is the Programme's study of the *values* held to by gang boys.

This enquiry[25] used a 'semantic differential' to test the values of both Negro and white gang, non-gang lower class, and non-gang middle-class boys. Contrary to expectation, the data showed surprising uniformity among all populations in their evaluation *and* legitimisation of behaviours representing middle-class pres-criptive norms, and marginal differences only in ratings indicating intolerance towards middle-class proscriptive norms. Neither the Cohen–Short, Cloward–Ohlin nor Miller hypotheses, which all view non-middle class or anti-middle-class values 'as an important link in a causal chain leading from social status to illegitimate behaviour', would have led one to expect this result. Middle-class behaviours were rated substantially higher than deviant behaviours on a 7–point scale, although the samples differed most in their attitudes towards the deviant behaviours, tending to form a gradient with gang boys most tolerant, middle-class boys least tolerant. Nor is there any get-out for subcultural theorisation in the Cloward-Ohlin distinction between the 'legitimacy' and 'moral validity' of a value-system for gang boys: images were tested on a 'smart-sucker' continuum to control for this factor. Probably inhibited by the unexpected nature of their findings, the investigators are excessively cautious in drawing conclusions from the data for subcultural theorisation, which can be reconciled with the data only if:

(*a*) the results sprang from some freak of methodology or from the nature of the stimulus arrangements: the one is extremely unlikely, since 17 factor analyses ruled out 'all but the most ingenious and most coincidentally patterned type of deliberately falsified scoring'; the second is possible, since the authors admit their main drawback to be the severance between the images

[25] R. A. Gordon, J. F. Short, Jr., D. S. Cartwright and F. L. Strodtbeck, 'Values and Gang Delinquency: A Study of Street-Corner Groups,' *Amer. J. Sociol.*, Vol. 69, No. 2, Sept. 1963, pp. 109–128.

judged and the contexts in which the judging normally takes place and is encountered. Replication will clarify the operation of these factors.

(*b*) if it can be shown that values do not strictly determine, or reflect, behaviour. Insofar as they do, the findings are as yet inexplicable; insofar as they don't, the findings are not quite so bizarre. Yet to invoke this as a face-saver for subcultural theorisation is to relegate it to that category of theory which is virtually 'unfalsifiable' and therefore inherently unscientific. The main implication of the findings is that, irrespective of adherence to middle-class prescriptive norms, certain lower-class boys are *forced into* delinquent gang behaviours by some peculiarities of their life-situation: both by *external* constraints—limitations on opportunity, female-based household pattern etc., leading in some cases (lower-class Negro in particular) to delinquency-promoting *internal* constraints. In the absence of replication studies, still under weigh, it would be useless to speculate further. It is enough to point to this single enquiry as the first to cast serious doubt on the reality of contracultural values in gang delinquency.

While the above studies have focussed on the values and dimensions of behaviour of gang delinquents in a metropolitan setting, two other sets of investigators have probed the variability of association between delinquency and ascribed social status. Reiss and Rhodes[26] studied the distribution of types of delinquent behaviour among 9,238 white school-boys aged 12–18 in Davidson County, Tennessee (1957). Their point of departure was that:

> residential areas . . . vary considerably in opportunities for cross-class contacts, ... Differences in the status structure of residential areas may mean that the effects of a class status position are not uniform from one residential status structure to another. The pressures for conformity on a lower-class boy may be greater in a middle than in a lower-class residential area.

For example, one possible deduction from Cohen's theory would be that the lower-class boy residing in a middle-class dominated neighbourhood experiences greater pressures towards deviance

---

[26] A. J. Reiss, Jr., and A. L. Rhodes, 'The Distribution of Juvenile Delinquency in the Social Structure,' *Amer. Sociol. Rev.*, Vol. 26, No. 5, Oct. 1961, pp. 720–732.

than the same boy residing in a lower-class-dominated neighbour-hood. Instead, they found that the more lower-class-dominated the community, the greater the delinquency life-chances for boys of *any* social status, though in the predominantly low social status 'contexts', the low-status boy had easily the greatest chance of becoming delinquent (both by official and self-report criteria, and for serious, petty and truancy offences). Moreover, the delinquency life-chances of a high-status boy in a low status context are greater than those of a low-status boy in a high status context. They conclude that 'there is no simple relation-ship between ascribed social status and delinquency', since the relative prevalence of the classes in an area, and the extent to which the class culture of each is diffused to the others, crucially affects the issue. However, while Reiss and Rhodes' study breaks new ground, it is weakened by its concentration on the white, in-school population (in a county where at least 25 per cent of the lower class are Negro, and in a situation where school drop-outs contribute an unknown quantity to the delinquency rates at the 'bottom of the heap'), and by its once-for-all allocation of delinquents to the most serious category of offence (thus elimi-nating 'versatility' and number of offences by individual delin-quents). With these reservations, it appears that the concept of 'social status context' has enriched, rather than invalidated, subcultural theorisation.

The same approach has been used by Clark and Wenninger[27] in their study of the social class-delinquency relationship between different types of community: Rural Farm, Industrial City, Lower Urban and Upper Urban. Holding ascribed social status constant, they show variations in the delinquency rate between community-types, much as Reiss and Rhodes did between 'status contexts'. They hypothesise that community-type differences will explain the apparent discrepancy between official and 'self-report' data on the distribution of juvenile delinquency by social class, the first locating the bulk of delinquency in the lower classes, the second asserting a much more even spread throughout both lower and middle classes. Since the 'self-report' researches of both

[27] J. P. Clark and E. P. Wenninger, 'Socio-Economic Class and Area as Corre-lates of Illegal Behavior among Juveniles,' *Amer. Sociol. Rev.*, Vol. 27, No. 6, Dec. 1962, pp. 826–834; and 'Goal Orientations and Illegal Behavior among Juveniles,' *Soc. Forces*, Vol. 42, No. 1, Oct. 1963, pp. 49–59.

Short and Nye[28] and of Dentler and Monroe[29] had been conducted in rural and small city areas, this conclusion seemed likely, and was confirmed by Clark and Wenninger's own 'self-report' study of 1,154 state school students representative of their four community-types. They found that 'nuisance-value' offences were committed by 80–90 per cent of the students irrespective of class or community, but that only 20 per cent or under—with significant class and community variations—admitted committing more serious offences. The Lower Urban group were most likely to commit 'real delinquent acts', whose incidence and seriousness grow with movement from Rural Farm (RF) through Upper Urban (UU) to Industrial City (IC—pop. c. 35,000) and Lower Urban (LU—both UU and LU groups were Chicago-based). Inter-class differences *within* community-types were estimated, but on a much less refined basis than that adopted by Reiss and Rhodes: some categories were combined or ignored due to small numbers, so that—unlike the Reiss–Rhodes study—they found that the same community background eliminated any significant differences of illegal behaviour rates between the various social classes within it. But the central finding was that the lower-class delinquency rates were much higher in LU and IC communities than in RF and UU communities. Their findings therefore echoed those of Reiss and Rhodes that within a given community-type or 'status context' the minority social-class groups conform closely to the norms of the dominant social class. Clark and Wenninger stress our ignorance as to what size—both relative and absolute—a social class minority must attain before it begins to assert its own normative influence. They also stress the need to combine the traditional social class concept with that of the 'cultural area'.

A similar emphasis emerges in their study of goal-orientation by social class (based on the same populations as above).[30] Here they infer from Miller's theorisation that the lower-class are oriented to goals markedly different from those of the middle class, as distinct from the Cohen-Cloward-Ohlin approaches,

[28] F. I. Nye, J. F. Short, Jr., and V. J. Olson, 'Socio-Economic Status and Delinquent Behavior,' *Amer. J. Sociol.*, Vol. 63, Jan. 1958, pp. 381–389.

[29] R. A. Dentler and L. J. Monroe, 'Early Adolescent Theft,' *Amer. Sociol. Rev.*, Vol. 26, Oct. 1961, pp. 733–743. (For more detailed consideration of Nye and Short's approach in another paper, see pp. 96–97.)

[30] It is not clear whether or not their work includes both sexes, or boys only.

which stress differential and unequal chances of attaining similar goals. By scoring responses to an inventory of 'goal orientations' based on (*a*) 'American' values, (*b*) 'lower-class' values, and (*c*) 'middle-class' values, they hoped to clarify the relationship between goal-orientation and delinquency rates. ('Values', 'goals', 'standard' and 'focal concerns' were used interchangeably). They found a broad relationship between affirmation of lower-class values or goals and seriousness of involvement in illegal behaviour, but this willingness to testify to the importance of lower-class values did not involve rejection of both 'all-American' and middle-class values. *All* communities rated the lower-class items only about half as important as American and middle-class values, though the LU and IC samples rated the lower-class items higher than did the RF and UU samples. Clark and Wenninger tend to ignore this global result, and concentrate on indicating finer points of difference between the communities, and between social classes within the communities. Inter-community differences were much slighter than inter-item-type differences, e.g. twice as many respondents in all populations rated 'having good manners' as of 'great importance' than rated 'being tough' as the same (83% cf. with 40%). They establish a weak relationship between illegal behaviour rates and opposition to middle-class/preference for lower-class values and goals. Only the UU sample were at all optimistic about their chances of attaining the goals without the employment of illegitimate means, the data suggesting that 'regardless of the goals juveniles desire to reach and the importance attached to them, the extent of illegal behaviour is more highly related to the chance they perceive themselves having of reaching these goals without resorting to illegal means.' Ultimately, Clark and Wenninger find support in their data for both the Miller and the Merton-based approaches to goal-orientation and subcultural delinquency. The main weakness of their approach, however—apart from their exclusion for the most part of school 'drop-outs'—was their initial assumption that the Miller- and Merton-based approaches were mutually exclusive. It has been argued above that these approaches can be aligned if Miller's work is seen as the definition of the 'hard core' of lower-class culture which demarcates it most clearly from middle-class culture, but which does not exclude the sharing of certain common values and goals by both classes.

Sykes and Matza argue along the same lines in their assertion that class culture differences should be viewed as differences in the 'distribution of frequencies' rather than as totally opposed and complete value-systems. Also, it is questionable whether 'focal concerns' can so easily be seen as 'goals'. It is this very attachment to lower-class 'focal concerns' which serves to handicap the lower-class boy in his pursuit of status in middle-class contexts.

The Reiss-Rhodes and Clark-Wenninger enquiries have much more relevance to Cohen's theorisation than to that of Cloward and Ohlin, who limit their hypotheses to gang delinquency in one community-type only, the metropolitan slum. Clark and Wenninger assert that Cohen's work is similarly limited, but the data do not justify this statement. Rather, it appears that these two investigations have fastened upon and elaborated Cohen's assumption that 'there is no one-to-one correlation between social class location and value-system.' The Reiss-Rhodes and Clark-Wenninger studies have introduced two concepts to the discussion of ways in which that correlation is made more or less likely to apply: 'status context' and community-type. A good theory should not be jettisoned as long as apparently contradictory evidence can be feasibly incorporated into its schemata. So far, only one study—that of the Chicago Youth Studies Programme on values in gang delinquency—can be said to have thrown real doubt on the subcultural issue.

(d) 'Basic' validation

The defining characteristic of any theorisation is that it can be proven false by empirical evidence. Since Cohen first proposed his theory of the delinquent subculture in 1955, has any evidence been presented that could seriously undermine or even negate it? Certain propositions central to the subcultural theorisation of Cohen and Cloward and Ohlin *have* been tested since 1955, and have not been proved false or even seriously weakened. This provides a form of 'basic' validation for subcultural theorisation, a form of testing which is different in kind to that outlined above.

Probably more basic to subcultural theorisation than any other proposition is that the structural location of most juvenile delinquency is the male, urban, adolescent sector of the working-class population. In 1957, Cressey[31] concluded that—even employing the utmost caution and making all allowances for 'dark' numbers, variations in reporting between countries, states, areas and types of offence, administrative changes, legislative innovations and leaving aside the thorny question of socioeconomic level—four broad relationships emerged between *age, sex, race, urban* residence and crime. The disparities surrounding these variables are stable enough to warrant *some* attribution of validity. Most assaults on the official statistics are, however, reserved for the picture they give of an overwhelmingly greater concentration of crime and delinquency at the lower-class level. Since 1955, the device of 'self-reported' delinquency has been adopted in the attempt to by-pass the strong probability of bias on a class basis. In a typical piece of 'self-report' research, Short and Nye[32] attempted to assess the extent of distortion. They dealt with: (1) types and frequency of delinquent behaviour (as indicated by 23 delinquent acts ranging from driving without licence to grand larceny) and derived delinquency scales from these items; (2) comparison of delinquent behaviour between students in a Western and a mid-Western high school, and institutionalised delinquents in a training school; (3) comparison of unrecorded delinquency with official delinquency records. They found that—while delinquent conduct in the non-institutionalised populations was 'extensive and variable', and this held true for both populations in a stable manner—reported delinquency corresponded to that treated officially with reference to sex ratio; arrest rates for both sexes, and proportion of crimes 'cleared up' by official FBI figures. It was also found that 'significantly greater proportions of training school boys and girls admit committing virtually all delinquencies, and admit committing them more frequently, than do high school boys and girls', e.g. the offence 'taken part in gang fights' was reported to have been committed by 24·3 and 22·5 per cent of mid-Western and Western high school boys in contrast to 67·4 per cent of training school boys; respective percentages reporting commission 'more than once or twice' were 6·7, 5·2 and 47·4. It

---

[31] D. R. Cressey, 'The State of Criminal Statistics,' *NPPA Journal*, Vol. 3, No. 3, July 1957, pp. 230–241.

[32] J. F. Short, Jr., and F. I. Nye, 'Extent of Unrecorded Juvenile Delinquency: Tentative Conclusions,' *J. Crim. Law. Criminol. Police Sci.*, Vol. 49, No. 4, Nov.–Dec. 1958, pp. 296–302.

was, however, found that on the basis of the 7–item (less serious offences) scale, 14 per cent of 'delinquent' boys were less delinquent than 14 per cent of 'non-delinquent' boys. Also, within the non-institutionalised populations, delinquency was found more 'evenly distributed throughout the socioeconomic structure of society than are official cases.' Yet the overall results of this research are—if anything—a vindication of the validity of the official records, assuming the 'random sample' limitations, rather than a demonstration that official records are 'seriously biased'. The one main objection—that the records are 'weighted' with lower-class adolescents—is in part sustained, but this has been a perennial objection, and Short and Nye reveal it to be a less serious bias than has often been feared.

Another proposition central to subcultural theorisation is Sutherland's theory of 'differential association'.[33] In essence, it holds that 'criminal behaviour is learned in interaction with persons in a pattern of communication' and 'a person becomes delinquent because of an excess of definitions favourable to violation of law over definitions unfavourable to violation of law': '. . . persons become criminals. . . because of contacts with criminal behaviour patterns and also because of isolation from anti-criminal patterns. . . . These contacts may vary in frequency, duration, priority and intensity'. The implications of differential association for subcultural theory are self-evident: it articulates the mechanisms by which a cultural adaptation is shared and maintained. If its utility as a broad organising principle were seriously invalidated, the efficiency of the subcultural process would be open to considerable doubt. Glaser[34] put differential association to a negative test by deducing from it hypotheses which, if proved more efficient than inefficient as predictors of criminality, would amount to a negative if not final validation— providing the operations testing the hypotheses *could* have proven them false. The hypotheses deduced by Glaser from the theory of differential association concerned intimacy of criminal associates; prior criminal experience; frequent, lasting and serious criminal

[33] E. H. Sutherland, *Principles of Criminology*, ed. D. R. Cressey, (5th ed. 1955). Also: D. R. Cressey, 'The Theory of Differential Association: An Introduction,' *Soc. Problems*, Vol. 8, No. 1, Summer 1960, pp. 2–6.

[34] D. Glaser, 'Differential Association and Criminological Prediction,' Ibid., pp. 6–14.

associations, and alienation from anti-criminal influences: these were then arrayed against the most efficient predictors discovered by the Gluecks, Ohlin and Mannheim and Wilkins in their prediction studies. Of the 15 most accurate predictors of *Unraveling Juvenile Delinquency*, 13 dealt with intimacy of delinquent companionship, alienation from school or parental influence; of the ten least accurate predictors, only one—that of 'Feeling of not being taken care of'—could conceivably have been deduced from the hypotheses as an index of anti-criminal parental influence. Of the 13 best predictors in the Borstal study by Mannheim and Wilkins, all but two omnibus prognosis items were readily deducible from differential association theory; of the 17 worst, 6 were derivable from the theory. Ohlin used 27 predictors and retained 12 as most efficient and reliable, a verdict derived from 20 years' parole prediction experience: of these 12, only 6 were deducible from differential association—Type of Offender, Home Status, Family Interest, Social Type, Work Record and Community. Of the 15 rejected, 6 were relevant to the theory—time served on sentence at parole, nature of prior criminal sentence, whether employed at arrest, and neighbourhood at offence and parole. Like those of Mannheim and Wilkins, however, none of those rejected by Ohlin were without *some* significance for parole outcome. Two successful predictors throughout which had no bearing on differential association—type of *offence* and non-criminal employment opportunities—point to inadequacies in differential association theory rather than any inherent flaw. Similar conclusions emerge from Short's[35] 'operationalisation' of a portion of differential association theory concerned with the 'frequency, intensity, priority and duration' of friendships of delinquents and non-delinquents: questions related to friends with whom they associated most often; their best friends; those they had known first; and those they had known longest. Intensity was found to be the strongest delinquency factor and the most delinquent associations were reported by older, institutionalised boys than any other age-group, sex or category. These findings confirm rather than cast doubt on differential association theory; to that extent, they supply negative validation for subcultural theorisation.

[35] J. F. Short, Jr., 'Differential Association as a Hypothesis: Problems of Empirical Testing,' Ibid, pp. 14–25.

(e) Conclusion

The discrediting of the multi-factor approach and the sense of the inadequacies of the 'cultural transmission', 'culture conflict' and 'differential association' theories of the 1930's and early post-war years are the context within which the contribution of Cohen to the understanding of juvenile delinquency can best be understood. *Delinquent Boys* was the most seminal post-war work in the sociology of juvenile delinquency, but the danger now is that too much will be hoped for from subcultural theorisation. It must be impressed that such theorisation is designed to account for the emergence of certain patterns of group delinquency: individual deviance is outside its etiological scope. The subcultural process is at present more a way of *looking at* these forms of delinquency rather than an established social structural fact. The most hopeful characteristic of this theorisation is that it can be analytically compartmentalised and tested proposition by proposition. It is flexible and capable of considerable elaboration and mutation. Yet it is doubtful if it will ever be amenable to the subtle factorial analyses employed ecologically by such investigators as Lander and Schmid.[36] It can act, rather, as a vehicle for the analysis of the empirical variations of delinquent behaviour, which are too diverse and complex to be handled adequately by any single analytic concept. In Yinger's view: 'Surely the evidence is rich enough for us to state that delinquency is a multi-variable product. The task ahead is not to prove that it stems largely from cultural or subcultural or contracultural influences, but to spell out the conditions under which these and other factors will be found in various empirical mixtures.'

[36] B. Lander, '*Towards An Understanding of Juvenile Delinquency*' (1954); and C. F. Schmid, 'Urban Crime Areas', (2 parts), *Amer. Sociol. Rev.*, Vol. 25, Aug.–Oct. 1960, pp. 527–542, and 655–678.

5

DELINQUENT SUBCULTURES—
THE ENGLISH EXPERIENCE

WHAT aspects of American theorisation are substantiated by post-war findings on juvenile delinquency in England? Any attempt to answer this question involves a revelation of the paucity of English work on the sociology of crime. Apart from the work of Mays, Morris, Jephcott and Carter, there has been no systematic empirical enquiry into the relationships between delinquency and social class. Apart from Fyvel's reportage, there is little data on the Teddy Boy phenomenon, and only in the Bristol Social Project was there an attempt made to study and work with a delinquent group over time. Beyond a paper by Scott, there is little data on the structure of delinquent gangs and groups. Concentration on penology, the psychology of crime, and legal and statistical studies of delinquency, has not only left huge gaps in our knowledge of what Short terms the socio-cultural context of delinquency: it has involved the almost complete neglect of the very questions with which American sociologists pre-occupy themselves. In many ways, the sociology of crime in England is much at the stage where Mayhew left it when—as Morris argues—he 'went far to demonstrate . . . that crime was essentially a social phenomenon which was perpetuated by antisocial attitudes and ways of behaving being transferred from one generation to the next in a social setting characterised by poverty, drunkenness, bad housing and economic insecurity'.[1] Despite the almost single-handed efforts of Mannheim, the sociological study of crime and delinquency slowly revived only during the 1950's, almost a century after the publication in 1862

[1] *The Criminal Area* (1957), p. 61.

of Mayhew's massive documentation of the London 'underworld' and slums.

I THE WORKING-CLASS 'SUBCULTURE'

The common theme which emerged during the 1950's was that the bulk of delinquent behaviour represented adolescent conformity to the sub-group norms of working-class—and especially the unskilled, slum working-class—communities. Mays, in his Liverpool study, argued that: 'Delinquency (in "underprivileged neighbourhoods") has become almost a social tradition and it is only a very few youngsters who are able to grow up in these areas without at some time or other committing illegal acts. . . . Delinquency is not so much a symptom of maladjustment as of adjustment to a subculture in conflict with the culture of the city as a whole.'[2] Liverpool reproduces the classic Chicago pattern in that 'an area covering about one-quarter of the entire city produces slightly over three-quarters of all delinquents'.[3] Mays' theorisation, however, is closer to that of Miller than to the ecological analyses and 'social disorganisation' theory of Shaw and McKay. He shares with Miller the view that the bulk of working-class delinquency stems from the co-existence rather than the interaction of distinctive working-class and middle-class cultures. While Mays nowhere suggests the prevalence of the 'female-based' household pattern, at least on an occupational basis—the male is still the 'bread-winner'—this does not undermine the thematic parallel: lack of any pressing need for 'masculine identification' could be held to explain the relative mildness of the offences committed by the boys investigated by Mays.

Mays studied 80 boys in mid-adolescence on an unstructured interview basis. The boys had in common attendance over time at the same youth club and residence in the same inner-Liverpool dockside area. Mays' tendency throughout is to stress environmental and 'social setting' factors in a descriptive way rather than cultural and social class factors in an analytic way, but while this approach dwells on the boy's role in his milieu at the expense of the milieu's role in the total society, this method may well be a function of the extent to which the milieu *is* insulated from the larger society rather than merely reflecting the author's own

[2] J. B. Mays, *Growing Up in the City* (1954), p. 147.
[3] Op. cit., p. 82.

predilections. The most striking fact about Mays' boys is their uniformity, and this uniformity is that of the 'corner-boy' culture as distinct from that of the 'delinquent subculture' or 'delinquent contraculture'. Yet, of the 80 boys studied, 42·5 per cent had been convicted on one or more occasions (41 larcenies, 10 break-ins, 3 wilful damage was the pattern of the city as a whole); 27·5 per cent of the group admitted the commission of a variety of undetected offences; another 8 per cent confessed to the peccadillo of 'lorry-skipping', thus bringing the total of technically delinquent boys to 78 per cent of the 80.[4] Again, technically, the majority of these boys were multiple offenders in the indictable category. But 'although the percentage of delinquency for the whole group is unusually high, judged by court statistics . . . the extent and continuance of delinquent acts is not very marked. . . . Delinquency is for the majority a phase and an episode',[5] begun at 11, reaching a peak at 13 and tapering off at age 15 on school-leaving. These figures are not valid for the country as a whole—the Albemarle Report found age 15 to be the peak year—but the decade since 1951 has seen some increase in delinquency among late adolescents. Mays' implication is clearly that those who persist in delinquency after age 16 are the more criminally inclined minority who are psychologically 'maladjusted' or 'disturbed'. This relation of delinquency to school-life is barely explored by Mays, who views it as an accidental coincidence with the working-class boy's maturation process: in 'growing up', he 'grows out' of delinquency, and settles into a job, girl-friend and marriage routine.

While Mays asserts that most of the boys with whom he was dealing could hardly be termed 'maladjusted' for conforming to those elements of the neighbourhood code which stressed toughness, daring and defiance of authority, he regards the code itself as essentially deviant and delinquency-producing. The code itself is a product in part of social factors—generations of low ascribed social status, poverty, unemployment and overcrowding —in part of ecological factors—slum streets, walled-in dockside milieu, lack of play facilities, deteriorating property, etc. The only element of frustration in the delinquent behaviour of Mays' boys is a function of environmental as distinct from social or cultural factors: asphalt rather than alienation is seen as the

---

[4] J. B. Mays, *Growing Up in the City* (1954), pp. 76–82.
[5] Ibid., p. 77.

motivating force. As Mays shows in a later, more general study of education in a similar Liverpool area, the community and the children are at odds with the school, and have great difficulty in coming to terms with it and deriving any benefit from it, but there is barely a hint of antagonism towards it.[6]

Mays' original sample, while highly delinquency-prone, were thought to be less so than other adolescents in the area. Their consistent attendance at a single youth club implies an ability to 'temporise with' the rules more characteristic of 'stable corner-boys' than 'delinquent' culture, and

> the very fact of their membership implies acceptance of standards of discipline and conduct higher than those obtaining at the street corner. Moreover, the particular club they derive from makes demands of an exceptionally high order on its members in the way of conformity with rules and attendance at cultural activities. Any findings . . . can be presumed to be below rather than above the norm for the district as a whole in respect of anti-social behaviour and delinquent proclivities.[7]

In a later study, Mays describes the work of the Dolphin Club, an attempt to assess the effects of group-work on delinquent and near-delinquent boys aged 8–13. The aim was to attract boys into a club at an age younger than that at which they normally joined, and to buttress the leader-member relationship with home visits to the parents.[8] Out of 66 households, 42 were 'broken' or 'disturbed' on account of either one or both parents: 21 from desertion, divorce or death; 9 from step-parentage; 8 from continual absence at work (seamen etc.), and 4 from chronic illness. Over half the boys were recommended to enter the Club by social agency workers, the rest by relatives: of the 89, only 3 joined of their own volition. The majority of the boys went to either local authority or Roman Catholic secondary modern schools: only 2 went to technical schools, none to grammar. After 2 years of operation, the wastage rate reckoned by loss of members was exactly 50 per cent; over 50 per cent were classified delinquent by the Club, the majority of whom were officially delinquent, although over half of these were court cases prior to joining; the wastage applied equally to delinquent and non-delinquent members.

[6] *Education and the Urban Child* (1962).
[7] Mays, op. cit., p. 32.
[8] *On the Threshold of Delinquency* (1959).

The sub-cultural background to the depressing-sounding chronicle of the Dolphin Club is that of the classic dockside slum, a familiar history of urban slum features plus 'the aliens and immigrants to add cultural confusion, colour clash and religious antagonism'.[9] All but a few of the boys had fathers in unskilled manual work, fathers absent at work or no fathers at all. Large families, unplanned childbirth, sexual promiscuity, ignorant baby and child care, haphazard child care making for a boy's early and 'long apprenticeship in street play and street society', physical and inconsistent punishment, bad diet, absence of family activity and a state of social apartheid between husband and wife: the main features of 'inadequate socialisation' are present. There is also a general, diffused nihilism about the behaviour used to display aggression: 'An almost aimless destructiveness . . . in the spectacle of bottle-smashing which is characteristic of the neighbourhood. Milk bottles are removed from doorsteps by children and deliberately smashed while the adults have a partiality for breaking empty beer bottles.' Also, 'the children will attack any empty house with tremendous ferocity. Almost instantaneous destruction takes place.' A crabsquashing episode was the high-peak of the children's 'almost aimless destructiveness'.[10] Mays also reports the behaviour of 'groups and gangs of adolescents . . . at once a gesture of defiance at the world and a demonstration of group solidarity'. To Mays, these are the 'pathological features of the district', yet even the 'socially constructive forces' are undermined by spendthrift habits of economy, deeprooted prejudice against education and the social services, religious fatalism, slavish conformity to slum codes of behaviour and a basic insecurity.

It is open to question whether this description applies to any recognisable social group at all, or whether it refers to the social isolates who, in Goodman's phrase, have 'dropped out' of society altogether, or who are—at best—hanging on by their fingernails. Mays himself has difficulty in deciding 'whether we are speaking about a sub-cultural or a sub-sub-cultural type; . . . whether the factors that have been identified are characteristic of those who live in the slums or more particularly of those who have fallen below even the norms of the traditionally slum

[9] Mays, op. cit., p. 154.
[10] Ibid., p. 156.

environment. . . .'[11] There is a strong case for viewing much 'inadequate socialisation' delinquency as Wilson views 'neglect-delinquency . . . not as a manifestation of a specific sub-culture, but as an index of breakdown of a culture'.[12] There is as much social distance between the 'mucking-in' of the slum and the 'ethic of reciprocity' of the stable working-class, as there is between the latter and the middle-class 'ethic of individual responsibility'. The question at issue is how far the cultural patterns inferred from observations of slum-life can be generalised to those stable, urban working-class neighbourhoods more typical of the population as a whole.

Four main points, then, emerge from Mays' work in Liverpool: firstly, the rarity of the non-delinquent boy; secondly, the commonplace nature of group—but not gang[13]—delinquency; thirdly, the confinement of this 'social' delinquency to early and mid-adolescence; fourthly, the preference for an out-group as distinct from a family, peer or community target. This last point in particular is reiterated with force by Kerr, in her study of 61 families in an Irish slum in Liverpool,[14] which serves as a social psychological counterpoint to Mays' research.

While Kerr's main concern was with the effects of deprivation on personality structure, her detailed portrayal and analysis of the Ship Street way of life confirms Mays' picture of the culture of the slum. The street attracted immigrants and the lowest social strata, and Kerr concentrated on the 'hard' core of residents of 2–3 generations, who were mainly Irish and, therefore, Roman Catholic in origin. These people 'are not interested in abstraction, or status, but only in personal relationships centred on their family groups'.[15] They have no awareness of the deficiences of their social situation, and display even an overt preference for slum-dwelling which at times intensifies into the 'inverted snobbery' of exalting 11 + failure and distrusting all outsiders. In Ship Street, people must play their traditional roles, because owing to the rigidity of the culture pattern, alternative ones are unthinkable. The Ship Streeters' refusal to 'get on', their desire to 'stay put'—despite, above all, a 'dreary and decrepit' housing

[11] Mays, op. cit., p. 171.
[12] H. Wilson, *Delinquency and Child Neglect* (1962), p. 158.
[13] See pp. 116–123.
[14] M. Kerr, *The People of Ship Street* (1958).
[15] Ibid., pp. 3–11.

situation—makes them a magnet for middle-class social reformers who 'make little headway in a culture alien to their ways'. Ship Street is a matrilocal, mother-dominated society which shuns the conventional world and its agencies. Work for men is manual and for teenagers 'blind-alley': yet Ship Street is woman-dominated to the extent that men are expected to hand over their wages and be given back pocket-money. 'Keeping up with the Joneses' is conspicuously absent as a goal: competitive attitudes do not influence conduct, as 'getting on' would involve moving out of the warmth of their families—often spread over several households in the street—and away from a familiar way of life. Hence, educational grants are turned down, jobs and houses in new places refused: all the pressures are against people getting 'big-headed' and 'above themselves'. This is not to imply non-materialism, as pools and horses—pursuits not really thought of as 'gambling'—are a constant investment.

Yet Ship Street's reputation for criminality is a 'projected fantasy' of those above it. While adults regard 'whipping' as legitimate, they avoid connection with both the peddling of Indian hemp among the coloured in the area and the various rackets run in connection with the ships through certain cafés. Just as doing the pools is not gambling, so 'whipping' or 'fiddling' things from work is not theft: these are two definitional disparities between Ship Street and the conventional world.[16] 'Delinquent behaviour shades off in a graduated manner into genuinely planned crime. The latter is rare in Ship Street . . . the crimes they commit are generally impulsive. . . . The violence is spasmodic and impulsive . . .' and is chiefly confined to family rows (p. 128). 'In Ship Street, the attitude of splitting what appears to be similar behaviour into quite differently evaluated sub-groups is general.' Hence stealing from your mother is wrong, shoplifting clever. The individual is loyal to his group—indeed, in-group disloyalty is strongly disapproved of—but the out-group of the rest of the world is fair game. 'Honesty doesn't pay, does it?' appears as the norm of the district. There is a

---

[16] While the manual worker has made an art of the practice of 'fiddling', he probably gains less from it than any other section of the community, and stands to lose more if discovered: the office worker who takes home paper, biros, note-pads, etc., and the sale rep. who 'jacks up' his 'ex's', are as commonplace as the 'whippers' of Ship Street: it is simply that the latter's depredations, taking place in a different social context, are seen as more heinous.

rather vague perception that people in other social areas consider stealing wrong, but parental reaction to their children being 'sent away' is mainly indignation at their bad luck in being caught rather than at their bad behaviour in law-violation involvement. Truancy is also rife: ' "How do you expect the boys to go to school when the nuts are in the docks?",' was one parent's explanation. Girls got into trouble with much less frequency: only 2 out of the 61 families were in institutions, in both cases for consorting with men. The 'mother-dominated' structure of the family meant that the 'over-indulged' boy was more frequent as a delinquent type than the 'affectionless' child. Because Ship Street has its own culture, because that culture can make distinctions between 'robbing' a private person and 'thieving' from big stores—the former is infinitely worse—Kerr's analysis is that this group is not 'sick' but rather 'socially immature', lacking associations and regarding the outside world with fear and even hostility. This conclusion is also deriveable from the material gathered on delinquency in a quite different community by Jephcott and Carter.[17]

'Radby' is a small mining and industrial town with a population of about 23,000 some 10 miles outside Nottingham in the Midlands. About 70 per cent of the town's 151 offenders in the decade 1942–52 resided in five small and well-defined areas, which were estimated to contain about 50 per cent of the town's juvenile population. Within each area, however, certain streets carried an abnormally high delinquent population, while adjacent streets were almost delinquency-free. While Jephcott and Carter do not make sufficient allowance for the considerable differences in the population at risk for the streets they compare, these differences in themselves are the main criteria for making distinctions between the 'paired' streets. For example, Dyke Street ('black') housed 474 people, of whom 136 were children aged 0–14, in 108 dwellings; Gladstone Road ('white') housed 316 people of whom only 68 were children aged 0–14, in 102 dwellings.[18] With twice the population at risk, Dyke Street's delinquency ratio of 3:1 as compared with Gladstone Road does not seem too outrageous, but participant observation indicated a huge disparity

---

[17] A. P. Jephcott and M. P. Carter, *The Social Background of Delinquency*, University of Nottingham (1954, *unpubl.*).
[18] Ibid., pp. 122–3.

of 16:1 between the two streets in 'unofficial' delinquency. The greater density of population on Dyke Street, however, was a corollary of basic differences in the way of life between the two streets, differences which were duplicated in the other four areas of study. The hypothesis tested was 'that within working-class areas different standards are upheld, and that the differences between the norms of behaviour contribute to the differential rates of delinquency distribution'. From the comparative study of contrasting streets, the authors were led to erect a typology of family standards. Grades I–III families predominated on 'black' streets, grades III–V on 'white'. Four key factors emerged from the polar types:

(1) Housekeeping standards: Grade I—permanently squalid

Grade V—house-proud

(2) Husband-wife relationship: Grade I—extremely unstable

Grade V—sense of partnership

(3) Relationship with children: Grade I—indifference to all but control

Grade V—definite plans for their future

(4) Education: Grade I—unconcern about school

Grade V—valued school as the road to status

This polarisation between the 'rough' and the 'respectable' is virtually that commonly supposed to apply to working-class and middle-class standards. Yet grades I and V accounted for only 11 per cent and 7 per cent of the sample respectively: 42 per cent of the families attained grade III standards, and about 20 per cent of the families fell into grades II and IV each. Grade III families aspired towards grade V standards but did not dissociate themselves from grades I and II. As 'Radby' is almost entirely a working-class town, the intra-working-class differences emerge exceptionally clearly. Jephcott and Carter assert a strong correlation between the distribution of delinquency, adult crime and matrimonial court cases with that of families of grades I and II standards in the areas they studied (though they did not show the distribution of grades I and II families to be confined to those areas). It is not so much that stealing, for example, is encouraged by parents in 'black' streets, but that they do not teach their children *not* to steal. With no internalised prohibition against stealing, the child has no guilt problem to cope with, and the only factor to be considered is that of risk and 'trouble'. Yet 'Radby's lower-lower' class do not resent their social isolation, and this leads to some doubt as to the appropriateness of invoking Merton's typology in explanation of their deviance, as the authors attempt: Jephcott and Carter stress throughout the insulated nature of the 'black' streets' way of life, their solidary community spirit in the face of social isolation, the absence of any aspirations or even expectations to achieve or be helped towards a better way of life. Their money-mindedness is not particularly excessive or acquisitive: careless and casual with money (often as much as £30 a week went into one household), they expect it to come as easily as it goes. Hence their institutionalisation of theft from institutions or the rich, though Carter noticed there was no pilfering from the factory. In explanation, 'bosses' were accused of theft: 'We steal in farthings, they steal in fucking pounds' was offered by one worker. As a recognition of the contradictions of the larger society, this is on a par with the 'Honesty doesn't pay, does it?' of Ship Street. The only real difference between Ship Street and Dyke Street is the apparent absence in the latter of woman-domination: otherwise, the replication in 'Radby' of the 'slum-culture' of Ship Street and Mays' Dolphin Club area is almost complete.

A strikingly similar picture emerges from Morris's study of Croydon.[19] Whereas the Liverpool and 'Radby' studies had been pursued by a combination of residential participation and informal interview, Morris employed the techniques of statistical and case-history analysis, spot-maps of crime commission and of criminal and delinquent residence. While crime commission predictably coincided with the opportunities available, and concentrated most heavily in the commercial centre and the satellite shopping districts (over 2/3 were larcenies without violence), both adult and juvenile offenders resided principally in either centrally situated deteriorating slum areas or council housing estates to which slum residents had been directed under clearance

[19] T. P. Morris, *The Criminal Area* (1957), Chs. 7–11.

schemes. Seven well-defined pockets within these areas carried almost half of all offenders. To Morris, these clusters had little 'ecological' significance: rather, 'the physical characteristics of the area are of little relevance save as an indirect determinant of the social status of an area',[20] and in Croydon the physical deterioration of an area pointed to the presence of the core of the 'social problem group'. The direction of housing by social policy undermines the basic concept of ecology, that the spatial distribution or 'spread' of an urban population mirrors its socio-cultural characteristics on a determinist basis. Morris's analysis of the case-material for all probation and Approved School cases for 1952 in Croydon showed that the only factors which related strongly to delinquency were membership of Social Class V and its corollaries, i.e., secondary modern education, low educational attainment, non-membership of a youth group and lax, severe or inconsistent home discipline. Of the remaining 18 factors, only one omnibus item—'Maladjustment/emotional disturbance/ enuresis'—related to more than 25 per cent of the 64 cases for boys (it occurred in 45 per cent of the cases). From several appalling case-histories cited by Morris, it appears that a minority of the children suffered from a hefty combination of the 17 separate psychogenic factors, suggesting that the remaining majority were relatively stable psychologically. Morris puts forward the idea that in each occupational group 'there is a hard core of 'psychiatric delinquency' related to serious emotional disturbance in the family, or mental ill health, which accounts for between 1/5 and 1/4 of all cases.'[21] The remainder can be regarded as 'social delinquency', 'related to the cultural milieu of the offender'. Correlations between rates of delinquent residence, overcrowding and social class (as measured by negative correlations with per cent middle class households) strengthen the earlier statistical indication that 'serious delinquency occurs more frequently among the families of unskilled workers (Soc. Cl. V) than among semiskilled, white-collar or skilled workers'. Thus Morris has arrived by a different route at the especial concern in particular of Kerr and Jephcott and Carter: the culture of the slum, or the workingclass 'social problem group'. The gradual erosion of 'workingclass culture', especially those standards relating to the socialisa-

---

[20] T. P. Morris, op. cit., p. 130.
[21] Ibid., p. 168.

tion of the child, is throwing into increasingly sharp relief the unplanned, squalid and violent version of it which persists among the unskilled, slum-dwelling or slum-clearance sector of the working class. The encouragement of spontaneity and autonomy from an early age leads the working-class boy to resist the assertion of middle-class authority he is bound to encounter via school and the law. Working-class culture is at once rigorously defined and sufficiently at odds with the controlling middle-class culture to make a head-on clash almost inevitable. That most working-class boys survive the age-cycle from 8 to 21 without becoming 'officially' delinquent is a function in part of the milieu in which that clash takes place—it could be rule-breaking in school as distinct from law-breaking at large—in part of detection risk—the clear-up rate for the MPD* in 1952 was an overall 31·9 per cent, for Croydon 35·4 per cent[22]—in part of differential standards within the working-class strata. On all three variables, the unskilled working-class boy is more liable to prosecution: his connection with school is minimal; he is more prone to impulsive and unplanned offences; and his parents are almost certain to be 'rough' as opposed to 'respectable' working class. These inferences from Morris's descriptions of difference within the working class are supported by his proof that delinquency-proneness increases as the socio-economic scale is descended, and his analysis of the tendency—strengthened by housing policy—for the most 'anti-social' working-class families to cluster together. 'Perhaps the most important fact about areas of delinquent residence is that they tend to be small and highly localised.... The net effect of segregation is to create enclaves covering a relatively small area, but which contain a disproportionately large number of families belonging to the social problem group . . .'[23] who are more likely than any other group in the population to contain delinquents of both 'social' and 'psychiatric' origin.

The descriptions of 'slum culture' given by Mays, Kerr, Jephcott and Carter, and Morris are strikingly uniform, as Trasler[24] has emphasised. In an attempt to erect an 'omnibus' theory of 'inadequate socialisation' as the origin of delinquent behaviour, Trasler links the social class location of delinquent

---

* Metropolitan Police District.
[22] T. P. Morris, op. cit., p. 121.
[23] Ibid., pp. 186–188.   [24] G. Trasler, *The Explanation of Criminality* (1962).

behaviour—as proposed by these investigators—with psychological theorisation on 'avoidance conditioning responses'. Because Trasler's theorisation represents something of a return to 'social disorganisation' theory, and contains parallel inconsistencies, it is important to distinguish it clearly from the work of Mays and Morris, who stress the degree of social organisation inherent in the working-class 'sub-culture'. To paraphrase crudely Trasler's theory, experiments with rodents have suggested that behaviour is most forcefully learnt by 'conditioning reactions of an autonomic (anxiety) kind'.[25] By inference, the child will internalise prohibitions against sanctioned behaviour, e.g. theft and violence, most permanently in situations where the parents utilise their relationships with the child as an anxiety-provoking instrument. 'Where there is a strong dependent relationship between a child and his parents, the sanction of withdrawal of approval will evoke intense anxiety.'[26] The middle-class 'love oriented' approach to child socialisation is much more successful in inculcating desired norms of behaviour than the haphazard, physical control practice characteristic of working-class parents. The lower the family's occupational status, the less willing—in general—are parents to modify their children's behaviour by consistent 'withdrawal of approval', an assertion which is consistent with the fact that Social Class V children are most delinquency-prone. While Trasler's theory has significance insofar as Social Class V parents *want* to control their children along middle-class lines, but fail to, it tends to assume—against the grain of his own 'social context' sources—that slum parents have roughly the same control and socialisation 'goals' as middle-class parents but adopt different, and disastrous, means to achieve those goals. Trasler's own sources argue that the working-class child *is* adequately socialised, but into a 'sub-culture unambiguously defined and in some aspects blatantly at variance with widely accepted middle-class norms'.[27] Also, if Trasler's one-to-one correlation between inefficient socialisation and delinquency held largely true, the delinquency rate variation over time would be sluggish and predictable—even allowing for his 'broken home' and 'unconditionable' categories. This is not to deny the impor-

[25] Ibid., p. 63.
[26] Ibid., p. 71.
[27] Morris, op. cit., p. 177.

tance of inefficient socialisation as the principal source of delinquency for certain groups, e.g. Wilson's 'social problem' families; it is simply to dispute its validity for working-class delinquents in general.

The evidence presented so far—which practically exhausts the supply of systematic work on the socio-cultural context of delinquency in England since World War Two—appears strongly supportive of Walter Miller's theory that the bulk of delinquency represents straightforward adolescent conformity to the expectations of lower class culture. Trouble, toughness, smartness, excitement, fate and autonomy: the 'focal concerns' deduced by Miller from his observation of lower-class, adolescent street-corner groups in Boston could well be duplicated in the work of Mays, Jephcott and Carter, and Kerr in particular. Yet how valid is the 'slum culture' view as a description of: (*a*) working-class culture in general, and (*b*) the most delinquent sector of the social-class system?

With 'slum culture'—to Miller, 'lower-class culture'— investigators are faced with forms of deviant behaviour which are both dramatic and uniform. Kerr in her Ship Street study had access to comparative material from her research in Jamaica and from Spinley's work[28] in London (itself comparative), and concluded that '. . . Deprivation, whether in London, Ship Street, Jamaica or New York, produces very similar personality configurations, both as regards structure *and as expressed in behaviour*'.[29] If this conclusion is stretched to apply to Mays' Dolphin Club area in Liverpool, Dyke Street in 'Radby', and the Waddon estate in Croydon, it appears that these investigations, diverse as they are in technique and locale—though not in time—have been focussed on a common problem, that of 'slum culture', which is atypical for the working class as a whole, and which— while its structural location is in some studies held to be responsible for as much as 50 per cent of the delinquent population—is not synonymous with the entire delinquent universe. A difficulty here is the scanty information at our disposal on the precise social origins—and hence social structural location—of offenders. Of writers on delinquency of a socio-cultural orientation, Morris is the only one to conduct an investigation since the war and to

[28] B. Spinley, *The Deprived and the Privileged* (1954).
[29] Kerr, op. cit., p. 154.

supply figures of social class origin. Of his delinquent sample of 64 boys in Croydon, none came from Classes I and II, 17 per cent came from Class III, 28 per cent from Class IV and 55 per cent from Class V.[30] While Morris's figures seem to leave no doubt but that the concentration of delinquents in Social Class V is overwhelming, the sample is a small one and is based on all boys put on Probation and sent to Approved Schools in 1952 in Croydon. The exclusion of boys who were absolutely or conditionally discharged, or who were fined, or remanded (102 boys altogether),[31] might well have reduced the disparity between the grades of working-class distribution. The work of Hood[32] suggests that magistrates in middle-class areas are more severe with low-status working-class offenders than magistrates in working-class areas, and Croydon—as Morris demonstrates—is relatively a middle-class dominated area, with more Class II residents than Classes IV and V combined—16,535 as against 7,238 and 8,252 respectively.[33] This may well have involved some 'weighting' of the Probation and Approved School sample with Social Class V boys, which category was already slightly inflated by the inclusion of boys in foster homes and Institutions (6.25%),[34] although these probably stemmed anyway from Social Class V homes. The net effect of these factors is an unknown quantity, but the Croydon figures probably exaggerate the disparities in delinquency distribution without distorting them. Some statistics from Little and Ntsekhe[35] suggest that either this is the case, or that the situation has changed since 1952 in London towards a more normal distribution of offenders throughout the social classes, a tendency for delinquency to be a property of more than the 'submerged tenth'. Apart from Croydon, however, there is little evidence for either view. Also apart from Croydon, there is a certain atypicality about the locales of the studies so far mentioned. Mays and Kerr both worked in a Roman Catholic-dominated, racially-mixed, dockside slum area. 'Radby' is a compact and almost entirely working-class mining town.

[30] Morris, op. cit., p. 144.
[31] Ibid., p. 133.
[32] R. Hood, *Sentencing in Magistrates' Courts* (1962).
[33] Morris, op. cit., p. 112.
[34] Ibid., pp. 143, 144.
[35] W. R. Little and V. R. Ntsekhe, 'Social Class Background of Young Offenders from London,' *Brit. J. Delinq.*, Vol. 10, No. 2, October 1959, pp. 130–135.

Manchester, Birmingham, Glasgow,[36] Leeds, Sheffield, Newcastle, Brighton, metropolitan and surburban London have been strangely untouched by social enquiry into delinquency. This applies even more strongly to research on group delinquency.

More recently, however, work based on a nation-wide sample, which adopts a more sensitive definition of social class than current occupational status of the head of the household, contradicts the near-normal distribution found by Little and Ntsekhe and points to a 'bottom-heavy' distribution of serious delinquency in particular. For break-ins, as distinct from larceny, the 'lower manual' contribution is even more pronounced.

THE SOCIAL CLASS (ACCORDING TO BOTH PARENTS' EDUCATION AND SOCIAL ORIGINS) OF ALL BOYS IN THE NATIONAL SURVEY AND THE BOY DELINQUENTS—POPULATION ESTIMATES

| | | Delinquent boys | |
| | *All boys* | *All* | *Repeaters* |
Social Class	%	%	%
Upper Middle	5 ⎫	1 ⎫	— ⎫
Lower Middle	15 ⎬ 24	11 ⎬ 15	3 ⎬ 5
Middle Self-employed	4 ⎭	3 ⎭	2 ⎭
Manual Self-employed	5 ⎫	2 ⎫	2 ⎫
Upper Manual Working	16 ⎬ 72	12 ⎬ 83	9 ⎬ 92
Lower Manual Working	51 ⎭	69 ⎭	81 ⎭
Unknown	3	3	3
Total %	99	101	100
Actual nos.	2402	288	62

[36] Fergusson's studies consist of factorial analysis. See *The Young Delinquent in his Social Setting* (1951).

(Provisional figures from an article for the *British Journal of Criminology* (forthcoming), quoted by kind permission of Dr. J. W. B. Douglas, Director of the National Survey of Health and Development Study, Medical Research Unit, London School of Economics. For detailed definition of the social class categories, see J. W. B. Douglas, *The Home and the School* (1964), pp. 39–45.

II THE NON-EXISTENT GANG

Research on delinquent gangs in England is a fair reflection of their absence. The only attempt at systematic enquiry was made in London by Scott—a clinical psychologist—in interviews with boys on remand known to have committed group offences, and on general experience.[37] Scott divides the 'sort of group in which these young people commit offences' into three essential categories: adolescent street groups, structured gangs, and loosely structured (diffuse) groups. The latter he sub-divides into the 'fleeting, casual groups'; the 'groups of customary friends and siblings'; and 'loose antisocial groups'. 'Adolescent street groups'

> are not really much concerned with delinquency, but . . . many people seem to think they are. The members of such groups admittedly sometimes get into trouble, but not usually as members of these groups, which in the great majority of cases bear no more relation to the actual offence than would any youth club or evening class which the individuals happen to attend together. . . . They look very fearsome, and may behave abominably, but they are not often actually charged with offences . . .

None of the boys in Scott's series offended as members of such a group. Their typical membership is anything between 5 and 30 youths aged about 14–18 'with girls occasionally tolerated'. While there is 'usually a territory, some sense of "we-ness", and a considerable degree of opposition to conventional standards' these groups are 'averse to the very concept of firm leadership. There is little loyalty, no firm control or persistence of membership. . . .' Such groups seem the equivalent of Miller's adolescent 'street-corner group' and, like Miller, Scott comments that they are 'perhaps necessary and useful'.

[37] P. Scott, 'Gangs and Delinquent Groups in London,' *Brit. J. Delinq.*, Vol. 7, July 1956, pp. 8–21.

'Gangs proper', i.e., 'with a leader, definite membership, persistence in time, a den, initiation procedure and criminal objectives', are extremely unusual. Police assert that they are both known and few. Those gang-members who come before the courts 'usually have a gross antisocial character defect' and come from chronically inadequate homes. Such gangs as exist are limited in membership to about 2–3 boys, apart from the leader. They exist on a leader-disciple basis, as distinct from a structured basis where each member is allotted—however vaguely—a role to play. It is 'a regular finding that (in London) even the most determined and successful leader of a delinquent gang can only manage to dominate those who are relatively handicapped. This seems to apply to all age groups.' In this situation, arrest and detention of the leader is enough to ensure the disintegration of the 'gang proper'.

Of the 'diffuse' groups, 'fleeting, casual delinquent associations' occur generally by chance where considerable predisposition towards delinquency is present, mostly in boys between 10–13; 'groups of friends and siblings' is the framework for 'most group offences', but their 'usual activities are not delinquent'. Such groups countenance rather than command delinquent activity, and some members can abstain from a common delinquent enterprise without losing face—'a situation which would be unthinkable in a gang'. Sibling-dominated groups are frequently under direct parental pressure to engage in theft; also, a delinquent may often involve his sib(s) in an offence out of jealousy or the need for support. Again, such groups have a regular nucleus, but rarely possess a leader or exert control over membership; 'loose antisocial groups' are more delinquency-prone than the other 'diffuse' groups, and their recklessness springs from 'unhappy' or 'disturbed' upbringing. 'In these groups, the role of leader means very little. A boy may be the follower in one offence in the morning and the leader of a different group in the afternoon.' Where one member impels the group into delinquent behaviour, it is as a 'catalyst' as distinct from a leader. Especially in this latter category, Scott's conception of the 'diffuse' group seems very close to that of Yablonsky's 'near-group'.

Of a sample of 151 boys on remand for group offences, only about 12 per cent were members of 'gangs proper'. Eighty-six per cent had offended in 'diffuse', unstructured groups. The average membership size for gangs was 2·5 members, that for all group offences was 2·6. As fas as both structure and motivation are concerned, Scott asserts that London juvenile delinquent groups differ markedly from those described in the overwhelmingly American literature. While Scott's clinical approach precluded the asking of those questions with which recent American theorisation had been concerned as regards motivation, his findings on group structure are the most definitive so far. Although he is limited to boys aged 8–17, there is no evidence for supposing that boys aged 17+ are radically different in the structure—or lack of it—in their groups. Scott's most relevant contention is that gangs on the classic Thrasher pattern are the preserve in this country of boys aged 8–12, for whom a leader who 'holds sway' and aggressive gang-fights are less unusual. The general picture which emerges from Scott's work is that delinquency—or kinds of delinquency—is not the preserve of any particular kind of group, save that most groups are 'unstructured', and that the 'gang proper' is an atypical form, springing from pathological rather than social pressures.

Apart from Mervyn Turner's work[38] with the Barge Boys Club 1947–51, and his later attempt to contact an East London (Hoxton) gang, the only attempt so far documented to locate and work with a delinquent group was that reported by the Bristol Social Project.[39] Group-work with adolescents was one of the Project's aims, but the group which was eventually studied was in part an artificial group selected from within an established Club, rather than an autonomous group located independently of the Club framework. An anonymous female worker divided a girls' Club into two sections—roughly corresponding to the 'respectable' and the 'rough'—and each was known respectively as the 'Tip-Tops' and the 'Teds'. The 'Teds' subsequently reassembled themselves as a group independently of the Club and called themselves the 'Calypsos', under the impetus of the worker. This process gave the group a coherence it might otherwise not have possessed, but even so the Calypsos developed into nothing

---

[38] M. L. Turner, *Ships Without Sails* (1953); with J. C. Spencer, 'Spontaneous Youth Groups and Gangs' in *Spontaneous Youth Groups* (1955), pp. 52–59.

[39] J. C. Spencer *et al.*, 'Preliminary Report of the Bristol Social Project' (1961, *unpubl.*) (IV) pp. 21–80, and (VI) pp. 13–17.

more structured than a sort of institutionalised adolescent street-group, in Scott's sense. The re-assembling of the group, dictated by the needs of action-research in the Project, went along lines different to those followed by street club-workers in the USA. In New York, for instance, the worker leaves the group structure intact and attempts to intervene in other ways; in Bristol, the methods of intervention demanded the virtual creation of the group from previously disparate smaller groups and individuals. The nature of the experiment precludes any conclusions as to structure, which was not the concern of the Project.

A major exception to the patterns of group structure suggested by the above evidence occurred in Britain in the mid-1950's: the Teddy Boy movement.[40] A strong sense of territory and the most bizarre teenage uniform yet devised were its most distinctive characteristics, differentiating it clearly from perennial, run-of-the-mill group rowdyism and aggression. The history of the Teddy Boy movement is that of two 'waves': it began in the inner urban areas of metropolitan London as a street-corner fashion, and soon became associated with large gangs of marauding and violent male adolescents. Slowly the fashion—and the delinquent associations—diffused outwards to suburban London, and—even more slowly—the provinces, so that by the time the movement had spread to the conurbations of the North, the original 'Teds' were gradually disappearing from London and making way for smaller, more purposeful but less overtly distinctive gangs. Preceding the Teds had been

> the old cloth-cap gangs of tough razor boys in the years immediately after the war.[41] Next came the Teddy Boys . . . strangely and expensively dressed up, moving about in large gangs, lawless and dangerous in their way, yet driven on by recognisable social urges and ambitions . . . By 1955–56, however, the height of the Teddy Boy cult was passed, certainly in London. The very word . . . had become a term of derision. 'Teds', 'a mob of Teds' was the more common description. The new wave of adolescents . . . were more sophisticated; they went about in much smaller, more purposeful gangs; their special clothes in the Italian style were not particularly formalised; but among those who tended towards criminality the lack of standards or restraints had become, if anything, more marked. . . . The Teddy Boys . . . possessed their

[40] T. R. Fyvel, *The Insecure Offenders* (1961).
[41] Also known as 'cosh boys', a term which retained currency for some time.

own code of conduct, and were obsessively loyal to each other. The new larger community of smaller gangs had few such scruples. . . .[42]

While Fyvel (p. 69) estimates the number of Teddy Boys at the height of the movement to have been at most 30,000, this figure is based on conjecture, and there is no means either of checking its accuracy or estimating what proportion of that number moved in gangs, 'near-groups' or mobs, cliques or pairs. The phenomenon was strangely neglected by academic research,[43] and Fyvel's sources are principally youth workers, teachers and ex-Teds themselves, and the picture of group structure which emerges is consequently blurred. Some gangs appeared to have 'leaders', others not; the term 'gang' appears in this impressionistic context to have emotive rather than structural significance, connoting delinquency and violence by large groups of working-class adolescents. The advent of the Teddy Boy garb seems to have forced these large groups into the cohesion of the gang, due to the dramatic reaction of adult, conventional society to the menace inherent in its distinctiveness. As such, the gang structure, the defence of 'territory' and the sporadic mass rioting seems to have been as short-lived as the Teddy Boy fashion in clothes.

Although Fyvel stresses the significance of the continental counterparts of the English Teddy Boys—the German 'Halbestarken', the French 'blousons noirs', etc.—since the Notting Hill race riots of 1958, there has been little recurrence in this country of the waves of destructiveness and violence which were their hallmark. Isolated incidents reminiscent of the movement occur, however, and the recent Finchley 'affray' was almost a microcosm of the dynamics of the Teddy Boy movement. One report captured the distinctive content of both Turner's descriptions of the gang he attempted to contact, and Fyvel's attempt to re-create the ethos of the movement. This case, which was pounced on by the press as a revival of 'gang warfare' and which was savagely repressed by the Bench, began in a crowded teenagers' café in North London where an 18-year-old youth named Vic Green took offence at a remark made at a younger boy called

[42] Fyvel, op. cit., pp. 76–77.
[43] The *British Journal of Delinquency* between 1953 and 1960 carried only one refererence to 'Teddy Boys,' and that referred to a German source.

Tommy Chamberlin. He hit Chamberlin and split his lip: six stitches had to be inserted. Chamberlin told one of his friends, Ron Fletcher (aged 20) about this attack, and Fletcher decided to round up a dozen or so friends and 'hangers-on' and have Green 'turned over'. On 4th April 1962, Fletcher and the 'Mussies'— as they came to be called—tracked Green to a church-hall dance in Finchley, and in assaulting him caused a mêlée in which several other boys were stabbed or knocked out. 'The fight was reported as a gang feud between the 'Mussies' and the 'Finchley Mob'. . . . The judge said: 'All of you have behaved in a way that would bring discredit on a pack of wolves. . . . This gang warfare has to be stamped out'.[44] He passed sentence of 5 years imprisonment on Fletcher, and of from 3 years imprisonment to 3 months in a detention centre on 14 other members of the 'gang'.

> In North London, as the police will tell you, the 'gangs' are no more than social gatherings in dance-halls and cafés of bored youths from the same area. They have no organisation, no accepted leader and no real name, just being referred to as 'the mob from Highbury' or 'the mob from the Angel'. They seldom get out of hand, and their fights are generally restricted to a bash on the nose to settle an argument. But the danger is that anyone like Ron Fletcher can quickly whip up a gang to 'turn over' any individual or group which has 'offended' him. Then the iron bars and the knives appear like magic.

Fletcher was aged 20, a plumber, and had nine previous convictions. The other 14 who were charged ranged in age from 15 to 19, employed mainly as labourers, but including clerks and trainees. There seems little doubt that the 'Mussies' constituted a 'gang' for the duration of the offence only, and the psychodynamics of their behaviour closely resemble those outlined by Yablonsky as the main criterion for 'near-group' as distinct from 'gang' structure: lack of persistence over time, manipulation of the periphery by a core-group of 2–3 seriously disturbed individuals (Fletcher is alleged to have had a 'lieutenant'), spontaneous mobilisation for a 'flare-up' rather than protracted organisation for continual gang warfare. Yet the notoriety of the incident is

[44] The *Observer*, 15/7/1962, 'Turning 'em over in Finchley' report by C. Brasher from which this and the following quotation are taken.

an index of its rarity,[45] and if the 'Mussies' are the nearest English equivalent to the American 'fighting' gang, it can safely be asserted that the structured gang is unknown in this country.

The available evidence indicates that delinquent group structure in England is different in kind from that of American metropolitan centres, insofar as the 'structured' gang is the ideal-type of the American 'gang proper'. This supremely predictable conclusion is based, however, on a certain absence of evidence, as we lack any kind of systematic data on the Teddy Boy movement —which is *supposed* to have been a gang phenomenon—and any comparative evidence for Scott's enquiry. The reasons for this non-existence of gangs are doubtless partly ecological—we have 'slums' but they are not 'teeming' slums—partly demographic—though we lack any research on the relationship, if any, between age-structure and delinquency rates between socioeconomically similar areas—partly racial—so far we lack the kind of ethnic ghettoes which sub-divide New York. Doubtless other factors operate more crucially, but an attempt has already been made (Ch. 2) to separate the 'delinquent gang' issue from the 'delinquent subculture' issue. Varieties of groups can 'carry' the same culture, or subculture; what matters is the integrative as distinct from the isolative pattern. In England, delinquent group structure is more fluid and less tangible than in the States. It seems clear that whatever the group structure, for a certain section of the male, adolescent, urban working-class sector, a kind of delinquent freemasonry operates. The question is whether this freemasonry amounts to a delinquent subculture, or whether it simply represents an intensified adolescent conformity to traditional working-class norms, allowing for the fact that we know little about the way normative structure varies within the working class. For on one point, the English evidence clearly corroborates the American, from Clifford Shaw onwards: the bulk of delinquency is group delinquency, and status within the group can take forms more subtle than the allotment of roles such as 'President' or 'War-Counsellor'.[46] But it is often overlooked that membership of a delinquent group is sought for the status *of*

---

[45] Cf. article in *The Guardian*, May 1961, 'The Jacobeans,' on teenage 'hooligans' who distinguished themselves by wrist tattoos, in Edinburgh.

[46] See Mays, *Growing Up in the City*, pp. 107–125.

the group, rather than for status *within* it: being 'one of the boys' takes priority over being '*the* boy'.

III DELINQUENT SUBCULTURES

It has already been argued that cultural disparities between the social classes are not synonymous with the concept of the delinquent subculture: they are simply a necessary basis for its emergence. To pose the question in two different ways:

(*a*) Does the 'delinquent subculture' represent—with Miller— a polar extreme of the 'corner boy culture', or does it—with Cohen—represent a radically different 'response' to the working-class boy's 'problem of adjustment'?

(*b*) Does the 'delinquent subculture' represent conformity— or over-conformity—with the traditional working-class normative structure, or does it represent a definite departure from that structure?

To approach this question at all, some knowledge is needed of the way the working-class boy reacts to the interpenetration of his world by middle-class institutions: school, youth club, police; and later, employment, youth club, police; and possibly, hospitals, courts, church. We also need to know how far the working-class boy's expectations and aspirations resemble those of his parents, both occupationally and otherwise. These questions are usually answered in question-begging ways; e.g., that the working-class boy regards the school as an 'alien' institution, but we have little more than conjecture as to why, how and what follows from this situation.

Lowson is one of the few English investigators to argue that the adolescent street 'gang' or group 'needs prestige' and

> may seek significance in a set of *contra* standards.[47] The Teddy Boy—hair short and sprouting at the front, long elsewhere, in contrast to the traditional 'short back and sides', his long jacket and short, tight trousers, his over-large shoes—seems to spring from his awareness of having chosen an opposite standard, *opposite to the older people of his group* as well as to broad society. . . .

Similarly, Fyvel[48] cites the opinion that the Teddy Boy movement

[47] D. Lowson, 'Delinquency in Industrial Areas,' *Brit. J. Crim.*, Vol. I, No. 1, July 1960, pp. 50–55.
[48] Fyvel, op. cit., p. 63.

combined the 'usual adolescent rebellion, although . . . the Teddy Boys represented a concentration of lads whose antagonism against teachers, employers and the State was quite abnormally tense', with 'the outlook of the typical criminal area where law-breaking was part of ordinary life and the police were always the enemy'. By fusing two distinct anti-social attitude-sets, 'by associating the spirit of adolescent rebellion with criminal traditions, by giving it the special glamour of a special uniform and gang life, the Teddy Boys were in fact spreading this criminal area outlook far beyond its usual confines. . . .' While this view —that working-class 'criminality' and 'adolescent rebellion' are mutually reinforcing—is not new, the Teddy Boy aura which accompanied it in the mid-1950's was unprecedented. What constituted this 'aura' is the hub of Fyvel's reportage—the dissatisfaction with the drabness of street-corner life, the move into the cafés, the threat of violence in defence of a new-found *persona*, a cynicism about the world-view of their own as well as of other classes, the self-romanticism with overlapped with the newly created 'teenage' culture, the low-ceilinged and narrow-focussed range of occupational aspiration. How did this combination of elements survive the school system, with its allegedly uniform attempts to inculcate sensible aspirations and ambitious industriousness, to endow skills and to 'mould character'?

Subcultural theorisation depends not only on the by now accepted fact that the school system has institutionalised 'culture conflict', but also that the value-system of the working-class boy is affected to some degree by that conflict. Mays summarises the position that

> the general trend appears to be in the direction of . . . 'middle class culture' . . . Grammar schools were, and still are, the pace-setters for most other kinds of schools. . . . Most of the teachers derive from or aspire to the same tradition and hope that their own children will follow a similar educational pattern. Thus it is fair to say that, in the down-town neighbourhoods, education is increasingly an introduction of an alien culture, and, in so far as this is true, a source of potential conflict.[49]

In Mays' 'Crown Street' survey area,[50] a mixed working-class

[49] J. B. Mays, *Education and the Urban Child* (1962), p. 8.
[50] Mays, op. cit., p. 85.

neighbourhood in Liverpool, the conflict is muted by a kind of cultural co-existence:

> There was no evidence whatsoever which in any way gave credence to any idea of a 'Blackboard Jungle' existing in the Inner City areas. Discipline was generally found to be well-maintained and there were no signs of rebellious pupils or incidents of children assaulting teachers[51] ... There is a rather sour joke current amongst teachers that the children are in reality bi-lingual, having one vocabulary and diction for school and an entirely different one for outside.[52]

But the 'assault and battery' criterion is too extreme as an index of 'conflict'. A well-run, well-regulated and disciplined secondary modern has mastered the techniques of control and eliminated hooliganism; but we learn little from Mays about the pupils' attitudes towards the teachers, the curriculum and the educational apparatus as a whole, although Mays fully documents the parents' apathy and—at times—hostility, towards the very idea of education in general and the demands made by the school in particular. If Mays is correct, however, then the Crown Street schools embody the familiar pattern of 'Them' and 'Us', with the pupils' essentially passive, and no element of frustration, resentment or any kind of reaction. This view gives very powerful support to Miller's 'lower-class' culture' view of the delinquency process.

A diametrically opposing view to that of Mays is taken by Webb in his study of 'Black School', a run-of-the-mill, urban secondary modern, although he draws heavily on Mays' observations on adolescent behaviour in *Growing Up in the City*. To Webb,[53] 'hostility (between teachers and boys) is the key factor at Black School. It is present whenever teachers deal with boys, but varies in intensity ...' from flick-knife exhibitionism and playground derision to 'playing him up' in minor ways in class. For the boys, it is 'almost guerrilla warfare against the teacher's standards—a ragged, intermittent fight to be oneself by being *spontaneous* and *irrepressible* and by *breaking rules*.' These forms of

[51] Or, it might be added, of defecating on teacher's desk. (See Cohen, *Delinquent Boys*, Ch. II.) But some recent fiction takes the opposite view of Mays. See, e.g., *The Teachers* by G. W. Target, and *Term of Trial* by James Barlow, both of which purport to be 'socially realistic' in their treatment of the school.

[52] Mays, op. cit., p. 92.

[53] J. Webb, 'The Sociology of a School', *Brit. J. Sociol.*, Vol. 13, No. 3, Sept. 1962, pp. 264–272.

behaviour militate against the teacher's most urgent priority: the need—and the desire—for order. Because he fears playground chaos spilling over into the classroom, and because the indiscipline and individualism lead to 'copying' and 'helping' over work, the teacher is forced to adopt the techniques of control more appropriate to the drill sergeant and his squad, which in turn limits the scope of his teaching: 'Only certain work and conduct standards can be conveyed by drilling', and the reiteration of the more mechanical skills in turn increases the pupils' dislike and hostility and the need to *maintain* drilling. Yet the school is *not* a closed system, 'and some functional harmony exists otherwise the school would not survive'. Webb finds such harmony in (*a*) the street gang, (*b*) the fundamental continuity between school and work, [54] and (*c*) the teacher ideology.

(*a*) The street gang: 'Its two-way relationship with the school is harmonious, because the values the school hostility makes for *are very similar to those that confer prestige in the gang*, in its constant war against Them. It is not a long step from rule-breaking, to law-breaking . . .' although Webb asserts that not many boys make that step (cf. Mays). Webb is not saying that Black School is the crucible of delinquency, but that 'by providing the gang with a very tangible enemy (the drill-sergeant teacher and his standards) it helps the gang to define itself'. Quantitatively the last year at school is the peak year for delinquency.[55] It is at this point that, as school-leaving approaches, 'social childhood' in school becomes increasingly incongruous with 'growing-up' outside it: 'rule-breaking' no longer suffices as an outlet for the school-engendered hostility and, moreover, the delinquent exploit 'supplies the gang with the event which reinforces a standard (of law-breaking)'.

(*b*) School and Work: The standards of Black School—if slavishly followed—would produce 'a neat, orderly, polite and servile' conformist, fit only for minor clerical or servile manual labour, of the kind which becomes increasingly redundant as mechanisation develops and job content decreases, so that the great majority of school-leavers at 15 enter semi-skilled jobs.

---

[54] See R. M. Titmuss on 'Industrialisation and the Family', pp. 104–118 in *Essays on the 'Welfare State'*, for examples of similar disparities between the roles of worker and citizen.

[55] Appx. 9, Albemarle Reports.

'Here there is continuity between school and work—*tedium.*' Sanity is possible only by the exercise of those very qualities developed in Black School—spontaneity, irrepressibility and rule-breaking.[56]

(*c*) The teacher ideology: The teacher's overall aversion for the boys further harmonises apparently irreconcilable disharmonies. This 'aversion' is compounded of two factors: firstly, the boys' collective hostility arouses in the teacher a feeling that they are—collectively—hateful; secondly, the impairment of the teacher's best qualities, compassion and detachment, owing to 'residual fatigue', a cumulative psychological and physiological weariness—induced by noise, stress and strain—which is not dispelled by free weekends and free periods. But the teacher develops an 'obsessional' attitude towards control not only because it minimises fatigue and dispels fear of chaos, but also because—in any school—he stands to be judged as a teacher and as a colleague by the criterion of how well he can assert ascendancy over the boys in an orderly fashion. In Black School, 'because of the strength of the hostility, control tends to be a sole end'. (' "Psychology" is a dirty word in secondary modern staff rooms.')[57]

Webb's analysis poses in very clear form the crucial differences between the positions of Cohen and Miller. Webb's description of the relationship between the street gang and the school is initially supportive of Miller's view of the delinquent gang as a polar extreme of the street gang, deriving directly from 'lower-class culture' and reinforced in that culture by their experience at school and—later—at work. A conjectural issue here must be at what point does a difference of degree, intensively pursued, become a difference of kind? Webb himself notes[58] that these values (i.e. spontaneity, irrepressibility and rule-breaking) can be seen as extreme working-class values along Cohen's lines, but thinks it more feasible to see them as *low rank* position values irrespective of structural location, in situations where upward mobility is unlikely, where the occupant has no stake in the

---

[56] Cf. Arthur Seaton in *Saturday Night and Sunday Morning* by Alan Sillitoe.

[57] Material giving powerful support for these views can be adduced from e.g., *The Young Devils* by J. Townsend, and *To Sir, With Love,* by E. R. Braithwaite. The latter stresses the high degree of charismatic and emotional feeling needed if the teacher is to be more than a 'caretaker' or a 'drill-sergeant'.

[58] Webb, op. cit., p. 270, n. 2.

system, and where occupants associate with equals, e.g. student, soldier, convict, assistant lecturer.[59] 'In short, all those in a position of social childhood, which is an important aspect of jobs of low rank. While all working-class jobs are of low rank, not all low rank positions are working-class.' Webb's disclaimer ignores the correlation between the particular low rank position he is discussing and the rate of delinquent behaviour. While it is too facile to equate 'spontaneity' with non-utilitarianism and short-run hedonism, 'irrepressibility' with malicious and 'rule-breaking' with negativistic behaviour, the Cohen-Miller dilemma is not purely of academic interest. If—in his basic assumptions— Miller is correct, then the form delinquency takes should be expected to fluctuate with changes in the lower-class sector and changes in lower-class culture, and should be checked with the erosion of crude class culture-conflict. If—similarly—Cohen is basically correct, then the delinquency pattern is much more unpredictable, for in a high-technology, 'open' society—increasingly stratified on the basis of 'achieved' criteria—the disparities between democratic ethics and social structure will intensify the problem of the 'bottom of the heap' boy, and increase the potential available for a 'delinquent solution'.[60] Perhaps the most challenging assumption of Cohen's theorisation is that the working-class boy *is* presented with a 'problem of adjustment': Miller's position is that no such 'problem' arises. The English experience seems to be a low 'achievement' orientation, a low ceiling of occupational aspirations and 'upward mobility' for the non-grammar school working-class boy, even within the working-class frame of reference. Fyvel talked with one West London 'gang' of 12 boys aged about 16–17:[61]

> Their picture of themselves was of a generation struggling against frustration. . . . Not one of them had thought of staying on the extra voluntary year at school, nor was anyone attending courses at Technical College. It stood to reason: any boy who did so would then not have had the money to go with the gang to dance-

[59] This comparison is facile, since the occupants of many low rank jobs *within* a system do have a stake in conformity, face only a *temporary* low rank: the convict and the 'Black School' child, on the other hand, are patently aware of their slim opportunities in achieving upward mobility within the system.

[60] In this connection, there should be some relationship between rates of delinquency and political apathy, as measured by total poll at local or national elections.

[61] Fyvel, op. cit., pp. 120–121.

halls. . . . One of them argued with conviction: 'Extra school won't get a boy any place. There's automation coming anyway. That means more work for a few people with brains and for the rest of us doing the same thing all day.'[62]

A club-leader reiterated a theme that Fyvel particularises many times: ' "They're not interested in their jobs—money is the only thing that counts".'[63] A systematic survey of adolescent aspiration in semi-rural, smaller urban and a London area showed much the same picture of stable, basically realistic and relatively unambitious aspirations about work.[64] Occupationally, adolescent aspirations —especially for the working-class 'corner-boy'—are notoriously, and realistically, low. While the jobs to which they have access are narrow in range and virtually interchangeable, the sole differentiating criterion is money, but even there the scope is limited. The uniformity of the juvenile employment market-place has not, however, simply led to a disillusionment with work. It explains in part the high importance which adolescents attach to leisure, and the way they spend their out-of-work time. It is here that they look not only for the status and excitement, but also for the freedom and dignity so conspicuously absent from their jobs.

IV 'TEENAGE' CULTURE

'Teenage' culture is largely synthetic culture: it is created for, not by, teenagers. Technically, the teenager 'status' belongs— irrespective of class—to anybody between the ages of 13 and 20. Commercially, however, teenage culture is aimed—more than at any other single target—at the unmarried working-class male aged between 15 and 25. The reason is not simply that his spending power is greatest, both individually and collectively; it is also that he responds to the values used to sell the commodities more than his middle or upper-class counterparts. This also applies to girls, as their spending-power grows, and their social differences with the boys diminish. But the working-class adolescent not only dominates the market and—to a certain

[62] The tragedy of this statement is simply that it isn't true—the unskilled worker is the first to be displaced by automation. Nevertheless, it was the image they held to.

[63] Fyvel, op. cit., p. 125.

[64] T. Veness, *School-leavers: Their Aspirations and Expectations* (1962).

extent—accepts its values; he lacks any real alternative to it. Despite the classlessness of teenage culture, and the attraction it possesses for both sexes, its pressures are greatest on the working-class 'corner-boy'. The working-class boy who is involved in higher or further education, or who is potentially socially mobile as an apprentice or a craftsman, is insulated to some extent against the seductions of teenage culture; the married teenager who has contracted into adult responsibilities, is similarly sealed-off from its pressures. It is the single 'corner-boy', who is 'at a loose end' between 'social childhood' and marriage, who is most vulnerable. 'Today's youth is not only starting younger, but finishing later. The glories of being a teenager are not easily given up.'[65]

It would be false, however, to stress too strongly differential response to teenage culture by social class. The concept of the teenage role is the product of external cultural forces, but the celerity with which it became rooted testifies to the immensely powerful 'generational' need it fulfilled. The logic of Abrams' work[66] on the 'teenage consumer' is that, in order to sell to this very prolific market, an image of the 'teenager' had to be created, the precise achievement of 'pop' culture, although it must be emphasised that not all 'pop' culture is 'teenage' culture. The normative expectation of a lack of understanding on the part of adults is the most clear-cut element of the teenage role. As teenagers demand increasingly that their charismatic 'idols' spring from their own ranks, this element finds more definitive expression. Helen Shapiro was established as a best-seller with the record 'Please Don't Treat Me Like a Child'; Susan Maugham's 'Bobby's Girl'—with its repetitive chorus 'You're not a kid any more'—is another example. In the words of the Albemarle Report,[67] 'a new market means new persuasions' and the sellers in this market have ensured that the adolescents have a clear image *of themselves* as teenagers. The growth of the teenage concept is in this respect a movement towards classlessness, or at least a movement in which lower-class and middle-class youth come together on a unigenerational basis. The material artefacts of

---

[65] R. Gosling, *Lady Albemarle's Boys*, Young Fabian pamphlet, January 1961, p. 9.
[66] M. Abrams, *The Teenage Consumer*, LPE Paper No. 5, July 1959, and *Teenage Consumer Spending in 1959: Middle Class and Working Class Boys and Girls*, January 1961 (Part II of above Paper).
[67] Albemarle Report, p. 24.

the culture are, moreover, quite classless—the pop record, the scooter, the coffee-bar. In other words, there are new social pressures operating which, aided by the mass media, advertising and the emergence of a mass market in consumer goods, are likely to produce profound changes in 'corner-boy' culture: it may not be so immutable as Miller appears to suggest. One of the most striking factors to emerge from Abrams' research is the similarity of spending patterns for male teenagers regardless of class. Both middle-class and working-class boys spend almost exactly the same amount per week, and spend it on the same category of goods in almost identical proportions: of the middle-class boy's 70s. a week, 8·3s. is spent on clothing and footwear, 5·3s. on entertainment; of the working-class boy's 72s., 7·2s. and 5·5s. are spent on the same categories respectively. The latter spends slightly more on smoking, slightly less on drinks of all kinds and food. The working-class girl, however, is much less 'affluent' than either her middle-class counterpart or her working-class boy-friend: she has only 47s. to spend on herself as compared with the middle-class girl's 68s., but she spends it in much the same proportion, except for clothing and footwear, where—with 14·6s. to the middle-class girl's 24·9s.—she has only about half the middle-class girl's freedom in a very important spending area. But the overall similarities may mask very important cultural differences within the categories, and Abrams' survey of periodical readership shows a real cultural difference:[68]

> The very high coverage . . . of *Reveille*, etc., and *Valentine*, etc., among teenagers is very largely due to their appeal to working-class teenagers; in the normal week the average working-class teenager reads between 2 and 3 of the 12 magazines (quoted), and of this high rate of reading three-quarters is made up of love-comics and Reveille type magazines. His (and her) level of reading these two types is nearly treble the level among middle-class teenagers . . . *The publications often described as typical teenage magazines . . . are really typical only of working-class teenagers*; they are largely without appeal for middle-class boys and girls.[69]

While this disparity may be a reflection of educational level—a function of social class—the socio-cultural differences in the responses to the '"teenage" thing' cannot be discounted.

[68] Abrams, Part II, p. 6.
[69] Abrams, op. cit., Part II, p. 10.

What is the highest common factor—or 'lowest common denominator', the more popular adult term—about teenage culture? At risk of plagiarism, the adoption of Miller's technique of observing 'focal concerns' may be of use. The central pre-occupations of teenage culture seem to be: (*a*) *status*—'belonging' rather than 'ranking', being popular, sociable, smart, two important elements in which are being 'with it' and 'up-to-date', not being 'square' i.e. old-fashioned; (*b*) *romance*—it is always assumed that the subject is in the middle of an emotional liaison, at the end of one, or just about to begin one: the supreme vice is not being interested in romance: (*c*) *fantasy*[70]—strongly linked with (*b*), refers to the constant addiction of the subject to pursuit of the unattainable: 'always dreamin'' etc., and usually with a sexual impossibility in mind; (*d*) *excitement*—the incessant plugging of the notion that youth is to be enjoyed, entails 'living for kicks'—in a generalised way—the antithesis to which is 'settling down': (*e*) *violence*—really a sub-type of (*d*), an undercurrent in teenage culture which combines readily with the lower-class predilection for 'trouble' and 'toughness': the 'ton-up', the 'punch-up' are culminations of the search for excitement.

Other elements obviously enter the picture, but the five 'focal concerns' figure crucially in teenage culture irrespective of class or sex, and in turn share a common assumption and impetus: the need for 'exploit', or conspicuous self-assertion.[71] It is in this connection that teenage culture can be related to delinquent activities, if not to the concept of the delinquent subculture. As Lowson has argued:[72]

[70] See Ray Gosling, 'Dream Boy' in the *New Left Rev.*, Vol. 3, May–June 1960, pp. 30–34, for a vivid evocation of the frustration inherent in teenage culture for the unattached, 'unclubbable' male working-class adolescent.

[71] Significantly, since the pop music charts have been dominated by singers and 'groups' who are recognisably young, British and working-class in origin (though the individuals involved would frequently have been upwardly mobile anyway, irrespective of the particular route chosen), rather than English or American adult, or American teenage, 'stars', there has been less need to synthesise 'teenage' appeal in a self-conscious way via the lyrics. This may eventually free 'pop' music for better things. Also, with the emergence of the 'beat' and 'rhythm and blues' groups, the Beatles, etc., the emphasis on 'exploit' has shifted from the content of the lyrics—which now reflect a more solidly-based set of romantic preoccupations than the previous 'mooning'—to the actual 'style of life' of the individuals and groups themselves.

[72] Lowson, op. cit., pp. 53–54.

Mere sartorial display of apartness is harmless, but there remains the need for action and too often they must seek this in destructive, violent acts—there is less competition in this sphere. Their violence is usually restricted to their own kind, fighting with representatives of gangs from neighbouring streets perhaps (loyalties are very narrow), but they commit public nuisance in their sometimes acquisitive, sometimes prowess-seeking acts against property, ranging from senseless destruction in parks, bus shelters, public conveniences and the like, to breaking-in offences, stealing cars and so on. However, these latter comments relate to the extreme of these gang activities, involving the cruder elements one could always find in society; the disturbing feature is that nowadays they seem to command prestige among the relatively inoffensive groups of young people, reducing the restraints which otherwise operate. But in all these groups a common feature is this random and aimless use of leisure out of which impulsive acts of lawbreaking so easily spring.

The call for 'exploit' arises most forcefully in leisure, and in this central respect, 'teenage' culture reflects the achievement orientation of contemporary adult leisure culture, e.g., the decline of craftsmanship in work which has led to the popularisation of 'do-it-yourself'. The growth of such outdoor activities as sailing and rock-climbing, which were previously the exclusive device whereby a leisure class exhibited their superiority, is due in part to increasing *adolescent* pursuit of these 'hobbies'.[73] Yet, in so far as legitimate 'exploit', which is now accessible to middle-class adolescents, is still economically denied to those of the working-class, the working-class boy—to the degree to which he responds to the enshrinement of 'exploit' in teenage culture—will be faced by a 'problem of adjustment' in connection with his 'leisure goals' equal in unpalatability to that which he is held to face in connection with occupational and educational 'status-frustration'. Moreover, this 'problem of adjustment' is a relatively new one, coinciding with the emergence of the 'teenager' as a status-conferring role, and with the commercial exploitation of a new market. Moreover, while the occupational and educational aspirations of the working-class boy are limited both relatively and absolutely, his leisure aspirations—in so far as he conforms to the classless 'teenage' role—are not only high in relation to his socioeconomic position: they are identical with those

[73] See Thorsten Veblen, *The Theory of the Leisure Class* (1899).

pursued by upper- and middle-class adolescents. The 'problem' is most severe for the 'corner-boy' who cannot temporise with either middle-class dominated leisure facilities, such as the Youth Club, or with adult working-class institutions, such as the pub or the working man's club: hence the move into the cafés so ably described by Fyvel, the overwhelming overlapping between the 'problem' of 'unclubbables' or 'unattached' and the new rise in delinquent 'gangs', the emergence of the 'Ton-kid' phenomenon (who monopolise their own cafés) and, more recently, the polarisation into 'Mods' and 'Rockers'. For the working-class 'corner-boy', the success-goals of Merton's paradigm are leisure-goals, and in a situation where he is baulked of legitimate access to them, he is confronted with the choice of boredom, i.e., absence of 'exploit', or—in Sykes and Matza's phrase—with the need to 'manufacture' his own 'exploit'. In this dilemma, he reacts against both middle-class *and* 'lower-class' culture, and arrives at the 'delinquent subculture' by pushing the legitimate values of 'teenage culture' to their logical conclusion.

V CONCLUSIONS

The English evidence lends no support for the existence of delinquent subcultures on the Cloward-Ohlin basis, and the material suggestive of Cohen's 'parent male' subculture is not clarified to the point where a definitive conclusion could be offered. Gangs of the distinctive 'criminal'/'conflict'/'retreatist' subcultural varieties clearly do not exist, and there is faint support for the clear-cut demarcation of delinquent activities which the Cloward-Ohlin typology delineates. Groups of the 'criminal' type, mainly composed of ex-reformatory delinquents, are undoubtedly scattered throughout the various conurbations, and will probably become recruits for professional crime, but these represent the end-product of the judicial and penal processes rather than a subculture of aspirants to adult, organised crime. The main factor militating against the emergence of 'criminal' subcultures in England is the relative absence of any demonstrably successful 'illegitimate opportunity structure'. There are no syndicated 'rackets' in the American sense, and what pale imitations exist—in racing, dogtracks, 'protection' and prostitution—are small and highly localised. 'Conflict' subcultures are similarly undocumented and almost certainly non-existent; although fighting between large 'gangs' on a territorial basis is not unknown, it is less frequent now than at the turn of the century or pre-war, and where it occurs approximates more closely to Yablonsky's 'near-group' concept than to the Cloward-Ohlin 'structured' formula. Ecological density, absence of large ethnic groups and full juvenile employment would appear to be crucial. Comment on the retreatist pattern must be tentative, but the fact that drug-use in the USA is the subject of severe social sanctions and cannot be regarded as anything but illegitimate, must alter any comparative analysis. While research by Schur[74] as recently as 1959 suggested that working-class adolescents not only avoided drugs but were barely acquainted with their lore and terminology, the strong relationship between retreatist patterns and jazz language, combined with the traditional addiction of some coloured immigrants to certain non-barbiturate drugs, are disseminating retreatist terminology, if not actually drug-use, to adolescents in these circles. There is probably more chance of the middle-class adolescent jazz enthusiast coming into contact with the genuine retreatist culture, and indulging in marginal addictive practices such as ether or gasoline sniffing—or smoking an experimental 'reefer'—than there is of the working-class adolescent 'double failure' taking to drug-use. The current retreatist pattern in this country is sophisticated, 'hip' and upper-class or middle-class or 'student'-class, rather than connected with working-class subcultural delinquency, though this is not to deny the probability of the drug-cult spreading down the socio-economic scale.[75]

In summary, the following points may be stated (*i*) Excluding from the analysis Morris's 'psychiatric', or Mays' 'maladjusted', category of delinquents, even Social Class V delinquency seems to be attributable to more than 'environmental' sources: the 'culture-less' 'problem family' and the lower-class 'slum culture'

---

[74] E. M. Schur, 'Drug Addiction in Britain and America', Ph.D. thesis, London School of Economics, 1959. Also *Narcotic Addiction in Britain and America: The Impact of Public Policy*, Tavistock, 1963.

[75] The 1964 'Purple Hearts' craze shows the extent to which it has done so since 1961–62, though the habit does not so far seem more prevalent among delinquents than non-delinquents, or even among males as opposed to females. Nor is there much 'lore' or 'sophistication' attached to its use. It could, however, be the embryo for more disturbing trends.

family—although probably both accommodated by Trasler's 'inadequate socialisation' approach—should be differentiated. For Social Classes IV and III, Miller's 'lower-class' culture theory seems most readily applicable, and this orientation is shared largely by Mays. It is possible that Social Class V delinquency is a constant, residual phenomenon, and that recent rises in the incidence of delinquency—and concurrent changes in age-distribution which stem from late-adolescent increases in delinquency—stem from the spread of delinquency to Social Classes IV and III rather than from increased delinquency by Social Class V adolescents. Hypothetically, these changes—plus the distinctive content of much contemporary 'fringe' delinquency—are due to new 'intervening' pressures making for a 'contracultural' response, as opposed to the spread upwards of 'lower-class culture' or 'slum culture'. (*ii*) Pending further data on the responses of working-class adolescents to 'status-frustration' in middle-class contexts such as the school, it is suggested that differential response by social class to the newly emerging 'teenage' culture can lead the 'corner-boy' to adopt a collective delinquent solution along 'contracultural' lines, although disdain for the limited job-opportunity market consequent upon educational 'failure' is a necessary basis for this sequence.

6

DELINQUENT SUBCULTURES IN STEPNEY AND POPLAR: STATISTICAL SURVEY

THE WORK of Reiss and Rhodes in America (Tennessee) has confirmed their axiom that 'there is no simple relationship between ascribed social status and delinquency'. The work of Cohen and Cloward and Ohlin—though not of Miller—does, however, lend itself to propositions about the distribution of certain kinds of juvenile delinquency between and within working-class areas. In particular, the Cloward–Ohlin theory stresses the importance of the adult 'illegitimate opportunity structure' in the neighbourhood, and holds that its availability and nature are crucial factors determining the type and prevalence of delinquent subcultures in the area. In brief, the adult crime situation heavily influences the type of 'delinquent solution' prevalent in an area, and any attempt to test the relevance of the Cloward–Ohlin theory in an English setting must incorporate an area where, at least reputedly, the adult criminal tradition is strong.

West Stepney seemed a natural choice for such an area: the Spitalfields and Cable Street areas, via both national and local press at least, have long since acquired a reputation for sheltering 'rackets' in vice, 'protection' and receiving. West Stepney is also a traditional 'reception area' for ex-cons, young offenders on the run, and habitual, if not professional, offenders. If the Cloward-Ohlin theory on the origins of subcultural differentiation hold broadly true, one would expect to find at least an exceptionally high degree of officially-designated 'deviant' behaviour at all age-levels in these two sub-areas. As a control, the rest of Stepney and the borough of Poplar were chosen for sheer convenience as areas which lack such a concentration of adult criminality, and hence should be expected to display different patterns of delinquent behaviour to those prevalent in West Stepney. For these reasons, a crime survey of Stepney and Poplar for one year—1960—was undertaken to discover if the patterns of delinquent behaviour inferred from subcultural theorisation coincided with the actual distribution.

There are several basic limitations in this approach. Firstly, the statistics for a single year provide too narrow a base for confident assertions. Fortunately, a survey over a 5-year period (1958–62) for Stepney, Poplar and Bethnal Green, is being carried out by the Social Medicine Research Unit at the London Hospital. Some preliminary findings[1] have already been published, and the completed survey will show how far 1960 was an atypical year, for offences committed by 8–16–year–olds. (The present survey covers the ages between 8 and 25). Secondly, data gathered from police files (as opposed to court records, the source for the London Hospital Survey) provide no evidence on parental socioeconomic background, and only unreliable evidence on family history. Thirdly, there are the limitations inherent in any use of official statistics: variable clear-up and reportage rates for different offences, age-groups, areas etc. The principal advantage of the approach is that the socioeconomic similarity of the areas means that each acts—to some extent—as a 'control' for the other. Where differences emerge, it can be assumed that their sources are not those of socioeconomic status, or of 'status context', but are related to other differences between and within the areas.

I PREDICTIONS ON DELINQUENCY DISTRIBUTION
INFERRED FROM THEORY

The crucial difference between the theorisation of Cohen, Cloward and Ohlin, and Miller, concern the norms, values and beliefs of working-class offenders, and are not amenable to validation via the official statistics. The theories of Cohen and of Cloward and Ohlin do diverge, however, on points which the statistics can illuminate. These differences revolve around (i) age-differences between patterns of offences, and (ii) area differences between patterns of offences:

[1] M. Power, 'Trends in Juvenile Delinquency', *The Times*, 9/8/1962.

(i) The Cohen hypothesis asserts discontinuity between delinquency at three stages: pre-adolescence to mid-adolescence; mid-to late-adolescence; and early adulthood. The Cloward-Ohlin hypothesis asserts exactly the opposite: '. . . The social milieu affects the nature of the deviant response whatever the motivation and social position (i.e. age, sex, socioeconomic level) of the participants in the delinquent subculture.' Cloward and Ohlin[2] insist on the continuity of delinquent and criminal patterns at all ages, whereas Cohen's theory, that the parent male subculture accounts for the vast bulk of delinquency until the age of about 16, lead us to expect that early-mid-adolescent delinquency patterns will bear little relation to late adolescent and early adult criminal patterns.

(ii) Whereas Cloward and Ohlin assert that subcultural differentiation is uniform at all ages, Cohen postulates its emergence in late adolescence and early adulthood only. Differences should—on this basis—emerge between the western third of Stepney—with its persisting adult criminal element—and the rest of Stepney and Poplar.

Different predictions about the distribution of delinquency between and within Stepney and Poplar emerge, therefore, from the two theories. These can be summarised as follows. (It is difficult to see how similar propositions could be derived from Miller's theorisation):

Cohen: Patterns of delinquency will be very similar for both Stepney and Poplar adolescents until the age of about 16. Variegated patterns will emerge from the age of about 17 onwards, dependent on the illegitimate opportunities of the area. Criminal behaviour along the lines of semi-professional theft will flourish alongside adult criminal behaviour; where the latter is absent, conflict offences will predominate. Retreatist behaviour will occur only in socially disorganised areas. This leads us to expect the predominance of semi-professional offences against property in the over-17 age-group in Spitalfields and Whitechapel, and the Stepney (Cable Street) areas; and the predominance of conflict—or offences of violence and rowdyism or hooliganism—in Poplar and the eastern belt of Stepney.

Cloward and Ohlin: Patterns of delinquency distribution will

[2] Cloward and Ohlin, op. cit., p. 160.

coincide with patterns of illegitimate opportunities. Throughout adolescence, the predominance of criminal behaviour is to be expected in Spitalfields, Whitechapel and the Stepney (Cable Street) areas. Elsewhere, but especially in Poplar, delinquency will assume the form of unruliness and vandalism, with semi-professional offences against property at a minimum. Retreatist behaviour is possible only in the criminal areas.

II   PATTERNS OF CRIME COMMISSION IN STEPNEY
AND POPLAR

A survey was made of all crimes known to the police—both detected and undetected—in Stepney and Poplar for 1960. (See Table 1, p. 141). While there is no necessary connection between high rate areas of crime commission and those of criminal residence[3], a high rate of crime commission can—within certain limits—suggest the physical, economic and socio-cultural charateristics of the high rate area. Some knowledge of the area is essential, but this fore-knowledge is itself an inducement to circular argument. But two concepts can indicate the factors making for a crime-attracting area; first, the concept of opportunity, second, that of social control.

The limitations on analysis of reported crimes are, however, too severe for any real degree of confidence. There is no link between the offence and the offender. The fact of a crime is, as Wilkins[4] has pointed out, no guarantee of an offender: the culprit may be a child under age 8. A large cluster of offences may be perpetrated by only a few individuals. (One man in Stepney in 1960 had 67 offences of larceny from telephone kiosks taken into consideration, offences whose locations were scattered over both Stepney and Poplar.) The line between crime commission as an index of opportunity and as an index of social 'disorganisation' becomes blurred when a large shopping centre is surrounded by slum residences. Even 'serious' offences have different rates of reportage, offences against the person being grossly under-reported, while offences against property are more likely to be brought to the attention of the police. Some offences, such as

---

[3] See T. P. Morris, *The Criminal Area*, Ch. 2.

[4] L. T. Wilkins, 'The Measurement of Crime', *Brit. J. Crim.*, Vol. 3, No. 4, April 1963, pp. 321–341.

receiving and unlawful possession can, only be reported and detected simultaneously. The differentials of crime reporting constrict analysis of even the most pronounced tendency.

TABLE I: CORRECTED DISTRIBUTION OF OFFENCES BY BOROUGH: 1960

Offence	Stepney		Poplar		Both	
	% Own Area	No. and % Both Areas	% Own Area	No. and % Both Areas	% Both Areas	Total
Break-and-enter	16·7	863 71·6	17·82	341 28·4	17·0	1,204 100·0
Larceny person/robbery	1·64	85 81·7	0·99	19 18·3	1·47	104
Larceny *of* vehicle	5·84	302 73·1	5·80	111 26·9	5·83	413
Larceny bicycle	4·15	215 67·75	5·33	102 32·25	4·48	317
Larceny *from* vehicle	13·1	676 81·6	8·0	153 18·4	11·71	829
Larceny dwellings/ meters/slot machine/ telephone kiosk	13·33	690 76·0	11·44	219 24·0	12·82	909
Misc. simple larceny/ larceny—trick/ shoplifting/frauds	26·2	1,354 70·1	30·1	576 29·9	27·25	1,930
Receiving	1·49	77 59·2	2·77	53 40·8	1·84	130
Take-and-Drive-Away	6·57	340 77·8	5·06	97 22·2	6·17	437
Other ind. and Non- ind. offences: against the person, malicious damage, etc., suspected person etc.	10·9	563 70·0	12·6	241 30·0	11·36	804
Totals	99·92	*5,165* *73·0*	99·91	*1,912* *27·0*	99·93	*7,077* *100·0*
cf. population		92,000 *58·0*		66,604 *42·0*		158,604
cf. acreage		1,770 *43·0*		2,346 *57·0*		4,116
Illegal gambling		34		3		37
Rowdyism, etc.		26		24		50
Soliciting (prostitution)		97		—		97
Possessing dangerous drugs		4		1		5
		5,326		1,940		7,266

Table 1 reveals little beyond the fact that the rate of crime commission is in rough proportion to the number of persons per acre (52·0 in Stepney, 28·0 in Poplar), and that Stepney, with 58·0 per cent of the population, has 73·0 per cent of the crime, i.e., the indictable and more serious non-indictable offences. (These figures differ from those of the Statistics department of New Scotland Yard. The crime report sheets are mainly division-based, and some 500 offences occurring in Stepney had been classified as falling within the local authority of Poplar. Officially, Stepney has 65·6 per cent of the crime to Poplar's 34·4 per cent.) Although Stepney has only 38 per cent more population than Poplar, 17 per cent more crime is committed in Stepney than in Poplar. The types of offences committed were, however, much the same proportionately for both boroughs. In only one instance—larceny from vehicles—is there more than a 5 per cent difference: 13·1 per cent of all Stepney offences were larceny from vehicle, which formed only 8 per cent of the Poplar total. When the totals for both boroughs are combined, Stepney consistently accounts for 70–80 per cent of the crime, to Poplar's 20–30 per cent. Only in the cases of Frauds, Receiving and Larceny Bicycle were over 30 per cent committed in Poplar (49 per cent Frauds). In only two cases—Larceny Person (including robbery with violence) and Larceny from Vehicle—were less than 20 per cent committed in Poplar. When four non-indictable offences are taken into consideration, only rowdyism (insulting behaviour, wilful damage, etc.) is equally distributed between the two boroughs. Stepney has a monopoly of prostitution, a near-monopoly of illegal gambling and possessing dangerous drugs, the last offence being officially almost non-existent. But the proportionate distribution of all indictable and the more serious non-indictable offences appears to be remarkably similar for both areas.

The locations of individual offences were plotted on spot-maps, and it is possible to gauge the extent to which the overall figures mask areas of real concentration of crime commission. (See map at end).

Break-and-Enter

The main areas of concentration are all in the western half of Stepney: Spitalfields (especially Brick Lane) and Whitechapel in general; also the rectangle formed between the south side of Commercial Road, Backchurch Lane, Cable Street and Watney Street. The only minor concentration in Poplar is around the Bow Bridge housing estate, the junction of Devons Road, Bow Road and Bromley High Street. Otherwise, offences occurred along the main road shopping and factory areas, especially the Mile End Road. Evenly and sparsely distributed in Bromley and Bow. Arbour and Stepney Green areas hardly touched. Very few break-ins were reported for Wapping and the Isle of Dogs, considering the warehouse/docks/factory nature of those areas.

Larceny Person/Robbery with Violence

Principal cluster occurs in the Wentworth Street Market area. Other clusters are on Batty Street, running off the south side of Commercial Road, a prostitution-café area; also, the west end of Cable Street, and the Cannon Street Road area, and the Mile End Road junction with Grove Road and Burdett Road. Very sparse distribution throughout the remainder of both boroughs, especially in the Isle of Dogs (only 2) and mid-Bromley. None occur in Wapping, and no concentrations at all occur in Poplar.

Receiving

Sparse, uniform distribution (except for a few located in the South West India Docks in Poplar).

Larceny of vehicles

Again, the main concentrations occur in Spitalfields and the belt between Commercial Road and Cable Street (west ends), although the remainder of Commercial Road and Mile End Road are quite heavily plotted. Poplar and the rest of Stepney display relatively light distribution, with no concentrations.

Larceny bicycle

Offences scattered uniformly throughout the boroughs. The only concentration is the East India Dock Road/Grundy Street market area of Poplar. If anything, inverse correlation with larceny of vehicle.

Larceny Simple and Miscellaneous, etc.
The hugest concentration occurs in Spitalfields, the central cluster being the Aldgate Woolworths (shoplifting). Also, all the main shopping and traffic arteries; especially the junction of Cable Street and Dock Street café areas; and Commercial Road, East India Dock Road, Whitechapel Road (especially the market), Mile End and Bow Roads; Roman Road and Old Ford Road in Poplar; Salmon Lane (seamen's hostel) and West India Dock Road in eastern Stepney. The biggest concentration in Poplar is the Grundy Street market area, and the belt between the east end of East India Dock Road and Poplar High Street.

Queen Mary College, Mile End Hospital and the London Hospital are institutions with a marked frequency of larceny. While St. Andrew's Hospital in Poplar has very few, this may be due to a different reporting policy. The same applies to the docks in both boroughs, which are the location of relatively few offences.[5]

After Spitalfields, the worst area remains the western part of Stepney (except Wapping), i.e. west of Sidney Street, though the predominance in relation to Poplar is less marked than for any other offence so far, except larceny bicycle. Stepney east of Sidney Street—Stepney Green, Bancroft, Arbour and Dunstan—are consistently light for all offences.

Larceny from vehicle
The main concentration for consistency is again the western half of Stepney, particularly Spitalfields and the western end of Whitechapel and Commercial Roads. Area of real density roughly ends at Sidney Street to the east, and the Highway to the south.

A peculiarity is the biggest single cluster at Wapping Wall, the situation of the 'Prospect of Whitby', a sophisticates' riverside pub, lying just inside Shadwell. These offences are probably responsible for Stepney's high larceny from vehicle rate for the 8–12 age-group, and the priority of Shadwell in the 8–12 age-group 'natural area' table. (See Table 9.) This cluster cannot be explained simply on the grounds of either opportunity or of social 'disorganisation'.

[5] See Note at end of chapter for some indication of the relationship between the Dock and the Metropolitan Police Forces.

Other big clusters occur around the Mile End Odeon cinema, and Tower Hill. The distribution throughout Poplar and the rest of Stepney is fairly even. The main traffic arteries are not particularly densely plotted, subsidiary roads providing equal opportunity for less risk.

Larceny from slot-machines and telephone kiosks
Evenly distributed, but none at all in Wapping, and very few in the Poplar areas of Bow and the belt between East India Dock Road and the docks.

Larceny dwelling and larceny from meters
Close correlation in distribution. Overwhelmingly concentrated, the biggest clusters being in the Brick Lane, Hopetown Street and Old Montague Street areas of Spitalfields; the rectangle formed by Commercial Road, Backchurch Lane, Cable Street, and Watney Street in western Stepney; and the western end of Cable Street with its junction with Dock Street, and Royal Mint Square (large and squalid tenement blocks). The only cluster in Poplar is also a tenement block area, Manisty Street, near the South West India Docks.

The remainder relatively sparse. Very little in Wapping, dockside Shadwell and Isle of Dogs. Large tracts of Bromley and Bow lack a single offence of this nature. Little in remainder of Stepney—east of Sidney Street—except in the north-east corner (Tredegar Square).

Violence against the Person and Possessing Offensive Weapons
Obvious close correlation. One massive cluster along the short, club-infested stretch of Cable Street between its junctions with Leman Street and Christian Street. Other—much smaller—clusters on Brick Lane (Spitalfields) and the club and restaurant portions of West India Dock Road (Limehouse), part of which—Ming Street and Pennyfields—falls within Poplar.

Large sectors of Stepney and Poplar lack a single offence of violence or weapon-carrying, including Wapping, Isle of Dogs, Bancroft and Arbour. Except for prostitution, violence is the most concentrated offence geographically; apart from Cable Street, small clusters occur on Cannon Street Road (coloured area, as is Cable Street), and the café areas running off the south side of Commercial Road between Batty Street and Cannon Street Road. Very sparse in Poplar, save for the West India Dock Road area.

Take-and-Drive-Away

Includes a large minority of offences where unauthorised borrowing was accompanied by theft of articles worth less than £50, mainly car radios and accessories. Take-and-drive is the most disseminated offence of all, although relatively few occurred in the Isle of Dogs and the north-eastern tip of Poplar near Victoria Park. Distribution is not simply a matter of opportunity: only four offences occurred on Wapping Wall, cf. larceny from vehicle. The biggest cluster is around the Mile End Odeon cinema; also the environs of London Hospital on Whitechapel Road. Spitalfields and the area between Commercial Road and Cable Street show a distribution which is less than average. Big concentrations occur also along Mile End Road, roads running through the Ocean Estate (Mile End) and Limehouse. The Commercial Road/Whitechapel Road/Sidney Street triangle, and parts of Shadwell, are also areas of concentration. Three such areas in Poplar are the northern junction of Devons Road with Bow Road; Roman Road in Bow; and East India Dock Road. But these are tendencies only: most areas are evenly covered.

Non-Indictable Offences against Property

(Including suspected person, unlawful possession, and enclosed premises, and frequenting). Random distribution, although biggest cluster is Wentworth Street market (suspected person). Also the docks in both Stepney and Poplar (unlawful possession, cf. receiving). But tendency again is in Spitalfields and the Stepney (Cable Street) areas. Poplar and eastern Stepney very sparse, though no area is free of this offence-type.

Sexual

(Indecent exposure; indecent assault; rape). Almost random distribution, except a small cluster on Wentworth Street market (indecent exposure).

Illegal Gambling
Almost entirely Spitalfields (Brick Lane and Old Montague Street) and Stepney west of Sidney Street. The biggest concentration (raid) is Cable Street. Only one location occurs in the whole of Poplar.

Malicious Damage (over £20)
Well scattered. None in the Isle of Dogs or Bromley. No evidence of 'protection'. (This offence type includes arson and sacrilege.)

Attempted Suicide
Still recorded as an offence in 1960. Almost random distribution, though more in Spitalfields than elsewhere. (Congested tenement accommodation.)

Rowdyism
(insulting behaviour, wilful damage under £20, obstructing P.C., etc.) None in Stepney Green, Arbour, Bancroft and Dunstan areas of Stepney, where more around Cable Street than elsewhere. In Poplar, hardly any in Bromley, several in Bow and Isle of Dogs (Cubitt Town).

Possessing Dangerous Drugs
(5 cases only) 1 seaman at South West India Docks (Poplar), 2 in Old Montague Street and 2 in Cable Street area (Stepney).

Prostitution
Locations occur only west of Sidney Street in Stepney. Two main clusters, in Hessel Street and Sander Street, account for 48 of 97 convictions. Only 1 occurred in Spitalfields. The rest occurred around the Cable Street area, and between the west ends of Commercial and Whitechapel Roads.

Immoral Earnings
Only 3 east of Sidney Street. One cluster, amounting to about half the total, on one small sector of Cavell Street (south end). A few operated in Spitalfields and on and around Cable Street.

Summary
The Spitalfields and Stepney (Cable Street) areas account for 22·7 per cent of the combined populations of Stepney and Poplar. By rule-of-thumb reckoning, they must account for between 45–50 per cent of crime commission. 'Spitalfields' includes the wards of Spitalfields and Whitechapel; 'Stepney (Cable Street)' includes the wards of St. Mary's, Tower Hamlets and St. Katherine's. Wapping—a distinctive 'natural' area—is included in St. Katherine's Ward, and it is impossible to disentangle Wapping from the Stepney (Cable Street) area for census population reasons (1961). Unless otherwise stated, propositions concerning crime in the Stepney (Cable Street) area exclude Wapping.

From spot-map analysis, it is apparent that the portion of Stepney which stretches from the east of Sidney Street to Poplar has more in common criminogenically with Poplar than with the western half of Stepney. Set out below are those offences which showed pronounced tendencies to be concentrated in western Stepney:

Offences (Crime Commission) concentrated in W. Stepney

<u>Break-and-Enter</u>   [Spitalfields and Stepney (Cable Street)]

Larceny person/Robbery with Violence

Larceny of Vehicle

Larceny from Vehicle

<u>Larceny dwelling and meters</u> [Spitalfields and Stepney (Cable Street)]

<u>Violence against the person</u> [Stepney (Cable Street) only]

Non-Indictable Offences against Property

<u>Illegal Gambling</u>   [Stepney (Cable Street) only]

<u>Prostitution</u>   [Stepney (Cable Street) only]

<u>Immoral Earnings</u>   [Stepney (Cable Street) only]

<u>Drugs</u> (4 cases only)   [Spitalfields and Stepney (Cable Street)]

(Underlinings denote degree of concentration)

Offences (Crime Commission) concentrated in Poplar

Larceny bicycle

Statistical Survey

Even Distribution

Take-and-Drive-Away
Receiving
Rowdyism
Larceny simple and miscellaneous

Doubtful

Sexual
Malicious Damage (over £20)
Attempted Suicide

It is difficult to see how the concept of 'opportunity' explains this distribution. The strong concentration of break-ins, larceny from dwellings and meters, illegal gambling, prostitution, immoral earnings and drug-use in the same area (though Spital-fields accommodates only the first two and the last, to any real degree) cannot be understood simply by assuming that the opportunity there is greatest. It is more likely that—in this context—the concepts of 'opportunity' and 'social control' merge as explanatory tools, and the 'social disorganisation' itself is the primary source of opportunity. Why—otherwise—should break-ins, larceny from dwellings and meters be so concentrated within e.g. one stretch of Commercial Road and its sub-sidiary network of squalid, poverty-stricken streets? The Stepney (Cable Street) area especially is a demographic mixture of English, Irish, Jewish (still a minority), white foreign-born and coloured, the last group including West Indians, West Africans, Maltese, Arabs, Indians and Pakistanis. The 'social disorganisation' is a compound of culture conflict, transience, demographic upheaval, poverty and insecurity, overcrowding and racial tension. But it is also possible that the distribution of offence-types is a reflex of the presence of either one or two subcultures in the areas:

(*a*) remnants of the traditional Stepney criminal subculture, reflected in high rates of break-ins, larceny dwellings etc.

(*b*) the semblance of a retreatist-cum-violent subculture, generating the high rates of illegal gambling, violence, prostitu-tion, immoral earnings and drug-use (the official figures are a gross underestimate of the latter), its carriers being the unskilled manual coloured population, seamen, vagrants and rootless habitual offenders.

The other alternative is that the two subcultures merge empirically on a basis of petty, unsophisticated, unorganised and largely unprofitable—if often squalid and brutal—criminal and retreatist behaviour. This binary subculture is the source of Stepney's reputation as a 'criminal' area. Far from resembling the criminality of the American syndicate, it implies a rendez-vous for social agencies, a sum total of human deprivation and affliction found only in the crevices of our society. This consideration inevitably holds implications for the emergence of delinquent subcultures on lines different to those delineated in American theorisation.

III   PATTERNS OF DELINQUENT RESIDENCE IN
STEPNEY AND POPLAR

The main concern of the following survey was to discover the proportionate similarity/dissimilarity of the crime and delinquency patterns for the two boroughs, and for areas within the two boroughs. This involved the collection of data for three analytically distinct populations:

(a) Offenders resident in Stepney and Poplar and committing offences in Stepney and Poplar.

(b) Offenders resident in Stepney and Poplar and committing offences elsewhere.

(c) Offenders resident elsewhere and committing offences in Stepney and Poplar.

A fourth subsidiary to (a) and (b) is that of offenders resident in Stepney and Poplar, committing offences both in Stepney and Poplar and elsewhere. For most purposes, analysis concentrated on groups (a) and (b). Data were gathered on all offences committed in 1960, for which offenders came before the courts in 1960. Overlaps at the beginning and end of the year cancelled out. Data were collected on all offenders aged between 8 and 25 inclusive. Although the boroughs and areas surrounding Stepney and Poplar were 'combed' for Stepney and Poplar offenders (group b), the coverage is obviously not comprehensive for any except those areas. As the tendency is for delinquency to be a local pursuit, however (as opposed to semi- and professional crime), it is hoped that the number of offenders analysed by offence is as near the actual number as the 'clear-up' rates permit, and the official statistics allow.

Data were originally gathered from crime report sheets for 'clear-ups', i.e. offences for which an offender or offenders had been detected, not convicted; the 'clear-up' reports gave the name, age and date of court appearance of the accused, and in some cases a CRO or Search File number. This information enabled CRO (Criminal Record Office) to locate files of the individual offender. This process was applied to all offenders aged 25 and under in 'H', 'G', 'J', 'K', 'M' and 'R' Divisions. 'H' Division covers most of Stepney and Poplar, except the Spitalfields and Whitechapel areas ('G' Division) and the half-dozen streets in the NE tip of Poplar ('J'). 'G' also covers Shoreditch, Bethnal Green, Finsbury, Hackney, Islington and Stoke Newington (parts). The rest of Bethnal Green falls into 'H' Division. 'J' covers the Hackney and Mare Street stations adjacent to Bethnal Green and northern Poplar. 'K' covers the borough to the east of Poplar, stations West Ham, Plaistow, Canning Town and North Woolwich; 'M' and 'R' divisions cover the south side of the river to Stepney and Poplar: 'M' stations cover Rotherhithe, Lower Road, Deptford, Tower Bridge and Grange Road; 'R' Blackheath Road, East Greenwich, and Westcombe Park. The only area adjoining Stepney and Poplar which could not be covered in the survey was the City, which keeps separate records for convictions. Of 4,402 files examined, 1,242 applied to offences committed within Stepney and Poplar. Of the remaining 3,160, only 88 turned out to be residents of Stepney and Poplar (15 of these files were still not available after a year, the same applying to 4 files in the Stepney and Poplar list). These files show population (*b*) to be 10·6 per cent of the combined total of offenders resident in Stepney and Poplar. For a few non-indictable offences, notably gambling and rowdyism (excluding drunk and disorderly), the information was on charge-sheets only, and these were examined for 'G' and 'H' divisions alone. Of the 1,242 files concerning Stepney and Poplar offences, only about half concerned residents in Stepney and Poplar. The rest concerned residents elsewhere or of no fixed abode, 4 were not available after a year, and the rest were either not traced or duplicated (i.e. concerned the same offender). No trace of a file generally meant acquittal, in which event the file was—for a first offence—destroyed.

In the case of 32 offenders, cases dismissed are included in analysis, as it was thought their exclusion would render the survey less rather than more accurate. All were previous offenders, otherwise their files would not have been traced. Some were dismissed on a solitary count, some on one out of two or more counts. In all other cases, the offence was proven. The cases dismissed, however, fall disproportionately within age-groups and boroughs, and this tendency gives a slight bias to the trends shown in the following tables. They should therefore be taken into account when the tables are examined.

Cases Dismissed

Age-Group	Stepney		Poplar	
8–12	—		1	(1 larceny dwelling)
13–16	3	(1 susp. p. 2 take/drive)	1	(1 mal. damage)
17–21	13	(1 larc. person 2 robbery with violence* 2 susp. p. m/car 4 take/drive 1 mal. damage 1 larc. simple 1 break-in 1 receiving)	2	(1 murder 1 receiving)
22–25	11	(5 viol. vs. person† 1 murder 1 each of take/drive, soliciting, mal. dam., break-in, larc. of vehicle)	1	(1 receiving 1 larc. simp.)

* witness failed to appear.
† 4 in Cable Street area.

Stepney accounts for 27 of the cases dismissed, Poplar for only 5. Of the 24 dismissals in the 17–25 year-old Stepney group, 12 reside in the Stepney (Cable Street) area—4 aged 17–21, 8 aged 22–25. This slightly inflates the extent to which this area has the highest rate of delinquent residence in the older age-groups. Their inclusion in analysis is justified on the grounds that they provide an index of the extent of the 'iceberg' effect in an area, i.e. that they indicate the prevalence in an area of 'floating' unsolved crime.

Table 2 shows the patterns of crime and delinquency for each borough separately, and for the entire 8–25 age-group. While this table inevitably masks differences between age-groups, several factors stand out clearly. 13·9 per cent of Poplar offenders commit offences of 'rowdyism' as compared with only 5·57 per cent of Stepney offenders. 6·35 per cent Stepney, and less than 1 per cent Poplar, offenders indulged in illegal gambling. Less clear-cut differences are the greater liability of Stepney offenders to break-and-enter, take-and-drive, assault, steal cars and live off immoral earnings; and of Poplar offenders to commit petty thefts and fraud, larceny dwellings, etc. Differences of less than 1·5 per cent occur with receiving, larceny from vehicles, non-indictable offences against property, larceny bicycle, malicious damage (over £20), larceny person etc., possessing offensive weapons, and sexual offences. Prostitution figures for residence belie the fact that soliciting is confined to Stepney. For both boroughs, the three main offences are break-and-enter, simple larceny, and take-and-drive, to which rowdyism must be added in the case of Poplar. Stepney offenders show a greater versatility, over 5 per cent committing 11 types of offence, whereas in Poplar, over 5 per cent of offenders committed only 8 types of offence.

These figures must be seen in relation to (a) population at risk, and (b) per cent of offences cleared-up. In 1961, Stepney's total population stood at 92,000, Poplar's at 66,604. The 8–25 age-group accounted for 25·55 per cent of the Stepney total, and for 26·9 per cent of the Poplar total.[6] The crime rate per 100 for the 8–25 group for Stepney is—for both sexes—2.22: for Poplar, 2·01. Male-female distribution is almost equal, for both boroughs, for population and crime alike: females number 9·9 per cent of all Stepney offenders, 7·7 per cent of Poplar.

Differences in clear-up rates are so marked that any research into crime on a statistical basis suffers from huge, built-in limitations. Two crucial differentials—differences between areas

[6] Census 1961—County Report—London.

and between offences—are plotted in the official statistics. Two equally crucial differentials—those between age-groups and the sexes—cannot be stated by their very nature. The MPD Analysis of Crime in 1960 show that for all 'H' Division and station GC—i.e. Stepney and Poplar—percentages of all indictable offences cleared up by stations varied from a low of 24·5 per cent for 'GC' (Spitalfields) to a high of 39 per cent for 'HH' (the Ratcliffe and Limehouse areas of Stepney and Poplar). The average clear-up rate for the whole of Stepney and Poplar is about 30 per cent, about 5 per cent higher than that for the entire MPD. However, the average clear-up rate for all Stepney stations is about 25 per cent, for all Poplar stations about 35 per cent. The obvious inference is that we have a 10 per cent more accurate picture of crime in Poplar than in Stepney, and that Stepney's figures for resident offenders reveal a smaller portion of the 'iceberg' than is the case for Poplar. And even this guess-work is confined to indictable offences only.

TABLE 2: OFFENDERS RESIDING IN STEPNEY AND POPLAR BY NUMBER AND PROPORTION WITHIN EACH BOROUGH COMMITTING TYPES OF OFFENCE: 1960

Offence	Stepney		Poplar		Both	
		%		%		%
Undifferentiated	520	62·7	309	37·3	829	100·0
Break-and-Enter	127	24·4	64	20·7	191	23·0
Larceny, Simple and Misc.	107	20·5	76	24·6	183	22·1
Take-and-Drive	93	17·85	46	14·9	139	16·75
Rowdyism	29	5·57	43	13·9	72	8·8
Violence vs. the Person	45	8·65	18	5·8	63	7·6
Larceny dwellings, etc.	27	5·2	30	9·7	57	6·88
Receiving	28	5·38	19	6·15	47	5·68
Larceny *from* vehicle	28	5·38	17	5·5	45	5·43
Non-Ind./vs. Property	27	5·2	12	3·9	39	4·7
Prostitution	26	5·0	10	3·2	36	4·35
Illegal Gambling	33	6·35	2	*	35	4·22
Larceny bicycle	15	2·9	9	2·9	24	2·9
Mal. Damage (over £20)	14	2·7	8	2·6	22	2·65
Larceny person, etc.	13	2·5	7	2·26	20	2·41
Larceny *of* vehicle	11	2·1	3	*	14	1·7
Poss. Off. Weapon	7	1·35	6	1·95	13	1·57
Immoral Earnings	8	1·54	1	*	9	1·03
Sexual	2	*	3	*	5	*
Poss. Dang. Drugs	4	*	0	*	4	*
Offence Totals	644	123·8	374	121·0	1018	122·6

* = less than 1%.

When differences between the clear-up rates for offences are considered, the disparities are even more marked. The principal discrepancy is that between the rate for offences against the person—76·1 per cent in 1960 for the MPD—and the rate for offences against property—about 22 per cent in 1960 for the MPD. Unfortunately, clear-up rates for offences are not given on a divisional basis. In 2 cases, larceny bicycle and larceny from vehicle, the clear-up rate is under 10 per cent (9·8 and 9·4 respectively). As has already been stated, for certain offences the clear-up rate approximates unity, as detection and reportage coincide, i.e. the offence cannot be 'known to the police' prior to apprehension of the offender. This applies to all 'possession' offences: possessing housebreaking tools, unlawful possession, receiving, and—to a certain extent—shoplifting and larceny servant. Even with a fairly cohesive category of offences, such as all 'breaking' offences, the MPD rates for 1960 varied from 38·1 per cent for burglary to 15·9 per cent for housebreaking. The high clear-up rates for offences against the person—96·2 per cent for murder, 75·1 per cent for wounding and assault and 84·9 per cent for rape—might make it appear that we are on much safer ground in discussion about offenders against the person than offenders against property. However, it may well be that clear-up rates are in inverse proportion to reportage rates as the gravity of the offence increases. Radzinowicz's well-known assertion that probably only 5 per cent of sexual offences are known to the police,[7] Harvard's work on the detection of secret homicides,[8] and the experience of woundings at hospital casualty departments, make something of a mockery of the high clear-up rates for offences against the person, while serious cases of theft and robbery are usually reported. To the differentials of reportage and clear-up rates by offence-type and areas must be added the unknown quantities of differentials by age-groups and sex. As Morris[9] has recently stressed, there is no way of knowing the extent to which being a teenager is an element in being caught. Nor do we know how far being a male or a female teenager affects the clear-up issue. The sum total of these

[7] Cambridge Institute of Criminology, *Sexual Offences*, Preface by L. Radzinowicz, 1957.

[8] Cambridge Institute of Criminology, *The Detection of Secret Homicide*, by J. D. Harvard, 1960.

[9] T. P. Morris, 'The Teenage Criminal', *New Soc.*, April, 1963.

limitations is that we are at least three-quarters ignorant of the real crime situation.

It was hoped that, by studying two adjacent, working-class, dockside boroughs, most of these limitations would be cancelled out. Also, as Cressey has stated,[10] it has yet to be *proved* that the statistics give a distorted, as distinct from an incomplete, picture. As far as Stepney and Poplar are concerned, the main difference is the 10 per cent disparity between the clear-up rates. This must be kept in mind in considering the following observed differences, but Stepney's relatively low clear-up rate *vis-à-vis* that of Poplar is feasibly a reflection of Stepney's much greater volume of crime commission and—less tenably—a proportionately greater responsibility for crime by male teenagers in Poplar.

Table 3 does illustrate this latter assumption: in the 8–25 age-groups, 35·9 per cent of Poplar offenders are aged 13–16, 26·1 per cent being the proportion in Stepney. Sixty-one per cent of Stepney offenders are aged 17 and over, while only 48·45 per cent are aged 17 and over in Poplar. In the Stepney 22–25 age-group, there are nearly twice as many offenders as in the 8–12 group; in Poplar, the proportions are virtually equal. The implication is that, irrespective of delinquency *rates*, the peak delinquency age is mid-adolescence in Poplar, and late adolescence in Stepney.

TABLE 3: DISTRIBUTION OF STEPNEY AND POPLAR OFFENDERS BY AGE AND SEX: 1960:

Age-group		Stepney (N = 520)		Poplar (N = 309)		Both (N = 829)	
		N	%	N	%	N	%
8–12		67	12·9	48	15·55	115	13·9
	Male	65	12·5	46	14·9	111	13·65
	Female	2	0·4	2	0·65	4	0·25
13–16		136	26·1	111	35·9	247	29·8
	Male	131	25·1	108	34·95	239	28·85
	Female	5	1·0	3	0·95	8	0·95
17–21		206	39·6	101	32·6	307	37·1
	Male	172	33·1	90	29·1	262	32·0
	Female	34	6·5	11	3·5	45	5·1
22–25		111	21·4	49	15·85	160	19·3
	Male	101	19·4	41	13·25	142	17·15
	Female	10	2·0	8	2·6	18	2·15

[10] *Principles of Criminology* (6th edn., 1960).

TABLE 4: DISTRIBUTION OF GROUP (c) OFFENDERS BY AREAS OF RESIDENCE, AGE AND SEX:

Age group	Sex	East (N = 87)	North (N = 109)	South (N = 56)	West (N = 12)	Elsewhere (N = 59)	NFA (N = 63)	DK/NA (7)	T (393)
8–12	Male	Nil	7 (6.4)	5 (8.9)	Nil	Nil	Nil	Nil	12 (3.05)
13–16		15 (17.2)	16 (14.7)	16 (28.6)	1	8 (13.6)	1 (1.6)	—	57 (14.5)
	Male	15	15	16	1	7	1	—	55
	Female	—	1	—	—	1	—	—	2
17–21		42 (48.3)	48 (44.0)	20 (35.7)	4	27 (45.75)	35 (55.55)	3	179 (45.5)
	Male	41	36	19	1	26	27	3	153
	Female	1	12	1	3	1	8	—	26
22–25		30 (34.5)	38 (34.9)	15 (26.8)	7	24 (40.65)	27 (42.8)	4	145 (36.95)
	Male	30	28	14	7	24	25	3	131
	Female	—	10	1	—	—	2	1	14
8–25		87 (100.0)	109 (100.0)	56 (100.0)	12 (100.0)	59 (100.0)	63 (100.0)	7	393 (100.0)
	Male	86	86 (79.0)	54	9	57	53 (84.1)	6	351 (84.1)
	Female	1	23 (21.0)	2	3	2	10 (15.9)	1	42* (15.9)

* (i.e. 10.7% Female)

Group (*c*) offenders differ in their age-structure from those resident in Stepney and Poplar, reflecting the tendency for the offence to be more localised the younger the offender. Only 17·55 per cent were under the age of 17. In this table, designation of residence relates to the position of Stepney and Poplar. 'East' means West Ham, East Ham, Stratford, Dagenham etc.; 'North' Bethnal Green, Shoreditch, Finsbury, Islington, Hackney etc.; 'South' Southwark, Bermondsey, Deptford, Greenwich, Peckham; 'West' Kensington, Ealing etc.; 'Elsewhere' means outer London, the rest of Britain and abroad (and includes a large minority of seamen); NFA = no fixed abode; and DK/NA don't know or not available, which applied to only 7 charge-sheet cases. Table 4 seems to indicate that the most 'mobile' age for delinquency is 17–21.

The data in no sense indicate that outsiders committing offences in Stepney and Poplar were gang-members spoiling for a fight. Only 4 per cent committed offences of 'rowdyism' and only 7·4 per cent (over a quarter of whom were of 'no fixed abode') committed violence against the person. (It must be remembered that most non-resident offenders lived only as far from the *boundaries* of Stepney and Poplar as Stepney-Poplar offenders). But the pattern of offences committed by non-residents differs in several respects from that of local offenders. The three main offences remain—for all except offenders of 'no fixed abode'—petty larceny, breakings, and take-and-drive, but for this group, petty larceny (28·0%) is twice as frequent as breakings (13·7%) and take-and-drive (13·0%). Significantly, the most frequent offences of offenders of no fixed abode were non-indictable offences against property, 'suspicion' offences of loitering and 'frequenting' (23·8%), although this group had the highest rate for violence against the person (12·7%), and larceny dwellings (11·1%). The high placings of petty larceny and non-indictable offences against property suggest that non-residents are—if anything—less positively delinquent than local offenders.

Differences Between Age-Groups

Power, in an article[11] which is of especial relevance to the present study, has discussed the 'masking' of important trends in delin-

[11] M. Power, 'Trends in Juvenile Delinquency', *The Times*, 9/8/1962.

quency by the official statistics. By analysing non-indictable as well as indictable offences, and by adopting single-year analysis, he found that:

> ... offences almost without exception fell into one or other of two categories. The first affected mostly children, rose sharply to 14, then fell away. The second affected mostly young persons, was scarcely apparent till 13, and then rose sharply till 16 (and so far as we can see continues to rise). ... Most of the boys in the first were guilty of some form of stealing, commonly minor theft, but sometimes the more serious 'breaking and entering'. The second category consisted largely of the offences associated with hooliganism and disorder. ...

The well-known 'peak' delinquency age of 14 is shown to be the peak for the first category only: 16–17 would appear to be the peak for the second category of offences, which comprises taking and driving away, malicious damage, insulting behaviour, carrying an offensive weapon, various assaults on the police, etc. While the present study incorporates the very deficiency that Power criticised in the official statistics, i.e. the use of age categories as distinct from single-year analysis, the same trends have been found.

Before differences between age-groups (and boroughs) can be discussed, there must be some indication that populations at risk are comparable. In the cases of Stepney and Poplar, the 8–12 and 17–21 groups are proportionately almost identical, while there are relatively more young persons in the 13–16 group for Poplar than Stepney, and the reverse for the 22–25 group.

Age-group	Stepney	Delinquency rates (per 100)		Poplar	Delinquency rates (per 100)	
		All	*Male only*		*All*	*Male only*
8–12	26·3	1·08	2·07	26·4	1·01	1·89
13–16	22·8	2·54	4·76	26·0	2·385	4·56
17–21	27·65	3·16	5·41	27·05	2·08	3·62
22–25	23·25	2·02	3·68	20·55	1·33	2·21
8–25	100·0	2·22	3·97	100·0	2·04	3·12

The delinquency rates indicate one of the most substantial points of difference between Stepney and Poplar, for while the Poplar rates for 16 and under are only slightly below those for Stepney, the rates for 17 and over are considerably below, and this applies whether all or males only are considered. More significantly, the peak delinquency age-group for Stepney is 17–21, for Poplar 13–16.

Tables 5–8 show the proportions of each total offender population by age-group committing an offence, e.g., in Table 5, 35·8 per cent Stepney, and 47·0 per cent Poplar, offenders committed breaking-and-entering, in the 8–12 age-group. As Power found, the 8–12 age-group almost invariably committed petty larcenies and break-ins. The only exceptions are 'malicious damage' and one sexual offence, though Stepney children were more versatile in the way they committed their larcenies. It is worth remembering that children of this age (despite rare exceptions) have not yet acquired the necessary techniques for 'take-and-drive-away' and can commit with impunity offences which—if committed by a teenager—would be construed as 'insulting behaviour' or 'wilful damage'.

TABLE 5 : DISTRIBUTION OF OFFENCES BY AGE-GROUP AND RESIDENCE: (I) 8–12

F = Female

Offence	Stepney (N = 67)			Poplar (N = 48)			Both (N = 115)	
	N	%		N	%		N	%
Break-and-Enter	24	35·8		22	47·0		46	40·0
Larceny, simple and misc.	21	31·4	(2F)	21	45·0	(2F)	42	36·5
Larceny bicycle	6	9·0		3	6·1		9	7·82
Larceny from vehicle	9	13·4		0	0·0		9	7·82
Larceny dwellings, etc.	3	4·5		4	8·2		7	6·08
Malicious damage (over £20)	5	8·1		2	4·1		7	6·08
Receiving	1	1·5		2	4·1		3	2·61
Larceny person	2	3·0		1	2·05		3	2·61
Take-and-Drive	2	3·0		0	0·0		2	1·74
Non-Ind./vs. Property	1	1·5		0	0·0		1	×
Violence against the Pers.	1	1·5		0	0·0		1	×
Sexual	1	1·5		0	0·0		1	×

In the 13–16 age-group, taking and driving away emerges as the most frequently committed offence in Poplar, and second most frequent in Stepney. Breaking-and-entering is virtually the same, but from Power's analysis, it seems likely that take-and-drive is most committed by the 15–16 year-olds, break-ins by the 13–14 year-olds. Petty larceny is just as frequent in Poplar, but much less so in Stepney, compared to take-and-drive and break-ins. The frequency of larceny dwellings and rowdyism (i.e. wilful damage, etc. below £20, insulting and threatening behaviour) approaches that of the main three offences in Poplar, but barely emerges in Stepney. The more serious category of violence against the person is still quite small, and there appear to be no convictions in this age-group in 1960 for carrying an offensive weapon. In the 13–16 age-group, more than 10 per cent of the offenders committed three offences: take-and-drive, petty larceny, and break-and-enter, though in the case of Poplar, larceny dwellings and rowdyism must be included. In the 8–12 age-group, more than 10 per cent of the offenders committed only two offences, break-and-enter and petty larceny, though larceny from vehicle must be added for the Stepney group.

TABLE 6: DISTRIBUTION OF OFFENCES BY AGE-GROUP AND RESIDENCE: (II) 13–16:

F = Female

Offence	*Stepney* (N = 136)		*Poplar* (N = 111)		*Both* (N = 247)	
	N	%	N	%	N	%
Take-and-Drive	45	33·1	28	25·2	73	29·55
Break-and-Enter	50	36·8	22	19·8	72	29·15
Larceny, simple and misc.	28	20·6 (5F)	24	21·6 (1F)	52	21·0
Larceny dwellings, etc.	6	4·4	17	15·2 (2F)	23	9·31
Rowdyism	4	2·9	16	14·4	20	8·1
Larceny from vehicle	9	6·6	8	7·2	17	6·88
Larceny bicycle	8	5·9	5	4·5	13	5·26
Non-Ind./vs. Property	8	5·9	2	1·8	10	4·05
Receiving	3	2·2	6	5·4	9	3·64
Violence vs. the Person	4	2·9	2	1·8	6	2·42
Mal. Damage (over £20)	2	1·45	2	1·8	4	1·62
Larceny person, etc.	3	2·2	—	0·0	3	1·21
Sexual	—	0·0	1	×	1	×

In the 17–21 age-group, rowdyism has become the most frequent offence in Poplar, but remains relatively minor in Stepney. With this exception, take-and-drive, break-and-enter, and petty larceny remain the offences with the highest rate of commission, and while relatively more offenders committed take-and-drive-away in Stepney than in Poplar, almost a fifth of the Stepney offenders lived in Wapping, a self-contained area which bears more resemblance to dockside Poplar than to the Cable Street area of Stepney. In the 17–21 group, violence against the person becomes fifth in ranking, committed by slightly more than 10 per cent of offenders in both boroughs. Prostitution accounted for more female offenders than all other offences in Stepney combined. Larceny dwelling has receded as an offence of some importance for Poplar offenders. A small minority of Stepney offenders—but none in Poplar—indulged in illegal gambling. Immoral earnings was also confined to Stepney. Larceny bicycle, numerically small in the younger age-groups, virtually disappears as an offence-type.

TABLE 7: DISTRIBUTION OF OFFENCES BY AGE-GROUP AND RESIDENCE: (III) 17–21:

Offence	Stepney (N = 206)		Poplar (N = 101)		Both (N = 307)	
	N	%	N	%	N	%
Take-and-Drive	42	20·4	15	14·9	57	18·55
Break-and-Enter	39	18·9 (1F)	17	16·8 (1F)	56	18·2
Larceny, simple and misc.	33	16·0 (4F)	17	16·8 (3F)	50	16·3
Rowdyism	17	8·2 (4F)	23	22·8	40	13·0
Violence vs. the Person	21	10·2 (3F)	11	10·9	32	10·4
Prostitution	19	9·2 (F)	6	5·95 (F)	25	8·15
Larceny dwellings, etc.	13	6·3 (3F)	7	6·9 (1F)	20	6·5
Receiving	13	6·3 (1F)	6	5·95 (1F)	19	6·18
Non-Ind./vs. Property	11	5·3	4	4·0	15	4·88
Illegal Gambling	13	6·3	—	0·0	13	4·24
Larceny person, etc.	7	3·4 (1F)	4	4·0	11	3·58
Larceny *from* vehicle	6	2·9 (1F)	3	3·0	9	2·93
Possessing off. wpn.	5	2·4	2	2·0	7	2·28
Mal. Damage (over £20)	4	1·9	2	2·0	6	1·95
Larceny *of* vehicle	2	×	2	2·0	4	1·3
Immoral Earnings	4	1·9	—	0·0	4	1·3
Sexual	1	×	2	2·0	3	×
Larceny bicycle	1	×	1	×	2	×
Possessing dang. drugs	—	0·0	—	0·0	—	0·0

The most frequently committed offence in the 22–25 age-group is petty larceny, especially in Poplar, where both breaking-and-entering and take-and-drive-away have been almost eliminated. While more than 10 per cent of the Stepney offenders in this age-group committed break-ins, substantially more committed violence against the person and illegal gambling. Violence was less of a problem in Poplar, though more than 10 per cent of offenders were convicted of assaults etc. Receiving becomes an offence of relative frequency for the 22–25 age-group in both boroughs, as do the 'suspicion' non-indictable offences against property in Poplar. Larceny *of* vehicle becomes a noticeable offence in the Stepney group; larceny *from* vehicle is, alongside violence and 'suspicion' offences, the second most frequent offence committed by Poplar offenders.

As Power has shown, failure to adopt single-year analysis masks certain trends, or at least their detailed definition, but his findings for the ages of 16 and under give some indication of

TABLE 8: DISTRIBUTION OF OFFENDERS BY AGE-GROUP AND RESIDENCE: (IV) 22–25:

Offence	Stepney (N = 111)			Poplar (N = 49)			Both (N = 160)	
	N	%		N	%		N	%
Larceny, simple and misc.	25	22·5	(2F)	14	28·6	(4F)	39	24·4
Violence vs. the Person	19	17·1	(2F)	6	12·2		25	15·62
Illegal Gambling	20	18·0		2	4·1		22	13·75
Break-and-Enter	14	12·6		3	6·1	(1F)	17	10·62
Receiving	11	9·9	(1F)	5	10·2		16	10·0
Non-Ind./vs. Property	7	6·3		6	12·2		13	8·12
Rowdyism	8	7·2	(1F)	4	8·2		12	7·5
Prostitution	7	6·3	(F)	4	8·2	(F)	11	6·87
Larceny of vehicle	9	8·1		1	2·05		10	6·25
Larceny from vehicle	4	3·6		6	12·2		10	6·25
Take-and-Drive	4	3·6		3	6·1		7	4·37
Larceny dwellings, etc.	5	4·5		2	4·1		7	4·37
Possessing off. wpn.	2	1·8		4	8·2		6	3·75
Mal. Damage (over £20)	3	2·7		2	4·1		5	3·12
Immoral Earnings	4	3·6		1	2·05		5	3·12
Larceny person, etc.	1	×		2	4·1		3	1·87
Possessing dang. drugs	3	2·7		—	0·0		3	1·87
Sexual	—	0·0		—	0·0		—	0·0
Larceny bicycle	—	0·0		—	0·0		—	0·0

the trend of offences after that age. From the present study, it is obvious that take-and-drive-away is an offence peculiar to the teenage male group in both boroughs. From Power's analysis, it can be inferred that this offence is concentrated overwhelmingly in the 15–19 age-group. In the present study, single-year figures can be presented only for rowdyism, etc.:

Age	14	15	16	17	18	19	20	21	22	23	24	25	Total
Stepney	1	2	1	5	2	2	5	3	0	2	3	3	29
Poplar	1	6	8	10	5	5	2	1	2	2	0	0	42
Both	2	8	9	15	7	7	7	4	2	4	3	3	71

Rowdyism is thus concentrated in the 15–19 group in Poplar, rising to a peak at 17, and following a curve similar to that presented by Power for offences of 'hooliganism'. The frequency of rowdyism commission is not, however, particularly closely correlated with take-and-drive on a borough basis. Except in the 22–25 age-group where take-and-drive is a marginal offence, Stepney consistently displays a higher involvement in unauthorised vehicle borrowing than Poplar, although the distribution throughout is essentially similar. The dissimilarity between the boroughs emerges only via rowdyism—which is predominant in the Poplar 17–21 group and very noticeable in the Poplar 13–16 group, and of little importance throughout for Stepney—and via illegal gambling, prostitution and immoral earnings for the older Stepney groups. (The residence figures for prostitution belie its concentration in two or three sub-areas of Stepney.) But both take-and-drive and rowdyism consistently tail away in the 22–25 age-group, though the trend for rowdyism in Stepney is one of persistence into adulthood.

For analytical purposes at least, it is possible to distinguish three fairly clearcut stages of delinquency, in a hypothetical delinquent life-cycle. The first stage begins about the age of 9 or 10 and persists to 14–15, i.e. from pre- to mid-adolescence. It involves almost exclusively break-ins and petty larcenies. This holds for both Stepney and Poplar, although Poplar children concentrate on these staple offences more than Stepney children. The second stage begins around 15–16 and persists until 18–19, i.e. from mid- to late-adolescence. It involves take-and-drive-away, rowdyism, some violence and continuing concentration on offences against property is at a minimum. It is assumed here that the age-categories mask a trough in offences against property for the ages 15–18. In Stepney, this stage is less clearcut: it assumes clearer form in Poplar. The third stage is early adulthood, when any one of several adaptations is possible, such as petty, utilitarian theft of a conventional 'fiddling' nature; semi-professional or professional crime, with a concentration on break-and-enter, car-theft, hi-jacking, etc.; or a pattern incorporating petty theft, violence, gambling, immoral earnings, drugs, etc. The first stage corresponds to Cohen's conception of the 'parent male' subculture; the second to a pallid version of Cohen and Cloward-Ohlin's 'conflict' subculture; and the third to the varieties of response termed 'criminal' and 'retreatist' by Cloward and Ohlin, though in this connection the link is very tenuous indeed.

It has already been shown that the offences committed by outsiders in Stepney and Poplar differ markedly from those committed by residents, especially in their concentration on petty theft. Almost exactly two-thirds of these offences were committed in Stepney, one-third in Poplar, irrespective in general of the offenders' point of departure (e.g. 'North', 'West', etc.) Even 'East' offenders unexpectedly committed more offences in Stepney than in Poplar.

Offenders of 'no fixed abode' were overwhelmingly detected in Stepney, and for them the probability of being brought before the courts on suspicion charges was significantly high. Well over 90 per cent of these offenders were located in Stepney, an index of Stepney's magnetism for the 'double failure', the homeless young and the institutionalised recidivist perpetually on the fringes of crime and kept there by chronic unemployability.

Differences Between 'Natural' Areas
A breakdown of offences between boroughs gives no indication of the distribution of offence-patterns within the 'natural' areas the boroughs accommodate. No two observers would agree on the definition of 'natural' areas, particularly in the East End, and the division of Stepney and Poplar into ten areas is mostly subjective, although based in part on the need for ward population figures provided by the 1961 census. Unfortunately, while population figures are given for single years till 21, and for groups of five years after 21 by borough, only blanket totals are given for wards. Estimates of age-group populations for 'natural' areas have had to be made on the assumption that the age-structure of the boroughs is relatively uniform.

ESTIMATED POPULATIONS AND DELINQUENCY RATES (BOTH SEXES)

(See Tables 9–13)

	Sp/ Fds.	St. (C.S.)	Sh./ L.	St. (Gn.)	Dun.	Ban.	Bow	Brom.	Pop.	Isle/ Dɔgs
8–12	900 0·78	1510 0·79	840 2·74	517 1·35	673 0·74	514 0·58	1591 1·11	3217 0·59	600 2·5	645 1·24
13–16	780 2·69	1310 2·82	730 3·15	448 1·34	584 1·2	446 3·81	1569 1·85	3173 2·17	592 2·53	635 3·62
17–21	946 2·96	1590 4·85	885 2·6	544 2·76	708 2·82	541 1·11	1630 2·58	3297 1·97	616 2·27	660 2·58
22–25	794 2·27	1338 3·89	745 1·34	457 0·44	595 1·18	454 0·88	1240 1·77	2513 1·355	467 0·64	500 1·6
8–25	3420 2·16	5748 3·1	3200 2·46	1966 1·53	2560 1·52	1955 1·54	6030 1·81	12,200 1·53	2275 2·06	2440 2·3

It is apparent that the areas with the highest delinquency rates are not those with the highest late-adolescent and early adulthood crime rates. There is no simple continuity between a high delinquency and a high adult crime rate area. In short, the high rate crime area does not appear to be the forcing-ground for the high rate delinquency area.

The bare rates may, however, conceal distinctly similar patterns of offences—irrespective of rates—throughout the age-groups of the 'natural' areas. It is also more than probable that the age-structure of the natural areas deviates from that of the boroughs, although it would need widespread differences for the rates to be radically affected in the more populated areas. For example, if—in the 8–12 age-group—it was found that the Shadwell/Limehouse area had 200 more, and the Stepney (Cable Street) area 200 less, children of that age than was estimated, the respective rates would be 2·21 and 0·915 respectively. It would need a much bigger difference to affect radically the rates for both high and low extremes.

Tables 9–12 show the distribution of offenders for the 'natural' areas by age-group. The 8–12 table shows little difference between the areas, except for larceny from vehicle in Shadwell/Limehouse.

TABLE 9: DELINQUENT RESIDENCE: 'NATURAL' AREAS: (I) 8–12

	Spital-fields	*Stepney (Cable St.)*	*Shadwell/Limehouse*	*Stepney (Green)*	*Dunstan*	*Bancroft*	*Bow*	*Bromley*	*Poplar*	*Isle of Dogs*	*Totals*
Offenders	7	12	23	7	5	3	16	19	15	8	115
Offences:											
Breakings	2	5	7	5	2	3	6	7	5	4	46
Larc./simp.	6	1	6	—	2	—	7	9	8	3	42
L./*from* veh.	—	1	7	1	—	—	—	—	—	—	9
Larc. bike	1	2	1	1	—	—	—	1	3	—	9
Larc. dwell.	1	—	—	—	—	—	4	2	—	—	7
Mal. Damage	—	2	2	—	1	—	—	—	—	2	7
Receiving	—	1	—	—	—	—	—	—	1	1	3
Larc. person	—	1	—	—	—	—	—	1	1	—	3
Take/Drive	—	—	2	—	—	—	—	—	—	—	2
Non-Ind/Prop.	1	—	—	—	—	—	—	—	—	—	1
Sexual	—	1	—	—	—	—	—	—	—	—	1
Violence/p.	—	1	—	—	—	—	—	—	—	—	1
	11	15	25	7	5	3	17	20	18	10	131

	Wapping	Area	% Offenders	% Total Pop.
Offenders	3	Shadwell/Limehouse	20·0	7·9
		Bromley	16·5	28·4
Mal. Damage	2	Bow	13·9	14·2
Ind. assault:		Poplar	13·05	5·3
Sexual	1	Stepney (Cable St.)	10·45	14·3
Violence	1	Isle of Dogs	6·95	5·7
		Spitalfields	6·1	8·4
		Stepney (Green)	6·1	4·8
		Dunstan	4·35	6·3
		Bancroft	2·6	4·8
		Wapping	2·6	c. 2·5
			100·0	100·1
				(excl. Wapping)

The emphasis throughout is on either break-ins or petty larceny, or both. The Stepney (Cable Street) area includes Wapping offenders, but separate tables are given for Wapping, which contributes a differential amount by offence and age-group to the Stepney (Cable Street) total. (It was impossible to calculate population figures for Wapping.) If Wapping's offenders are subtracted from the Stepney (Cable Street) total, the latter's 8–12 delinquency figures look even more ordinary.

The main idea in setting up the 'natural' area tables was to disentangle the notorious Cable Street area from the rest of Stepney, and to follow obvious lines of division for the remaining parts of the two boroughs. Poplar falls readily into four divisions (see map at end): the docks and the two main traffic arteries of the Bow and East India Dock Roads form natural boundaries. While it would be possible to subdivide even further, e.g. the Isle of Dogs into Cubitt Town and Millwall, the numbers involved would be too small for any kind of analysis. In Stepney, the main roads again provide natural boundaries, though this is less so for the western end of Commercial Road, where the areas for prostitution has extended to Cavell Street on the north side of Commercial Road. Spitalfields is an amalgam of the wards of Spitalfields and Whitechapel combined. The Stepney (Cable Street) area combines three wards, St. Mary's, St. Katherine's and Tower Hamlets. Bancroft ward is more Bethnal Green than Stepney in atmosphere. Stepney (Green) is a fusion of Redcoat and Arbour wards, and is quite distinct from Dunstan, which is dominated by recently-built, multi-storey flat developments, such as the Ocean Estate. Shadwell and Ratcliffe (which incorporates the old Limehouse areas in part) were combined as a fairly coherent dockside sprawl. The Stepney wards of Holy Trinity, Limehouse and Mile End were included in Bow (Holy Trinity) and Bromley (Limehouse and Mile End wards). Burdett Road and Grove Road form a more realistic boundary between Stepney and Bow and Bromley than the actual borough boundary. It is impossible to validate the

TABLE 10: DELINQUENT RESIDENCE: 'NATURAL' AREAS: (II) 13–16

	Spital-fields	Stepney (Cable St.)	Shadwell/ Limehouse	Stepney (Green)	Dunstan	Bancroft	Bow	Bromley	Poplar	Isle of Dogs	Totals
Offenders	21	37	23	6	7	17	29	69	15	23	247
Offences:											
Breakings	9	14	9	1	4	8	5	15	3	4	72
Take/Drive	3	15	9	3	3	6	5	21	4	4	73
Larc./simp.	11	9	1	1	2	—	7	12	3	6	52
Larc. dwell.	—	2	—	—	—	—	10	3	4	4	23
Rowdyism	—	1	—	—	—	—	5	7	—	7	20
Larc/*from* v.	—	3	4	—	—	2	2	5	—	1	17
Larc. bike	—	1	2	1	1	—	—	5	—	3	13
Non-Ind/Prop.	1	2	1	—	2	—	—	3	1	—	10
Receiving	1	1	—	—	—	1	1	4	1	—	9
Violence/pn.	—	1	—	—	—	3	1	1	—	—	6
Mal. Damage	—	—	2	—	—	—	1	1	—	—	4
Larc. person	—	2	—	—	—	—	—	1	—	—	3
Sexual	—	—	—	—	—	—	—	1	—	—	1
	25	51	28	6	12	20	37	79	16	29	303

	Wapping
Offenders	8
Breakings	2
Take/Drive	5
Larceny bicycle	1
Larceny simple	1
Larceny *from* veh.	1
Non-Ind/Prop.	1

Area	*% Offenders*	*% Total Pop.*
Bromley	27·95	28·4
Stepney (Cable St.)	14·95	14·3
Bow	11·75	14·2
Shadwell/Limehouse	9·3	7·9
Isle of Dogs	9·3	7·9
Spitalfields	8·5	8·4
Bancroft	6·9	4·8
Poplar	6·05	5·3
Wapping	3·2	c. 2·5
Dunstan	2·8	6·3
Stepney (Green)	2·4	4·8
	99·9	100·1
		(excl. Wapping)

'natural' essence of an area: but at least the purpose was served of breaking the boroughs up into smaller units for comparative analysis.

TABLE II: DELINQUENT RESIDENCE: 'NATURAL' AREAS: (III) 17–21

	Spital-fields	Stepney (Cable St.)	Shadwell/ Limehouse	Stepney (Green)	Dunstan	Bancroft	Bow	Bromley	Poplar	Isle of Dogs	Totals
Offenders	28	77	23	15	20	6	42	65	14	17	307
Offences:											
Take/Drive	5	20	3	1	4	3	6	10	3	2	57
Breakings	8	12	6	3	1	2	10	12	2	—	56
Larc./simp.	5	7	3	2	5	1	10	13	3	1	50
Rowdyism	1	5	3	3	—	1	7	9	2	10	41
Violence/pn.	5	6	3	2	1	1	5	6	1	2	32*
Prostitution	2	16	1	—	—	—	2	3	1	—	25
L./Dwellg. etc.	3	5	2	2	—	—	3	2	—	3†	20
Receiving	3	3	—	—	5	—	—	7	1	—	19
N/I vs. Propty.	1	4	1	—	2	2	2	2	1	—	15
Gambling	1	5	3	4	—	—	—	—	—	—	13
Larc/person	3	3	—	—	—	—	2	3	—	—	11*
L./*from* veh.	2	1	—	—	—	—	2	3	1	—	9
Poss. off. wpn.	1	1	1	—	2	—	1	1	—	—	7
Mal. Damage	—	1	1	—	—	—	1	2	1	—	6
L./*of* vehicle	—	1	—	—	—	—	—	3	—	—	4
Imm. Earnings	1	3	—	—	—	—	—	—	—	—	4
Sexual	—	—	—	—	—	1	—	2	—	—	3
Larc. bike	—	—	—	—	—	—	—	1	1	—	2
	41	93	27	17	20	11	51	79	17	18	374

	Wapping	Area	% Offenders	% Total Pop
Offenders	11	Stepney (Cable St.)	25·05	14·3
Take/Drive	8	Bromley	21·15	28·4
N/I vs. Property	2	Bow	13·7	14·2
Receiving	1	Spitalfields	9·1	8·4
Larceny *of* vehicle	1	Shadwell/Limehouse	7·5	7·9
		Dunstan	6·5	6·3
		Isle of Dogs	5·5	5·7
		Stepney (Green)	4·9	4·8
		Poplar	4·55	5·3
		Wapping	3·55	c. 2·5
		Bancroft	1·95	4·8
			99·9	100·1

* includes 7 robbery with violence.
† all larceny slot-machines.

(excl. Wapping

Table 12 shows that the areas with the two highest crime rates for the 22–25 age-group, i.e. Stepney (Cable Street) and Spitalfields, possess radically different patterns of offences. Spitalfields' main offences are—for this age-group—the utilitarian property offences of breaking-and-entering and larceny.

TABLE 12: 'CRIMINAL' RESIDENCE: 'NATURAL' AREAS: (IV) 22–25

	Spital-fields	Stepney (Cable St.)	Shadwell/ Limehouse	Stepney (Green)	Dunstan	Bancroft	Bow	Bromley	Poplar	Isle of Dogs	Totals
Offenders	18	52	10	2	7	4	22	34	3	8	160
Offences:											
Larc./simp.	6	5	3	2	3	2	6	6	2	4	39
Violence/pn.	1	11	1	—	—	2	5*	4	—	1	25
Gambling	3	14	2	—	—	—	1	2	—	—	22
Breakings	6	4	1	—	—	—	2	3	1	—	17
Receiving	2	3	1	—	2	1	1	5	1	—	16
N/I. vs. Prop.	1	2	—	—	1	1	2	6	—	—	13
Rowdyism	—	6	2	—	—	—	2	1	—	1	12
Prostitution	1	4	—	—	1	—	2	3	—	—	11
Larc./of veh.	3	3	—	—	2	—	—	2	—	—	10
Larc. from veh.	1	3	—	—	—	—	1	2	1	2	10
Take/Drive	1	3	—	—	—	—	1	1	—	1	7
L./Dwellgs.	1	3	1	—	—	—	1	1	—	—	7
Poss. off. wpn.	—	2	—	—	—	—	1	3	—	—	6
Mal. Damage	—	3	—	—	—	—	—	1	—	1	5
Imm. Earnings	—	4	—	—	—	—	—	1	—	—	5
L./Person etc.	—	1	—	—	—	—	2*	—	—	—	3
P. D. Drugs	2	1	—	—	—	—	—	—	—	—	3
	28	72	11	2	9	6	27	41	5	10	211

	Wapping	Area	% *Offenders*	% *Total Pop·*
Offenders	1	Stepney (Cable St.)	32·5	14·3
Poss. off. wpn.	1	Bromley	21·25	28·4
Violence/pn.	1	Bow	13·75	14·2
		Spitalfields	11·25	8·4
		Shadwell/Limehouse	6·25	7·9
		Isle of Dogs	5·0	5·7
		Dunstan	4·4	6·3
		Bancroft	2·5	4·8
		Poplar	1·85	5·3
		Stepney (Green)	1·25	4·8
		Wapping	0·6	c. 2·5
			100·0	100·1

* includes 2 robbery with violence.   (excl. Wapping)

TABLE 13: DELINQUENT AND 'CRIMINAL' RESIDENCE: 'NATURAL' AREAS: (v) 8–25

	Spital- fields	Stepney (Cable St.)	Shadwell/ Limehouse	Stepney (Green)	Dunstan	Bancroft	Bow	Bromley	Poplar	Isle of Dogs	Totals
Offenders	74	178	79	30	39	30	109	187	47	56	829
Offences:											
Breakings	25	35	23	9	7	13	23	37	11	8	191
Larc./simp.	28	22	13	5	12	3	30	40	16	14	183
Take/Drive	9	38	14	4	7	9	12	32	7	7	139
Rowdyism	1	12	5	3	—	1	14	17	2	18	73
Viol./vs. pn.	6	18	4	2	1	6	11	11	1	3	63
L./dwllg. etc.	5	10	3	2	—	—	18	8	4	7	57
Receiving	6	8	1	—	7	2	2	16	4	1	47
Larc. *from* veh.	3	8	11	1	—	2	5	10	2	3	45
N/I. vs. Prop.	4	8	2	—	5	3	4	11	2	—	39
Prostitution	3	20	1	—	1	—	4	6	1	—	36
Gambling	4	19	5	4	—	—	1	2	—	—	35
Larc. bike	1	3	3	2	1	—	—	7	4	3	24
Mal. Damage	—	6	5	—	1	—	2	4	1	3	22
L./person, etc.	3 (3)	7 (1)	—	—	—	—	4 (3)	5 (2)	1	—	20*
Larc. *of* veh.	3	4	—	—	2	—	—	5	—	—	14
Loss. off. wpn.	1	3	1	—	2	—	2	4	—	—	13
Imm. Earngs.	1	7	—	—	—	—	—	1	—	—	9
Sexual	—	1	—	—	—	1	—	3	—	—	5
Drugs	2	1	—	—	—	—	—	—	—	—	3
	105	230	91	32	46	40	132	219	56	67	1018

	Wapping	*Area*	% *Offenders*	% *Total Pop.*
Offenders	23	Bromley	22·55	28·4
Take/Drive	13	Stepney (Cable St.)	21·45	14·3
Breakings	2	Bow	13·15	14·2
N/I vs. Property	3	Shadwell/Limehouse	9·55	7·9
Mal. Damage	2	Spitalfields	8·94	8·4
Larc. simp.	1	Isle of Dogs	6·76	5·7
Violence vs. pn.	1	Poplar	5·67	5·3
Larc. *from* veh.	1	Dunstan	4·7	6·3
Larc. *of* veh.	1	Bancroft	3·62	4·8
Larc. bicycle	1	Stepney (Green)	3·62	4·8
Receiving	1	Wapping	2·75	c. 2·5
Poss. off. wpn.	1			
Sexual	1		100·01	100·1
	—			(excl. Wapping)
	28	* figures in brackets = robbery/violence.		

The dominant offences in the Stepney (Cable Street) area are gambling, violence and rowdyism—the latter has almost disappeared from the Poplar areas for this age-group. Yet for the 17–21 age-group, the dominant Stepney (Cable Street) offences are (with the exception of prostitution) take-and-drive (even allowing for the disproportionate number committed by Wapping offenders) and breaking-and entering. For Spitalfields, take-and-drive and violence are committed as frequently as larceny simple. For the 13–16 age-group, Stepney (Cable Street) offenders committed break-and-enter, take-and-drive and larceny when the expected reflection of the older age-groups would have suggested the predominance of rowdyism and violence. For Spitalfields, offences against property again predominate in this age-group. There is thus no one sequence for any 'natural' area. The clearest point to emerge is the priority of rowdyism in the Isle of Dogs in the 13–21 age-groups.

What follows is a crude guide to offences which predominate by area or which are considerably less committed than would be expected from total population distribution. By calculating the difference between the actual proportion of each type of offence committed by residents in each 'natural' area, and the proportion one would expect from simple population distribution, those sharing disproportionately in the total offence make-up to the extent of a 10 per cent difference or more were highlighted. For example, the Stepney (Cable St.) area, with only 14·3 per cent of the population of the two boroughs, accounted for 55·5 per cent of those charged with prostitution, and 7 out of 9 of those charged with 'immoral earnings'. To take another offence, the Bromley area, with 28·4 per cent of the population, accounted for only 14 per cent of larceny dwelling offenders. However, the smaller areas could hardly show differences of this size, and to establish 'characteristic' offences for these areas, the actual distribution of offences by residents *within* each area was measured against that for the borough as a whole (see final column, Table 2). For example, in the two boroughs as a whole, 16·7 per cent of offenders aged 8–25 committed take-and-drive: in Wapping, 56·5 per cent; in the Isle of Dogs, only 12·5 per cent. Similarly, the overall proportion committing rowdyism was 8·7 per cent: in the Isle of Dogs alone, 32·1 per cent; in Bancroft, only 3·3 per cent of offenders, and so on. A combination of both approaches crudely reveals the offences most characteristic of each area. Without weightings, only extreme tendencies can be noted.

Area	*Characteristic Offences*	
	+	−
Spitalfields	Break-and-Enter	Mal. Damage
	Larceny simple, etc.	
Stepney (Cable St.)	Take-and-drive	
	(due to Wapping)	None
	Violence	
	Prostitution	
	Gambling	
	Larceny person, etc.	
	Mal. Damage	
	(due to Wapping)	
Shadwell	Larceny *from* vehicle	Larceny person, etc.
	Mal. Damage	
Stepney (Green)	None	Receiving
		Non/Ind. vs. Prop.
		Prostitution
		Mal. Damage
		Larceny person
Dunstan	Receiving	Rowdyism
		Larceny dwelling
		Larceny *from* vehicle
		Gambling
		Larceny person
Bancroft	Break-and-enter	Larceny simple
	Violence	Larceny dwelling
	Take-and-drive	Prostitution
		Gambling
		Larceny bicycle
		Malicious Damage
		Larceny person
Bow	Larceny dwelling	Gambling
		Larceny bicycle
Bromley	None	Violence
		Larceny dwelling
		Prostitution
		Gambling
		Malicious Damage

Poplar	Larceny simple, etc.	Gambling
	Larceny bicycle	
Isle of Dogs	Rowdyism	Prostitution
		Gambling
		Non/Ind. vs. Prop.
		Larceny person

Wapping is notable for its high incidence of take-and-drive and the absence of indictable offences against property. Larceny *of* vehicle, possessing offensive weapon, immoral earnings, sexual offences and possession of drugs are not included due to their low incidence.

The combination of characteristic and non-characteristic offences shows that Stepney (Cable Street) is the most criminal area, but the criminality is that of offences of morality and disorder rather then semi-professional acquisitive offences. The least criminal areas appear to be Stepney (Green) and Bromley—although, if the residence spot-maps are considered, Bromley accommodates a few clusters of offenders, especially at the northern end of Devons Road. Spitalfields appears to be the most utilitarian criminal area. The Isle of Dogs is the only area of which rowdyism is the characteristic offence, although in the 13–16 age groups, rowdyism is a significant offence for Bow and Bromley also. The patterns revealed demand some re-casting of theoretical assumptions about criminality in Stepney, which will be dealt with later. It is worth noting here, however, that the forms of disorder prevalent in the Stepney (Cable Street) area connote some form of organisation, while the relatively mild category of rowdyism connotes spontaneous disorder.

Miscellaneous

This section gives indication of the characteristics of Stepney and Poplar offenders *vis-à-vis* offence location, 'multiple' offences, accomplices, previous convictions, and certain socioeconomic factors; information on prostitutes was fuller than for other offenders, and is given in a separate set of tables.

Table 14 shows that relatively more Stepney offenders committed their offences locally than Poplar offenders. Only 6 per cent of Stepney residents offended in Poplar: 18 per cent of

Poplar residents committed their offences in Stepney. Also, while 11 per cent of Stepney offenders committed offences in Bethnal Green, Shoreditch, etc., only about 2 per cent of Poplar offenders were guilty of offences in Canning Town, West Ham, Plaistow, etc. Stepney was, therefore, not only the location for most of its own residents' offences: it was also a delinquency-attracting area for almost a fifth of Poplar offenders.

TABLE 14: LOCATION OF OFFENCES:

(a) Stepney Residents			(b) Poplar Residents		
	N	%		N	%
Stepney	413	79·45	Poplar	218	70·7
Poplar	31	5·95	Stepney	58	18·7
'North'	57	10·95	'North'	17	5·5
'East'	5 ⎫		'East'	6 ⎫	
'South'	5 ⎟		'South'	5 ⎟	
'West'	1 ⎬	2·7	'West'	1 ⎬	4·2
Gter. London	1 ⎟		Gter. London	— ⎟	
Elsewhere	2 ⎭		Elsewhere	1 ⎭	
DK/NA	5	0·95	DK/NA	3	0·9
	520	100·00		309	100·0

In table 15, 'multiple' offender means one who commits more than one distinct offence, as opposed to one who commits the same offence twice or more. As a possible index of 'versatility', it was found that slightly more Stepney than Poplar residents were 'multiple' offenders, 17 per cent and 15·5 per cent respectively. For both boroughs, the older offenders proved more 'versatile', about a quarter of the 22–25 age-group committing more than one distinct offence in 1960. In Stepney, however, the least versatile age-group was 8–12, in Poplar 17–21. In the 13–21 groups, about 5 per cent more Stepney residents were 'multiple' offenders than was the case for Poplar. Otherwise, this approach revealed little difference between the two boroughs.

Table 15 shows (a) the proportion of 'multiple' offenders committing each offence-type, and (b) the proportion of each offence-type coupled by 'multiple' offenders with another offence. For example, 53·3 per cent of multiple offenders committed—among other things—breaking-and-entering; and of all offenders committing breaking-and-entering, 38·4 per cent committed a different offence, which was either 'taken into consideration' or dealt with at a separate court appearance in the same year.

TABLE 15: 'MULTIPLE' OFFENDERS: BOTH BOROUGHS

Offence	N (N = 137)	(a)	(b)
Breakings	73	53·3%	38·4%
Take/Drive	39	28·5	28·3
Larceny simple, etc.	40	29·2	22·0
Violence vs. the Person	22	16·05	34·9
Rowdyism	6	4·4	8·3
Mal. Damage (over £20)	16	11·7	72·7
Poss. off. weapons	7	5·1	53·9
Poss. dangerous drugs	1	×	33·3
Non-ind. Offs. vs. Property	14	10·2	36·8
Illegal gambling	5	3·65	14·3
Receiving	17	12·4	36·2
Larceny dwellings, etc.	22	16·05	38·6
Larceny person	2	1·45	10·0
Larceny *from* vehicle	18	13·2	46·0
Larceny *of* vehicle	11	8·0	78·5
Larceny bicycle	5	3·65	20·8
Immoral earnings	2	1·45	22·2
Prostitution	4	2·9	11·1
Sexual	0	—	—

(For the overall totals for each offence, see final col., table 2.)

However, as the proportion of 'multiple' offenders committing offence-types is obviously weighted by the proportion of undifferentiated offenders committing each offence-type—although break-and-enter and malicious damage offenders exceed this proportion, while rowdyism, and prostitution, offenders do not —(*b*) is a less crude index of the extent to which an offence-type serves as a self-contained 'adaptation'. For example, 32·6 per cent of Stepney 'multiple' offenders—about a third—committed 'take-and-drive-away'. Of these, 58·5 per cent coupled the offence with 'breaking-and-entering' or were guilty of breaking-

and-entering in the same year. Of *all* Stepney take-and-drive-away offenders, 18·3 per cent—mostly in the 17–21 age-group—also committed breaking-and-entering (not given). The implication is that offence-types provide differential indices of offender-types. It must not be assumed too readily that the break-in offender and the take-and-drive offender are two different species, when in a fifth of the latter cases they are the same offender. On this basis, malicious damage (over £20) and vehicle theft cannot be generalised about as adaptations, since 75 per cent of such offenders are prone to commit other offences. If it can be shown that these other offences are of an essentially similar nature, then it can be assumed that the offence-type provides a meaningful basis for generalisation about an offender-type. If, for example, it can be shown that car-theft is linked with other offences of theft, then the distribution of car-theft offenders can be held to provide an index of utilitarian offences against property. Malicious damage (over £20) has a totally different distribution to rowdyism. The former is distributed fairly uniformly throughout age-groups: rowdyism is not. Malicious damage (over £20) includes not only offences involving destruction of property by physical force, but also by arson and other means; 'sacrilege' is included, and the possibility of property destruction as a means of reprisal in 'protection' is a factor to be considered. This heterogeneity of means, target and motivation for an offence-type as limited as malicious damage of over £20 of property is reflected in the high proportion of such cases occurring as 'multiple' offences. Rowdyism, on the other hand, is coupled with another offence in only 8·3 per cent cases, suggesting its accuracy as an index of an adaptation.

Tables 16–18 set out the number of accomplices per offender committing (*a*) all offences, and (*b*) selected offences. (For the actual number of offenders per offence, add 1 to all totals.) The accomplice rates clearly indicate the tendency for delinquent group size to diminish with increasing age. Poplar throughout shows a slightly higher accomplice rate than Stepney. But the most marked differences are between age-groups rather than between areas. Table 17 shows that only 15·7 per cent of 8–12 year olds commit lone offences, compared to 50·7 per cent in the 22–25 age-group. The characteristic delinquent group size for 8–12 years olds is 4–5 and 2; for the 13–16's, 2; for the 17–21 group, 2 and lone; and lone for the 22–25 group. Even in the 13–16 age-group, however, only 17·8 per cent commit lone offences. The over-riding trend seems to be for offenders to need at least one accomplice until the age of about 19 or 20.

TABLE 16: ACCOMPLICE RATE BY BOROUGH AND AGE-GROUP

(incl. lone offenders)

	Stepney		*Poplar*		*Both*	
8–12	1·78		2·44		2·12	
13–16	1·79		1·8		1·79	
		} 1·34		} 1·64		} 1·455
17–21	1·1		1·42		1·21	
22–25	0·79		0·815		0·8	

N.B. (*a*) Excludes gambling—nearly all 11+ 'accomplices'.

(*b*) Excludes soliciting prostitution—all charges individual.

(*c*) Re 'multiple' offenders, data on only one offence, either the principal offence or that committed latest in the year, was collected, due to coding.

TABLE 17: % ACCOMPLICE DISTRIBUTION BY AGE-GROUP:
BOTH BOROUGHS

	8–12	13–16	17–21	22–25	*Total*
Lone	15·7	17·8	31·2	50·7	27·8
1	27·8	42·0	34·5	29·2	35·0
2	21·7	14·9	24·2	13·1	18·9
3/4	28·6	18·1	8·6	6·9	14·4
5/6	6·1	5·2	1·5	—	3·15
7/8	—	2·0	—	—	0·65
	99·9	100·0	100·0	99·9	99·9

TABLE 18: ACCOMPLICES: SELECTED OFFENCES: RATES BY BOROUGH
AND AGE-GROUPS

(a) Breakings:	Stepney		Poplar		Both	
8–12	2·41		2·98		2·69	
13–16	2·84	2·15	2·22	2·16	2·66	2·155
17–21	1·08		1·22		1·13	
22–25	2·04		0·5		1·82	

(b) Rowdyism:	Stepney		Poplar		Both	
8–12	Nil		Nil		Nil	
13–16	2·12		3·72		3·4	
17–21	1·88	1·6	2·37	2·8	2·16	2·32
22–25	0·75		1·62		1·04	

(c) Violence vs. the Person:	Stepney		Poplar		Both	
8–12	Nil		Nil		Nil	
13–16	1·75		1·0		1·5	
17–21	1·45	0·98	1·54	1·26	1·48	1·06
22–25	0·37		0·83		0·48	

(d) Take-and-Drive-Away:	Stepney		Poplar		Both	
8–12	1·75		Nil		1·75	(2 cases only)
13–16	1·27		1·2		1·24	
17–21	1·19	1·28	1·07	1·15	1·15	1·23
22–25	2·75		1·00		1·87	(4 cases only)

Considerable variations exist between offences as well as between age-groups. When four selected offences are considered, although the pattern already noted broadly holds, it is found that rowdyism has more than twice the accomplice rate for violence against the person, and breaking-and-entering almost twice the rate for take-and-drive-away. Overall accomplice distribution by offence (not given) shows that only 5·55 per cent of rowdyism offences were lone, compared to 44·5 per cent of violence against the person. The proportions committing lone offences of break-and-enter and take-and-drive were virtually identical—16·9 per cent and 16·7 per cent respectively. Certain offences impose their own pattern on the accomplice rate: for example, taking-and-driving-away a car is unlikely to be accomplished by more than four in a group, and two if the vehicle is a motor-bike or scooter. Not surprisingly, 61 per cent take-and-drive's were carried out by groups of 2, compared with only 26·5 per cent of break-ins, 37·5 per cent of rowdyism and 14·3 per cent of violence against the person. The highest rate is the 13–16 rowdyism rate for Poplar, the average number of accomplices being 3·7, making the average group size 4·7. The rates for the boroughs are very similar for break-and-enter and take-and-drive, but Poplar's exceeds those of Stepney for violence, and for rowdyism. The break-and-enter rates reveal many points of difference between Stepney and Poplar, however: the Poplar rates follow the normal trend, declining in size from groups of about 4 in the 8–12 group to a pattern of lone and 1 accomplice for the 22–25 group; in Stepney, the 8–12 group has a considerably lower rate than both that for the same age-group in Poplar and the 13–16 group in Stepney, and the 22–25 group has a much higher rate than the 17–21 age-group, possibly indicating a greater element of criminal organisation for this particular offence in Stepney in the adult group.

A roughly comparable accomplices table is given for the MPD in the Analysis of Crime for 1960. This analysis applies only to arrests of groups 'whose members were all under 21 years of age' and who committed indictable offences only. This can be compared only with figures for Stepney and Poplar which include offenders aged 21, and include non-indictable offences, at least two of which—rowdyism and take-and-drive—exceed the average for all offences for both boroughs by a considerable margin. For the MPD, on the basis, 36·4 per cent of offenders had no accomplices operating with them: for Stepney, 25·8 per cent were lone offenders; for Poplar, only 19·8 per cent; and for both, 23·2 per cent. For the MPD, of the 63·6 per cent who committed indictable offences in groups aged under 21, over 87 per cent were of 2 to 3 persons: for Stepney, of the 74·2 per cent who committed both indictable and non-indictable offences, aged 21 and under, 78·1 per cent had 1–2 accomplices; for Poplar only 66·75 per cent, and for both only 73·4 per cent had 1–2 accomplices. The accomplice rate for the MPD is 1·54; for both Stepney and Poplar, 1·98. (88·2 per cent of the MPD groups comprised members *all* of whom were under 21.) It seems likely that—if the non-indictable offences were extracted from the East End calculations—the rates would be roughly the same as for the whole MPD. Stepney has a persistently higher rate for solitary offenders than Poplar, especially for violence against the person.

TABLE 19: PREVIOUS CONVICTIONS: ALL OFFENDERS: BOTH BOROUGHS

	8–12	13–16	17–21	22–25	Total
No previous	87 75·6	129 56·0	86 36·8	40 33·6	342 49·2
1: Same	14 12·2	21 9·1	12 5·1	4 3·4	51 7·35
2+ : Same	1 0·9	7 3·0	6 2·6	9 7·6	23 3·3
1: Same and Allied	7 6·1	23 10·0	15 6·5	7 5·9	52 7·5
2+ : Same and Allied	5 4·3	27 12·2	48 21·1	23 19·3	103 14·8
1: Different	1 0·9	6 2·6	13 5·6	3 2·5	23 3·3
2+ : Same, Allied and Different	— —	11 4·8	43 18·5	29 24·4	83 11·95
1+ : Less Serious N/ind.	— —	5 2·2	9 3·9	4 3·4	18 2·6
	115 100·0	229 99·9	232 100·1	119 100·1	695 100·0

Tables exclude: (*a*) Prostitutes convicted of soliciting only (see tables on Prostitution).
(*b*) Almost all gambling and rowdyism offenders: no data on previous convictions available from charge-sheets.

The same method of analysis, i.e. of all and of selected offences, is used for previous convictions as for accomplices, and similarly consistent trends emerge. The most obvious and expected trend is that the proportion of offenders with previous convictions increases with age. In the 8–12 age-group for both boroughs,

75·6 per cent of offenders had no previous convictions. In the 22–25 group, only 33·6 per cent offenders had no previous. Throughout all age-groups, however, Stepney had a higher proportion of recidivists than Poplar. Of all age-groups combined, 45·3 per cent Stepney, and 55·9 per cent Poplar, offenders had no previous convictions, and the disparity is consistent for all four age-groups.

As in the case of accomplices, a roughly comparable table on previous convictions for the whole MPD is given in the New Scotland Yard 'Analysis of Crime' for 1960. Although (as with accomplices) the MPD table refers only to indictable offenders, comparisons with the tables of the present study are more accurate than for accomplices, as offenders committing rowdyism, illegal gambling, and soliciting only have been excluded, and it is doubtful that take-and-drive, 'suspicion' and offensive weapon carrying offenders are atypical enough seriously to bias the comparison. For the MPD, only 9 per cent of children aged 8–13 who were arrested had previous convictions: for Stepney, 27 per cent of delinquent children aged 8–12 had previous convictions; for Poplar, the figure is 20·9 per cent. In the MPD'S 14–16 age-group, only 16·9 per cent had previous convictions: the figures for Stepney and Poplar are 47·5 per cent and 39 per cent respectively for 13–16 year-olds. Of 17–20 year-old offender in the MPD, only 35·2 per cent had previous criminal records: of 17–21 offenders in Stepney and Poplar, 68·8 per cent and 57 per cent had previous criminal records. In the MPD's 21–30 age-group, 44·3 per cent of offenders had a record: in the 22–25 groups in Stepney and Poplar, 68·8 per cent and 61·6 per cent had a record. The disparity between the rates for the MPD and the rates for Stepney and Poplar are most marked in the 8–12 age-group, whose offences are almost wholly indictable. The possibility of bias due to the inclusion in the East End figures of non-indictable offenders—such as those committing take-and-drive-away—occurs only from the age of 13 onwards. Also, less than 3 per cent of the East End sample had criminal records composed solely of the less serious non-indictable 'suspicion' offences against property, such as 'found on enclosed premises', 'suspicious person', 'frequenting', 'unlawful possession', etc. The gross disparities between the MPD and the East End situation appear, therefore, to be indications of a real difference in recidivism, despite the fact that exclusion of non-indictable offences would reduce the disparity by perhaps as much as 10 per cent. The only figure given for a specific offence in the MPD is that 37·5 per cent of break-in offenders had previous criminal records: in Stepney and Poplar, 62·5 per cent and 47·5 per cent of break-in offenders had previous criminal records, in the 8–25 groups.

When four selected offences are considered, it appears that 57 per cent larceny simple offenders, 43·2 per cent take-and-drive, 42·7 per cent break-in and only 27·4 per cent violence vs. the person offenders had *no* previous convictions. Moreover, 50 per cent violence vs. the person offenders, and only 13.4 per cent take-and-drive, 10·6 per cent break-in, and 7·1 per cent larceny simple offenders, had committed radically different offences at least once previous to their current offence. Three broad divisions were made between offenders with previous convictions who had committed the 'identical' offence once and more as that for which they were charged; offenders whose previous convictions were not necessarily 'identical' but broadly similar to that for which they were currently charged; and those whose record revealed the commission of at least one radically different offence. The two broad categories of offences 'against property' and 'against the person' were used, but incorporated in the latter were malicious damage, possessing offensive weapons, prostitution and immoral earnings. On the basis that offenders who combine both species of offence are the most serious and dangerous, if not necessarily the most 'professional', criminals, it appears that offenders committing violence against the person are the most serious offenders, those committing larceny simple, etc. the least. The tendency to combine both species of offence is also more marked in Stepney than in Poplar and grows with increasing age. Of Stepney and Poplar offenders, therefore—both of which boroughs display a recidivism distribution at least twice and, for some age-groups, treble that for the MPD as a whole—Stepney offenders have both longer and more serious records, and this tendency is most marked for violence vs. the person offenders, quite marked for break-in and take-and-drive offenders, and negligible for larceny simple offenders; it is also most marked for offenders aged 22–25.

The background data on each case showed that only 5·55 per cent Stepney, and 7·26 per cent of Poplar offenders, went through an educational process better than that of the secondary modern or equivalent, though the rest include those in primary education. 'Equivalent' refers to a small minority of delinquents who attend 'central' schools, i.e. secondary modern with a technical stream, who were mistakenly classified as wholly secondary modern. All these, however, left at 15. There are no comprehensive schools in Stepney and Poplar, but both boroughs are over-supplied with grammar-school places, many of which are filled by children commuting from Essex. It is unlikely that the 3 per cent of delinquents who were grammar-school boys merely reflect the grammar-school proportion of the population at risk. The table confirms already well-known facts, that the delinquent boy is overwhelmingly the secondary modern school 'drop-out'. Where he is not still at school, the delinquent is most likely to be an unskilled, semi-skilled or unemployed worker. Occupationally, as educationally, the delinquent is 'bottom of the heap' but the unskilled are only slightly in excess of the semi-skilled delinquents. As far as could be judged from bare, one-word descriptions of jobs, e.g. 'labourer', 'van-boy', etc., over 6/7ths of those at work in Stepney were in unskilled or semi-skilled jobs, or were unemployed: as were 3/4ths of those in Poplar. Of the total, however, about 7·5 per cent were either apprentices or boys who had relinquished their apprenticeships and were in semi-skilled or unskilled work. Of the 13–25 age-groups, 10 per cent more offenders were still at school in Poplar (27·5%) than in Stepney (17·7%), indicating that delinquency is more a problem of mid-adolescence in Poplar, and of late-adolescence in Stepney. Unfortunately, no comparative figures for population at risk are available for either education or occupation. The proportion of skilled manual workers and active and ex-apprentices in the total is not quite as high in Poplar (13·2%) as in Stepney (16·7%), but these proportions are not meaningful with reference to numbers at risk in each occupational group. These figures merely support known tendencies.

About 90 per cent of the 17–21, and about 60 per cent of the 22–25, groups were unmarried. The main difference between the boroughs is the greater proportion of married offenders in Poplar than in Stepney (36·6 per cent in Stepney, 52·3 in Poplar) in the 22–25 age-group. Comparative figures can be presented only for the 20–24 age-group: of all Stepney males aged 20–24,

28·1 per cent were married, 35·3 per cent for Poplar. The tendency for more offenders in this age-group to be married for Poplar is therefore reflected in the pattern for all males, but Stepney probably has a greater floating population of unattached males than Poplar, as reflected in the figures for offenders of 'no fixed abode'. If anything, offenders in this age-group were more likely to be married than non-offenders.

The material on offenders' home backgrounds is extremely suspect, mainly due to the sketchy police recording of data which, from their point of view, are of marginal importance only. Also, no information was available for rowdyism and gambling offenders, unless they had committed another offence in the same year and had a file to their name instead of simply a charge-sheet. Further information was available on prostitutes, and is presented separately below. For all other offenders, information was scanty and of doubtful validity, since discrepancies were frequent once an offender's record was long enough to provide cross-checks. Data on parental marital status were either not known or not available in 11·3 per cent cases: on family size in 70 per cent; and on parental occupational status in 90·2 per cent. According to the records, 67 per cent offenders had their natural parents at the time of the offence. Excluding the 'Not Known' category, 21·7 per cent had experienced a really 'broken' home, although this almost certainly underplays the instability of the home background situations, particularly as the step-parent rate is far too low (only 15 out of over 700 offenders were credited as having a step-parent: though a further 110 were recorded as having mother only or father only). Again excluding the 'Not Known' category, 24·4 per cent of Stepney, and 17·3 per cent of Poplar, offenders came from overtly 'broken' homes. If the data are seen as relevant only to the 8–16 age-group, since information on older offenders usually referred to the existing home background only, the overall 'broken' home rate is reduced to 15·75 per cent: 16·6 per cent for Stepney, 14.7 per cent for Poplar, offenders. These figures are of use, however, only because they indicate little difference between the two boroughs *vis-à-vis* family situation, though it appears that Stepney has a higher rate than Poplar of technically 'broken' homes in the older age-groups. In a wider context, however, the figures are meaningless, since the prevalence of 'broken' homes is not known either for

Stepney and Poplar non-offenders, or for offenders outside these two boroughs.

The tables for prostitution are presented separately mainly because of the nature of the offence, but partly to remedy on at least one sector of inquiry the two main deficiencies of the present study, i.e. lack of single-year analysis and lack of information about place of birth, nationality, etc. Only 3 out of 51 prostitutes operating in Stepney were, in a strict sense, local girls. Around 60 per cent came from outside London, about 30 per cent from outside England. Significantly, only 2 came from outside the UK, and those from Eire, none coming from abroad and none being coloured girls. Logically the proportion of East End offenders who were actually born in Stepney and Poplar would be expected to decline considerably with age, to a low proportion of somewhere around 30 per cent for Stepney and 50 per cent for Poplar in the 22–25 age-group. It is doubtful that the proportion of all offenders aged 17 and over who were born in Stepney and Poplar is anything like as low as the proportion of prostitutes born locally. Birth figures for the older age-groups would have been undoubtedly affected by the war-time evacuation policy in the dockside boroughs, and place of birth is no guide to length of residence in the East End. The coloured immigrant contribution to even the 22–25 offender age-group did not, it must be emphasised, appear at all disproportionate to their numbers, though detailed figures on ethnicity cannot be given.

Table 20 shows that 21 is the peak age for prostitution, and that just over half the prostitutes had previous convictions for other offences, mainly for petty theft, rarely for violence (although the 1960 figures alone show a predominance of violence among other offences committed by prostitutes). Few prostitutes earned money in any other way, half had overtly 'broken' family backgrounds, and over half had experienced at least one 'broken' relationship: only 20, i.e. 39 per cent, were single and childless. Twenty-eight, i.e. 55 per cent had children (more than one in 9 cases), and of the 5 who ostensibly had husbands to share this responsibility, 3 had husbands who were in prison. Thirty-three, i.e. 45 per cent, had undergone at least one separation, and were responsible for the child(ren). These figures alone suggest the social 'misfit' rather than the smoothly operative call-girl.

TABLE 20: PROSTITUTION

Commission: All in Stepney (N = 51).

Residence:

	N	%
Stepney	26	51·0
Poplar	10	19·6
'North'	13	25·5
'East'	1	1·95
N.F.A.	1	1·95
	—	———
	51	100·00
	—	———

Birthplace:

Stepney	2	Wales	2
Poplar	1	Scotland	8 (5 in Glasgow)
East London	8	Ulster	2
London e/where	8	Eire	2
South England	7	West Indies	0
Midlands	2	Elsewhere	0
North England	9	DK/NA	0
(5 in Lancs.)			

Age:

17	18	19	20	21	22	23	24	25	17–21	22–25	26+
—	4	3	11	15	6	3	3	6	33	18	10

10 prostitutes aged over 25 were charged in Stepney in 1960, their ages being 27, 28 (2), 29 (3), 30, 31, 39 and 40.

Previous convictions:

	0	1: S	2+: S	1: S/A	2+: S/A	1: D	2+: D/S/A	1+: N/Ind.
	4	7	11	—	1	1	27	—
No. of previous soliciting offs.		7	237		14		550	

i.e. 46 of the 51 prostitutes had been charged on 808 separate occasions, on average 17·5 times each, ranging between 1 and 115 previous convictions for soliciting alone.

Previous soliciting convictions	No.
1–10	28
11–25	7
26–50	4
50+	5 (60, 70, 85, 90, 115)

Of the 51 prostitutes, 29 had previous convictions for offences other than soliciting and its equivalents, such as 'committing gross indecency' and 'outraging public decency' and other euphemisms.

Past Offence Records	No.	
Break-and-enter	2	
Larceny, simple and misc.	22	
Larceny, dwellings, etc.	10	
Larceny from vehicle	1	
Receiving	6	Straightforward larcenies
Take-and-drive	3	and receiving predominate
Larceny person	2	(67·4%). Violence and non-
Violence against the Person	1	utilitarian offences are at a
Poss. off. wpn.	1	minimum.
Mal. Damage/Rowdyism, etc.	2	
Forgery (fraud)	4	
Obstructing P.C./insulting behaviour, etc.	4	
	—	
(Attempted suicide: 1)	58	
	—	

'Multiple' offenders: (1960):

Soliciting and equiv.	No.		Other	No.
2 convictions	7		Violence/pn.	3
3 convictions	4		(2 vs. police)	
4 convictions	6		Larceny simp.	1
7 convictions	1		Poss. off. wpn.	1
			Poss. dang. drug	1
			Ins. behaviour	1

Education:

Secondary Modern	41	(Of these, 14 became 'care and protection' cases, for at least a year, after school-leaving.)
Grammar	2	
Technical	3	
Convent	2	
In Care, L.A.	2	
More inst. than other	1	

Home Background

Own mother and father	25	Only child	—	
Step/parents	2	1 sib.	3	
Mother only	6	2 sib.	2	
Father only	6	3 sib.	5	
Foster/parents	4	4+ sib.	10	(4 (4), 6 (2),
Orphaned 0–5	5	DK/NA	31	8, 9, 11, 15)
Orphaned 6–16	3			
Parents Sep. /Div.	4		51	
DK/NA	4			

Only about half had a formally 'unbroken' home background. No information on parental occupations.

Occupations:

Prostitution only	44	
Casual, unskilled	5	(e.g. waitress in cafés)
Semi-skilled	2	(e.g. factory machinist)

IV CONCLUSIONS

The data show the need for a re-casting of the original basic assumptions on the criminal make-up of western Stepney which underlay the predictions inferred from theory. Stepney certainly possesses a larger adult criminal population than Poplar, and within Stepney, the Cable Street and Spitalfields areas have the highest rates in the 17–21 and 22–25 age-groups. But the nature of the criminality suggests Skid Row rather than professional crime, in the Cable Street area, whose characteristic offences are violence, illegal gambling, prostitution, larceny person, immoral earnings and a hidden incidence of drug-use. While prostitution and gambling require rudimentary organisation, it is not thought that any network of vice exists. Rather, any organisation is simply the minimum required for the commission of these offence-types. The offences characteristic of Spitalfields are, however, utilitarian in character, and suggest the operation of the remnants of an older criminal tradition which is fast becoming obsolete. The 1960 Pen Club murder, with its roots in the 'protection' racket, was likely an instance of a practice which has since shifted its ground rather than of an on-going tradition.[12] The higher criminal 22–25 rates for recidivism in Stepney, the presence of offenders of 'no fixed abode', the meths. drinker problem and the higher proportion of unattached males indicate 'disorganised' slum criminality rather than a successful criminal élite.

This picture is one of the 'unintegrated' slum area, whose adult crime 'tends to be individualistic, unorganised, petty, poorly paid and unprotected. This is the haunt of the small-time thief . . . the pimp . . . the unsophisticated con-man. . . .'[13] In this context, the expected adaptation is that of the 'conflict' subculture; however, offenders committing take-and-drive and rowdyism and individualistic violence against the person can hardly be said to embody the negativism and structured aggression of the 'conflict' subculture, since this behaviour is hardly 'wild' or 'untrammelled' in nature. However, Kobrin applied those terms to delinquent behaviour in the 'unintegrated' areas of American conurbations with the highest rates of delinquency and the most extreme problems of street-gang warfare. The analysis is not abortive simply because the UK does not share these extremes. But the 'mixing' of offences favours comparison with Cohen and Short's concept of the 'parent male' subculture rather than any of the Cloward and Ohlin variants.

Comparison between the London and New York situations is bedevilled by the full juvenile employment and absence of second-generation immigrant adolescents in large numbers in the former. These are probably the main reasons for the absence of structured delinquent gangs in Stepney and Poplar, or even of delinquent fighting gangs on the Yablonsky model. (Only 9 rowdyism offenders possessed 5 or more accomplices in Poplar and Stepney, and no violence against the person offender had even that number.) But the main determinant of the form of delinquency adopted by adolescent offenders in Stepney and Poplar—and, by implication, in other urban areas—does appear to be the fact that adult crime is *not* an alternative avenue for the materially upwardly mobile. It is generally the reverse: the pursuit of desperate social failures and discriminated against minority

[12] The boom in betting shops following the 1961 Gambling Act has, it appears, given the local 'protection' racket a boost. The shooting of Ted Berry in Stepney is a sign that it still flourishes; see the report in the *Sunday Times*, 19/1/1964.

[13] Cloward and Ohlin, op. cit., p. 173.

groups. As such, it is largely irrelevant to teenagers—except for the very poor and the educationally subnormal—most of whose socio-cultural problems are of a different order. (Criminals—in common with teachers, youth workers, etc.—are, after all, adults.) This divorce between the delinquency and adult crime situations has led in the East End to a pattern of delinquency in mid- to late-adolescence which bears more resemblance to the 'parent male' than to the 'conflict', 'criminal' or 'retreatist' adaptations. Also, pressures on the young male adult which conceivably make for the emergence of organised crime are weakened by the institutionalisation of 'fiddling', which in this connection performs a useful social function. (As, of course, does all crime in the Durkheimian sense.) The lack of an illegitimate opportunity structure is not only reflected in the absence of syndicated crime, but also in the absence of any conspicuously localised criminal class. The 'protection' racket appears to be small-time only, stifled largely by the legalisation of most gambling[14] in much the way that drug-peddling is staved off by the legality of medical treatment for addicts. (Though there are fears that experimentation with narcotics is filtering through to working-class adolescents.)

Male adolescent delinquency is, therefore, influenced in this important negative direction by the adult crime situation. The two trends stressed by Power may indicate a transition from the 'parent male' subculture to a 'conflict-oriented' adaptation. Alternatively, this 'break' may be nothing more than an indication of the greater versatility of delinquent 'exploit' available to the older mid-adolescent age-groups, and a differential arrest policy for teenagers as opposed to juveniles committing rowdyism. The discontinuity between age-group delinquency rates is not readily explicable in terms of the Cloward-Ohlin formulation, which asserts by inference consistency of incidence and patterning of delinquent and criminal behaviour at all age-levels. The Cohen formulation is more attractive as an explanatory tool for the uniformity of delinquency between areas until the age of 17–18. The trend is more clearly acted out in Poplar than

---

[14] See note p. 190; so lucrative has the betting shops' business become that they may be *reviving* the protection racket rather than the reverse. Stepney has one of the highest concentrations of betting shops in London. It is too soon to deliver any kind of assessment of this situation.

in Stepney, the former being characterised by emphases on rowdyism, take-and-drive, larceny from dwellings and slot machines, the latter by take-and-drive, break-and-enter only, while both display similar incidence of petty larceny, grievous and actual bodily harm, etc. This complies with Cloward-Ohlin theory, as Poplar adolescents are at a greater distance from adult criminal influence than Stepney offenders. But the over-riding tendency is for greater uniformity of juvenile delinquent behaviour than the Cloward-Ohlin theory will permit, if it is applied outside the framework of structured gang delinquency.

In their classic Chicago study, Shaw and McKay estimated that 'the proportion of unduplicated individuals who become police cases during their 7-year period of eligibility is approximately 3 times larger than the rate of police cases for a single given year.'[15] On this basis, the highest rate area in Stepney and Poplar—the 17–21 Stepney (Cable Street) area—possesses only a 15 per cent delinquent population, and this for a five-year period of eligibility is probably an over-estimate. Even allowing for undetected delinquents, the majority of the age-group cannot be held to qualify as serious offenders, though technically few would be non-delinquent. While most male adolescents probably temporise with the delinquent pattern that has been described, it is only for a time: only a minority persist with it. Some idea of this pattern has emerged from the official statistics: what makes for identification with the pattern remains unresolved.

Note

Section 128 of the Port of London (Consolidation) Act, 1920 gives the Port of London Authority power to appoint constables 'who shall be sworn in by two justices duly to execute the office of a

[15] Kobrin, S., 'The Conflict of Values in Delinquency Areas', *Amer. Sociol. Rev.*, Vol. 16, Oct. 1951, pp. 653–661. However, if the age-range of 8–21 or 10–25 is considered, the 'prevalence' rate for an area would obviously be much higher. A. N. Little, in calculating the 'prevalence' rate for England and Wales on the basis of the 1962 Criminal Statistics relating to male indictable offenders, established that the likelihood for males of at least one court appearance for such an offence by the age of 21 was between 15–20 per cent, though there are uncertainties about duplication involved. The rate for an area like Cable Street would be even more striking, though too much cannot be read into a single court appearance. It is the 'repeaters', with a much lower prevalence rate of around 3 per cent for the country as a whole, who command attention from the viewpoint of subcultural theory. See A. N. Little, 'The "Prevalence" of Recorded Delinquency and Recidivism in England and Wales,' *Amer. Sociol. Rev.* (forthcoming).

constable within the limits of the docks and works and within one mile of the same and when so sworn in shall have the same powers protections and privileges within the limits aforesaid and in relation to or on board any vessel therein and shall be subject to the same liabilities as constables have or are subject to by the laws of the realm'.

The general figures relating to the theft and kindred offences during the years 1960, 1961, and 1962 are as follows:

	LONDON AND ST. KATHARINE DOCKS (STEPNEY)			INDIA AND MILLWALL DOCKS (POPLAR)		
	1960	1961	1962	1960	1961	1962
Larceny—Cases						
Reported	77	59	74	187	137	143
Detected	32	18	33	133	97	81
Undetected	45	41	41	54	40	62
Unlawful Possession	2	—	3	4	2	1
Breaking and Entering	1	—	1	4	8	10

Statistics in respect of Other Crimes are not kept separately but are recorded in total figures relating to the Authority's Docks as a whole.

By the Port of London Act, 1962, Section 10(1) a constable of the Authority when 'pursuing a person from within the area of the constable's authority, that is to say, within the docks and works and within one mile thereof, shall have the same powers of arrest in respect of that person outside the said area as he would have within the said area.'

The 'docks and works' of the Authority referred to consist of five large groups of docks and a number of warehouses situated in the City of London and the Metropolitan Police District. Two of the five groups of docks are situated in the Boroughs of Stepney and Poplar, viz. the London and St. Katherine Docks which lie in Stepney and the India and Millwall Docks which lie in Poplar.

All persons arrested by the Port of London Authority Police in Stepney and Poplar are taken to the Metropolitan Police Station of the area in which they were apprehended to be formally charged. Therefore, the details of these offences are included in the Metropolitan Police crime statistics submitted to the Home Office. All other offences, unless of special importance, are not reported to the Metropolitan Police but are dealt with by this Force.

7

DELINQUENT SUBCULTURES IN STEPNEY AND POPLAR: INFORMAL OBSERVATION

PRIOR to work on the statistical survey of crime and delinquency in Stepney and Poplar, field-work was carried out in the two boroughs on the basis of 'informal observation'. This approach was thought to be the most feasible means of penetrating street-corner society in the neighbourhoods, outside institutions such as the school and the youth-club. 'Informal observation' is simply meant to convey the approach of 'hanging around', talking and sometimes going around with male adolescents and adults who seemed to be connected with delinquency and crime, although the original emphasis was on contact with delinquent male cliques or gangs. This approach differs fundamentally from that of 'participant observation'. The participant observer seeks direct involvement in the group(s) observed. The classic instance in the field of crime and delinquency is the work of W. F. Whyte with young adults in an Italian-American slum district of Boston. But for this method to work as a basis for research, as distinct from action-research and welfare work, there must be some degree of certainty that the observer is participating without unduly influencing or changing the life of the group(s). Whyte went to great pains to avoid changing the behaviour patterns of the 'Corner boys', but he was a young adult playing a role within a young adult—not an adolescent—group which was almost wholly non-delinquent. An equivalent approach with a delinquent adolescent group would entail not only the probable expectation that the observer participated in delinquent exploits, but also the near-certainty that the behaviour patterns of the group would undergo drastic change. It is one thing for an adult to become sufficiently friendly with such a group to be tolerated in their milieu; it is an entirely different matter for an adult to 'join' the group without some recasting of the group's attitudes and values, and some modification of their way of life. Thus, unless some intervention for delinquency prevention purposes is intended, it is essential for the observer to avoid playing any role *within* the group, the central notion of 'participant observation'.

Likewise, 'residential participation' fails to describe the approach made in the present research. This term connotes the complete sharing by the observer of the environment, if not the behaviour, of the group(s) observed. In this case, while residence within the boroughs was taken up for several months, this was not synonymous with sharing the environment of the boys or adults in question. 'Informal observation' implies also that no attempt was made to gain information by the use of interviews, whether structured or unstructured, questionnaires or any kind of projective technique. At a later stage, unstructured interviews were attempted, but the approach proved abortive for the purposes in mind. The results of this type of observation are impressionistic and are akin to reportage. The role adopted—that of a writer working on a book about teenagers in London—was not unfamiliar to the adolescents involved. No role is without disadvantages, but that of writer appeared to have less than those of youth worker, student etc. The attempted interviews illustrate the difficulties involved. With a view to more extensive interviewing, a 'pilot' sample of 10 names was chosen at random from the electoral registers of Stepney and Poplar. All were 21 year-old males: of these, four were successfully interviewed; two refused; two more consistently not available; one was on 'holiday'; and one had moved elsewhere. The interviewees were approached at home, and on the basis of a survey for London University on how far young people were satisfied with the jobs they were doing. In this respect at least, the refusals were of interest. Those who agreed to be interviewed were a university student, a technician and a skilled craftsman; the other interview gained was with a youth undergoing occupational therapy who had little idea what the interview was about. The direct refusals came from individuals who were in unskilled work, and who reacted against the mention of 'London University'. As there was no reason to assume that more extensive interviewing would reveal a different pattern of acceptance and refusal, the idea was dropped. If contacts refused to talk freely about employment, there was even less chance that they would—on the basis of a doorstep introduction—be drawn into comments on delinquency, their views on the law, the police, etc. Unless large-scale infiltration into the lives of *families*—as opposed to one adolescent—is envisaged, as with the Gluecks' research, and that of the Cambridge Institute in Camberwell—it appears that adolescents can be contacted individually only on their own terms in their own milieux on an informal basis. The only exception to this applies where the population is 'captive'; i.e. in prison, school, or youth-club, but forces of selection operate in these instances which defeat the purpose of sampling the population at large. But there is a more compelling reason why interviews with an East End young adult sample in the home would have been essentially unscientific, even if the response rate had been 100 per cent. Even in the four interviews completed, there were marked differences in the interview situation. Two were interviewed alone, one with both parents present, and one with his wife present. The interview situation is obviously determined by factors such as family size, housing, household leisure interests, marital status, etc. Data gained in such diverse interview situations will be of interest, but cannot be quantified in any meaningful way, particularly when the focus is on attitudes, not simply factual information. As the object of interviewing was to compare impressionistic with systematically-gathered evidence, and the only way to locate a random sample was by home contact, the interview situation—as much as the refusal rate—led to the abandoning of this approach. Significant here is the success of the Institute of Community Studies in interviewing Bethnal Green adults on family and kinship, with a refusal rate of only 5·5 per cent.[1] Three factors were probably crucial in securing this high response rate: (a) the enquiry was family-, not problem-centred; (b) family heads, and not adolescents, were approached; (c) the Institute was situated locally. However, a later enquiry on behalf of the Institute by Ralph Samuel, into adolescents' attitudes

[1] P. Willmott and M. Young, *Family and Kinship in East London* (1957), p. 168.

towards employment, met with a refusal rate of only 4 per cent. If this had been the case in Stepney and Poplar, a programme of interviewing would have been desirable. In the event, however, all the data available were extracted on the basis of 'informal observation'.

Field-work was carried out over a period of six to seven months in Stepney and Poplar. Owing to the way field-work developed, the data do not make for easy comparability between the two boroughs. In Stepney, fleeting contacts were made with adolescent individuals and groups mainly in youth clubs, and with coloured adults in pubs. In Poplar, work centred almost entirely around one 'street-corner group' with whom acquaintance was maintained over the period of several months, and contacts were restricted to the single 'caff' where the group hung out. Fyvel's work has by now familiarised the typically drab caff which all too often is the only resort for teenagers outside the pub, the cinema, the youth club and home. This particular caff conformed to the pattern. Between 8 and 11 p.m., it usually contained about 30 teenagers, mostly male, and the contacted group of 5–6 supplied much of the following information, though where appropriate, data from other sources are presented. At no time throughout the research did observation suggest that this group was especially unrepresentative of adolescent groupings in the two boroughs. This chapter is concerned with relating observed behaviour to concepts central to subcultural theorisation on delinquency.

(a) 'Gang' or Group?

Delinquent groups in the East End lacked both the structured cohesion of the New York gangs described by Cloward and Ohlin, and the fissile impermanence of Yablonsky's 'near-group'. If the definition of delinquent gang is that of a group whose central tenet is the requirement to commit delinquent acts—i.e. 'delinquent subcultures' as defined by Cloward and Ohlin—then observation and information combined point to the absence of delinquent gangs in the East End, except as a thoroughly atypical collectivity. The possible exceptions that were heard of were—by repute—conflict-oriented and 'near-group' in structure, and neither criminal- nor retreatist-oriented gangs were mentioned by respondents even in the legendary sense. The groups responsible for the bulk of delinquency were simply small cliques whose members committed illegal acts sometimes collectively, sometimes in pairs, sometimes individually, in some cases regularly, in others only rarely. Delinquency was no more the central requirement for membership than the experience of sexual intercourse, though the group and the peer group gave collective support to the commission of delinquent acts, much as they would to sexual prowess. Average group size was 4–5, with a few individuals on the periphery. While these street-corner groups persisted over time, and invariably possessed a dominant personality, all the other features commonly attributed to the delinquent 'gang' were absent: i.e. leadership, role allocation, hierarchical structure, consensus on membership, uniform, and name. Girls were attached to the groups only in so far as they were acquainted with individual members, but rarely took part in any delinquent activity. The norm, then, is the fluid, street-corner clique, averse to any form of structure and organisation, but with persistence over time.

Undoubtedly, exceptions to this general pattern existed, but the exceptions also conformed to a distinct type, and it is doubtful if this type conformed to the Cloward-Ohlin criteria. In general, these exceptions were heard of in connection with street forays, and descriptions of the action suggested close parallels to Yablonsky's delineation of the delinquent 'near-group'. The evidence suggests that short-lived mobilisation of groups numbering up to 20–30 is feasible in any urban working-class area for reprisal against a single target, but that such 'near-group' formations can be easily dispersed by police action, and disintegrate even if unscathed once the single act of reprisal is over. For example, a teacher at one of the East End's rougher secondary schools mentioned an incident in which the 'S—— Street boys' converged on the school one afternoon to 'get' an individual Cypriot boy who allegedly had beaten up one of their number. Two squad cars dispersed them before they even reached the school, but in fact nobody had ever heard of the 'S—— Street boys' before or since this incident. They were simply a heterogeneous group of boys living on or around S—— Street, mobilised for the temporary purpose of reprisal by a few friends of the boy who was beaten up. This is not to say that these groups, with their show of violence—they carried bike-chains, etc.—are not dangerous: the legends generated by such occasional acts of mobilisation for conflict purposes are indeed a pure example of the Durkheimian logic that crime serves as normative reinforcement for conventional society. Another example was given by one of the Poplar boys:

> 'The other night . . . I got off the bus down here, and outside the post office there were fifty of 'em having a fight. . . . Honestly, they've got gangs of 25 round here. They walk along in a big gang, they come up against another gang in the street, they have a punch-up.' The boys in the café weren't a gang, 'not really' though 'Ray, he's got a black jacket with a skull painted on the back'. Tony knew nothing about these gangs except 'they get the leader's name. Like Johnson's boys. That's Barry Johnson. They're fairly young, he's only 18.'

From observation, however, in no part of the East End did gangs even obtrude, let alone dominate an area, despite stories such as the following:

> 'I can't see no sense in a big gang going round beating up a couple of fellers. I been beaten up myself. It happened to me and Bill. In Plaistow. We was just walking along, three of us, and three fellers come up towards us, looking for trouble, so we thought well alright, there's three of them, three of us, then twelve more comes round the bleeding corner and kicks us to death. The trouble is, get any one of them on their own and they're bleeding cowards, but put 'em in a gang with all the boys behind 'em, then it's different. I was walking down the main road last Saturday, and there's a kid lying there with his face all smashed in. The boys had come over from the Castle. There's a few of 'em round here. . . . They've got leaders, but take the leaders away and you won't find the gangs no more. . . . Over in Plaistow there were two gangs and two leaders. Now one's in Ireland, the other's in the nick. You go over to Plaistow you won't find the gangs no more.'

Paradoxically, it appears that the Teddy Boy movement brought the gang as a unit into very low repute, especially among working-class people. The view was frequently expressed that 'They're the lowest of the low', 'They're the real morons', etc., so that to move in a large crowd became, for a time at least, an index of cowardice rather than toughness.

The most general attitude towards gangs in the East End was

that they were a thing of the past, even though 'There's a rough lot in every district' and 'There've always been Teds. There always will be. It doesn't make any difference what clothes they wear.' The most that happened was the occasional dance-hall fight, 'no *West Side Story* stuff', just 'the Canning Town boys' coming over to a Stepney dance, 'we expected them to come'. There would be fights in defence of some vaguely defined 'territory', but nothing serious. In the 1950's, each gang had a leader—'all gangs have'—but the names were either vague references to area—the Canning Town boys, the Whitechapel boys, the Roman Road boys—or simply the name of the 'leader'. But even this was dying out. The most usual attitude was that whatever 'gang' problem had ever existed in the East End had both disappeared and shifted to areas like St. Pancras. 'The East End isn't a trouble spot any more. 'It's more Paddington and King's Cross now'; this is the view of most youth workers in the East End. Adolescents themselves thought much the same, that 'Kids aren't in gangs round here' or 'It's like a police sergeant once said: "Go round in twos and you're alright, go round in threes and you're a gang". There's one or two gangs round here, but . . . they don't bust places up, or anything like that', or 'About once a month you'll get a real fight between two of the boys here, but nothing like gangs fighting'. These beliefs were reiterated many times by both adolescents and adults. Chain-swinging, knife-carrying Teds were apparently eliminated in the boroughs of Stepney and Poplar almost before they began, the local community and the police combined taking immediate action against the threat of the institutionalisation of violence in gang form. The feeling against gangs is deep enough for most adolescents themselves to react against the idea of going around in a gang, even though the rare 'punch-up' between groups which resemble mobs rather than gangs takes place; 'You just get into trouble that way'. Preventive work by the police took the form of 'beheading' a gang. 'If they always go round together, the police'll bust them up', and this policy was remarkably effective, if only because other factors in the East End situation worked against the emergence of structured gangs. However, gangs of a conflict-oriented and near-group variety are reported to exist in areas more highly urbanised than the East End, such as Paddington and St. Pancras, which are dominated by the main-line termini and characterised by appalling housing, extreme poverty, immigrant Irish and coloured populations on a large scale, property racketeering, and a prostitution-gambling-drinking club network which appears much more organised than the same elements in west Stepney. But even there incidents are infrequent, though the reports which filter through to other parts of London about gang-activity serve to preserve the delinquent gang myth.

The non-existence in Stepney and Poplar of both gangs and groups based on the pursuit of delinquent activity *per se* is not, however, necessarily a proof of the non-existence of delinquent subcultures. The bulk of delinquency is committed by groups: but the delinquency is one aspect of the group's way of life, not the controlling factor in its formation. The issue now at stake is not what gangs there are, but why none—or very few—exist. What relevance have the Cohen and Cloward-Ohlin concepts to this type of delinquency situation?

(b) Non-utilitarian

The assertion that the bulk of working-class male group delinquency was non-utilitarian is central to Cohen's concept of the parent male subculture, and was consistently borne out by the observation with the Poplar group, even though they were aged 16–17, and would theoretically have been expected to conform to some more distinctive adaptation, such as semi-professional theft or conflict-oriented delinquency. There were obviously exceptions to the pattern, but little of the group's delinquent activities appeared to be consciously and deliberately motivated by the desire for gain, or by any other rational utilitarian purposes. This tendency is more pronounced with younger boys, once it is disentangled from the petty theft endemic to traditionally 'rough' working-class neighbourhoods. For example, a tremendous amount of vandalism takes place in certain East End primary and secondary schools. But it would be naïve to assume, in very poor areas, that all delinquency is non-utilitarian. Poverty —i.e. the lack of many stealable things—is still a real force for crime, and in most parts of Stepney and Poplar it would be abnormal for a boy to refrain from stealing throughout childhood and adolescence—unless he belonged to the fast-disappearing respectable Jewish population. Groups of children stealing from the docks and the big stores may be a commonplace in both working-class areas, but crime as a part of everyday life for children stops at peccadilloes. Essentially non-utilitarian delinquency is a separate tendency.

The delinquent mode for the Poplar boys was usually non-utilitarian:

'Pete told me Bill and the boys were out "joy-riding" and the police would probably be in after them tonight.' He dangled a car-key and said it was a Ford Consul, brand-new model. 'The bloke just left it lying around (at work). Well, that's just asking for it, ain't it?' They had been joy-riding 'only just lately. They just got the craze. We do it for enjoyment, you know. There's nothing else to do around here. Anything round here you can get enjoyment from you're breaking the law.' They had this particular craze for only three days, then stopped: 'Best to give up while you're lucky.' Pete had received two years probation at the age of 14 for breaking-and-entering. He had broken into four or five shops a week 'for months' before being caught. They did it 'just for laughs. That's all we do it for. We take a few things, but nothing much.' The next development had been stealing bikes: 'We must have stolen hundreds of the things. People just leave 'em lying about. I did it with Lennie and the boys. When I'd ridden 'em round for a bit, I dumped 'em in the canal or sold 'em at the Lane. Just walk up and down the Lane with a bike and somebody'll give you a couple of quid for it.'

Also, rowdyism—though not vandalism—was a feature of their behaviour in the street and in the cinema, though not so much in the café, due to the threat of a ban by the proprietor. A trip to the cinema was typically 'just for laughs': it had nothing to do with the film. Inside, often by the back exit, activity took the form of races round the aisles, frequent door-banging trips to the lavatory, shouting up 'birds', cat-calls, etc. but nothing serious, no seat-slashing or violence. Later, however, they became more money-minded:

'We had three look-outs. We were after one of those cig. machines. They hold ten quid those things. . . . We get the whole thing off the wall and take it away. I'm going for the money now. I'm ten quid in debt. We're off doing things just for a laugh now. Last laugh I had, it cost me twelve weeks' (i.e. two hours a week in an attendance centre). Pete also left his job—his eighth—for a scrap-firm as '. . . It's no good now. They stopped all the fiddling. I used to fiddle six or eight quid a week out of that, but the other silly buggers had to go and get caught. One of 'em's due for a stretch. I just got warned.'

'Fiddling' is the adult practice of enlarging income tax-free by theft from one's work-place, the childhood version being theft from stores and school, the justification being that 'Everybody does it'. It is associated with the docks in particular, but is not regarded as a crime, simply as an occupational risk. Non-utilitarian offences are generally reserved for out-of-work hours. Exceptions were reported, but the pattern of delinquency for the Poplar group seemed to be one of pointless break-ins, joy-rides, rowdyism and larcenies for small returns. They rarely capitalised on their law-breaking abilities. For example, although adept at borrowing cars, they apparently made no attempt to sell them, even though they knew of sources for purchase. But the rate of theft of car accessories in conjunction with take-and-drive points to a limited form of utilitarian delinquency.

There is a point which springs from Cohen's treatment of this concept. He states that the objects stolen may often be valued by the delinquent, but the treatment of the object is in no rational proportion to the risks run in its illegal acquisition, i.e. it is the act of theft, not the object stolen, which is the principal motivating force. It may be objected to this that the delinquent steals for imagined utilitarian ends, but possession of the object stolen reveals the illusory nature of the original impulse; e.g. he steals a car because pressurised by commercial-ideological forces into thinking he needs one, but soon realises the falsity of the need and discards it. While this would account for a single car-borrowing, it would not account for a car-borrowing career, for disenchantment with the object stolen would be final, and the delinquent would cease to pursue car-borrowing.

(c) Malice

A tendency, but not a marked one, and refuted more often than confirmed. With the Poplar boys, it was possible to infer the element of active spite from certain activities—the cinema rowdyism, the discarding of bikes in the canal—but they did not display the 'gratuitous hostility towards non-gang peers as well as adults' which Cohen postulated as one hallmark of the delinquent subculture. Only one incident of active malice was observed, which involved the teasing of a girl in the café by throwing around and damaging a newly-bought under-skirt, but the incident was exceptional and sexually-derived, not the rule. On the other hand, many incidents of vandalism in school were reported, and it is axiomatic that in a middle-class institutional atmosphere, the element of active malice emerges much more clearly. (Cf. the 'irresponsibility' of 'Black' school, as analysed by Webb.) In joy-rides, however, the Poplar boys never took girls along, because 'It'd be wrong to risk anybody except yourselves'. They denied any connection with an episode of vandalism in Poplar, both on their own behalf and for the rest of the boys in the caff: 'What would they get out of it?' They thought that if adolescents had done it, it was 'out of boredom. They get nothing to do round here, and once they get into a gang, they'll do anything.' The attitude towards seat-ripping in provincial cinemas—following an account in the Press—was that it was 'stupid, there's no sense in that kind of thing, is there?' Moreover, youth clubs relied in general on self-discipline by adolescents who frequently had delinquent records: 'If there's a riot, there's nothing we could do about it.' This reliance has considerable point: if the element of malice was so marked in the delinquent subculture, few youth-clubs would be left standing. Possibly the most archetypal piece of 'malice' witnessed in Poplar was that of a group of school-boys throwing stones and systematically breaking glass in a deserted tenement block. No harm was done—the block was due for demolition—and the impulse worked itself out in twenty minutes.

(d) Negativism

To establish the reality of the element of negativism in delinquent subcultural behaviour, the concept of 'inverse polarity' must be strongly exemplified as a determinant of the delinquent's value-system, i.e. that the delinquent turns the rules of conventional society upside-down, as distinct from simple engagement in rule- and law-breaking. No such evidence can be offered in the case of the Poplar boys; the only episode indicative of negativism is that of cinema rowdyism, where the behaviour of the boys in the cinema exactly opposes that thought desirable by a conventional cinema audience. It should be noted here that on a subsequent visit, barely any rowdyism occurred. The trouble with the concepts of non-utilitarianism, malice and negativism is that they hang together simply as negatives, i.e. the presence of one such element in a delinquent act implies the other two from the view-point of a middle-class observer. Yet the vast majority of the delinquent acts committed by the Poplar group were surreptitious: there was no overt 'flouting' of the rules, no display of prowess to the world at large, only to the peer group. There was no assertion resembling that of Arthur Seaton's 'Rules are there to be broken by blokes like me.'[2] Again, there is the strong probability that these elements are much more noticeable among secondary modern school-boys in the poorer working-class areas (cf. Webb's disclaimer on this point). But no such value-system was encountered with post-school-leaving adolescents, despite their immersion in a social climate conducive towards delinquency.

(e) Versatility

This characteristic was fully borne out. In a short acquaintance, the Poplar group engaged in take-and-drive-away, larceny from slot-machines, rowdyism and some violence. In the past, they had committed break-ins, a variety of simple larcenies, larceny of bicycles and trespass. (Receiving almost goes without saying.) But the avoidance of vandalism, and the periodicity of indulgence in delinquency of all kinds, means that the behaviour of the Poplar group cannot be equated with the 'generalised, diversified, protean "orneriness"' which Cohen attributed to the delinquent gang proper.

(f) Short-Run Hedonism

This strain was very marked in the life of the Poplar group and, as far as could be seen, of all other similar groups encountered. As Cohen asserts, it is a characteristic of working-class life in general, but 'in the delinquent gang it reaches its finest flower'. The Poplar boys spent most evenings—and earnings—hanging around in the caff, with the occasional visit to the cinema, skating or swimming, 'outside' to pick up girls or commit an offence, and—even more rarely—a trip to the West End. They rarely planned for more than the evening ahead, and bouts of

[2] A. Sillitoe, *Saturday Night and Sunday Morning* (1959).

activity came spontaneously. With jobs and school, they had displayed the same inability to think ahead that they revealed with leisure. Throughout the period involved, they planned months ahead for one event only, Bill's eighteenth birthday party. They would 'chuck in' their jobs without any alternative to hand, 'it's like being on holiday', but soon be compelled to take one only fractionally different. Pete, asked what he would do if the boys didn't come in, replied that he had nothing to do: 'There's nothing to do around here, see? Nothing at all.' They did not 'work at' delinquency, least of all in a planning sense: most of the 'enjoyment' stems from improvised illegality. They soon lost interest in any form of regulated activity, even a game of darts or snooker. Cohen's point that only a small fraction of the delinquent gang's time is spent looking for 'fun' via delinquency is carried by definition. 'Hanging around' creates its own tensions only gradually. A corollary is the difficulty of 'hanging around' with them for any period of time. The role of 'writer' eventually caused suspicion owing to lack of an immediate end-product.

(g) Group Autonomy
As all authoritarian settings were avoided, the kind of situation in which the Poplar group's autonomy would have been tested never arose. This avoidance in itself indicated the group's desire for an autonomous existence. Individual members were subject to parental regulation and a modicum of discipline restricting behaviour in the caff. For example, Pete and Lennie had to be in by 11 p.m. and paid £2 10*s.* a week rent to their parents. They obeyed the café owner in several instances regarding misuse of property in the caff. Stan, a 19-year-old on the fringe of the group, was barred from the caff for swearing at the owner. But in no case was the *group* reprimanded, and in no case did the group have to face any threat, whether verbal or physical.

Summary: No group is in stasis. In the period of time—relatively short—in which the Poplar group were contacted, their delinquent behaviour appeared to lack two elements crucial to Cohen's construct of the delinquent subculture, i.e. malice and negativism. The absence of these elements signifies the 'corner boy' rather than the 'delinquent boy' adaptation, although their

involvement in delinquency was far greater than Cohen postulated for the typical corner-group, whose delinquent activities
implicitly stop at truancy and do not involve property or personal
aggression.[3] However, this is not to deny that the group had
been subcultural delinquents at an earlier age and while still at
school, the forcing-house for the delinquent subculture. According to Cohen, the parent male subculture tapers off at about
age 15–16. In this way, the Poplar group can be viewed as en
route from subcultural delinquency to young adult 'corner boy'
conformity. The question of interpretation must remain open.

(*h*) *Criminal*

The three categories of the Cloward-Ohlin typology are discussed here not as delinquent subcultures, but as patterns of
behaviour generalised throughout the social and geographical
areas studied. The ultimate criterion for the existence of a
criminal opportunity structure in an area must be that such a
structure has a separable existence as an institution within the
area. By this criterion, Stepney can hardly be considered a
'criminal' area, and Poplar even less so. While there are in the
East End several well-known (to the police) criminal cliques, and
families of a 'professional' nature, i.e. solely engaged in the
utilitarian pursuit of break-ins, robbery, and drug-trafficking,
these groups are largely independent of each other, and are not
organised in such a way as to constitute a visible, coherently
patterned criminal opportunity structure on a quasi-bureau-
cratic basis, as are the big American syndicates. The set-up of
adult crime in the East End seems to be that of small autonomous
groups, some with their own 'guv'nor', some recruited on a
completely *ad hoc* basis. Allerton[4]—in one of the few 'life-histories'
of an East End professional criminal available—describes his
recruitment for a specific 'job' into just such an *ad hoc* clique.
This adult set-up is naturally reflected in the structure and aims
of adolescent delinquents, among whom there are very few
groups dedicated to deliberate and positive criminality, and these
are almost certainly composed of boys with much Approved
School and Borstal history. Small pockets of organised crime
undoubtedly exist in Stepney, and it has traditionally acted as a

[3] Cohen, op. cit., pp. 129–130.
[4] R. Allerton and T. Parker, *The Courage of his Convictions* (1962), pp. 78–80.

magnet for ex-cons and receivers, as well as for the social 'inadequates' who fill the hostels and whose last resort is the bomb-site. Traditional Stepney crime comprises 'screwing', the used-car racket, H.P. rackets, dog-doping, and—more recently—drug-trafficking, as well as prostitution and illegal gambling and small-time 'protection' exercised against cafés and betting-shops. In a continuum of adult crime in west Stepney in particular, the most organised activities—'screwing', robbery, doping, drug-traffic—would have least personnel involved; more numerous would be those engaged in prostitution, immoral earnings, illegal gambling, drug-use and proneness to violence; mid-way would be larger numbers purposefully engaged in crime as a supplement to their jobs; and finally even more would take the opportunities inherent in their jobs to 'fiddle' extras in a fairly systematic way. The last category, which includes such activities as dockers 'whipping' goods, cannot be considered a criminal 'career', but is rather what Sykes and Matza might term a 'subterranean' aspect of conventional job-routine. 'Fiddled' goods are generally consumed personally or by immediate family, or are sold cheaply on a kind of informal community network, in which those who will buy suspected stolen goods, and those who would disapprove, or who might even 'inform', are known in advance. Where goods whose origin is fairly anonymous are concerned, such as nylons or canned soup, the risk is sometimes taken of hawking them round local pubs. There is little interaction between this kind of amateur crime—where recourse is rarely had to established 'fences'—and the first two categories mentioned. This is not to say that the promising dock 'whipper' or car-borrower never progresses to more ambitious and better-organised crime: but in the cases where this happens, the process is largely one of self-recruitment to a way of life, rather than attraction into a stable hierarchy which provides an alternative route to upward mobility. The latter feasibly occurs more frequently in those activities which are essentially crime-promoting but technically legal, such as property-racketeering and certain forms of bookmaking, and gambling.

The absence of a conspicuously successful adult criminal élite is reflected in the lack of any perceptible aspiring towards professional crime among adolescent delinquents; it is also reflected in the areas of adolescent congregation—which are

restricted to stable working-class or wholly teenage locales—
and their avoidance of specifically 'criminal' milieux. The self-
image of the Poplar boys, for example, was that of the 'hooligan',
not the criminal. This is not to say that they had no contact with
individual adult criminals—a relative of the café owner was
'inside' for dealing in stolen cars—or that none of them had
ever envisaged a full-scale 'job':

> I asked Pete what he'd be doing in ten years time. 'Swinging by the
> fucking neck', he said. I asked what for. 'Well, if I ever run out of
> money again, I'm going to go out and do a job for some.' He told
> me that last weekend a kid had offered to go in with him on a
> job they'd get £200 each from, 'but why should I?' said Pete.
> 'If I got caught I could get five or ten years for that. Five years
> for two hundred quid, it's not worth it. Anyway, the next job I
> do I'm going to do by myself. I've been to court four times but
> I've never been caught yet, have I? I've always been split on.
> Every single time one of my mates has given me away. . . . But
> there's one job I'm gonna do, as soon as I break up with my girl.
> I'll get a couple of thousand quid out of it'—The pub radio gave
> out a bulletin on a mail-van raid when the bandits got away with
> £4,000—'Good luck to 'em, mate', said Pete vehemently. 'Behind
> every robbery like that, there's a brain. They do the job and he
> pays them off. The bloke who gives the inside information gets
> £500. They don't have to worry about getting rid of the stuff.
> The brain does that. I read it in the papers.'

This story shows—for one boy at least—intense sympathy for,
if not identification with, the adult professional criminal. It also
testifies to the efficiency of the various media as vehicles for the
dissemination of criminal techniques. This example of aspiration
towards the 'big score' was atypical, and probably paranoid. But
it serves as a reminder that the tendency for offences to be non-
utilitarian declines with age and growth of the appreciation of
risk.

A factor which feasibly serves to deflect adolescents from
certain offences in the East End, such as prostitution, poncing,
drug-use and illegal gambling, is the association of these offences
with the 'blacks', although long-established working-class
families in the area are traditionally antipathetic towards prostitution. Prostitution is the notorious 'Stepney problem', a term
which was actually used in one survey to differentiate the Stepney

prostitute from the West-End type: ' "Stepney problem" is a special connotation used to describe those girls who were mainly the failures of Approved Schools and Borstals, and went to live in the coloured quarter of Stepney; mentally, physically, and morally they were in a lower grade than the ordinary prostitute.'[5] It is no longer so true that the Stepney prostitute is a pathetic and feeble-minded amateur, absconded from an institution or newly arrived by lorry from the North, sharing a bed often for nothing as the only means of finding one. Since the early and mid-1950's, the girls have been more organised, and a pattern established. There seems to be a distinction between the Cable Street and Spitalfields areas *vis-à-vis* prostitution, the former being centred on the caffs, the latter being much less public and tightly controlled by ethnic cliques, centred in all-night caffs and drinking-clubs. The clubs in Spitalfields are near the City, and cater for businessmen during the day, locals and 'tourists' at night. Many caffs rely on respectable trade during the day, and open at night simply as rendezvous for the girls, ponces and clients. Clubs which are closed simply re-open under a different name and management, on the by now well-established pattern. The Maltese reportedly run the girls in Spitalfields, and have been held to sell them to other cliques, such as Pakistanis, for sums around £10. Few girls are from Stepney or Poplar, and no attempt is made to recruit locally: the influx from the Northern conurbations is consistent. The occasional caff is 'queer' or lesbian, but these circles shift within short periods of time. Underlying the prostitution situation, and in partial explanation of community attitudes towards the 'slags' and the 'blacks' are two main factors. First, the shrinkage of the native resident Cockney and Jewish population of Stepney from about 200,000 in 1939 to just over 90,000 in 1961, due to massive re-housing schemes and migration to the suburbs, both during the war and after, so that while the influx of coloured immigrants is well under 10,000 in number, they stand out disproportionately in the young male population. Second, the housing situation has left west Stepney in particular with tracts of slum, condemned property, some of which is not scheduled to be pulled down until 2005. But the property crucial to prostitution and property racketeering is especially that in re-development areas, with

[5] C. H. Rolph (Ed.), *Women of the Street* (1955), p. 245.

only a decade at most to stand. Whole areas have been bought up cheaply by agents and let off at exorbitant rents, or leased at high rates of interest, to landlords—often coloured—who connive at maximum short-term profits either from the girls and their ponces or sub-letting at exorbitant rents. Since the mid-1950's, therefore, prostitution has spread from the coloured enclave of Cable Street to Cavell Street, Spitalfields and, more recently, to Mile End, a pattern pre-determined by the ownership of crumbling property. Illegal gambling and drug-use has spread correlatively. Local white residents are bitter, but are now resigned to the spread of prostitution and the lack of official action apart from the occasional police raid. Neighbourhood organisation to tackle the problem came to an end with the break-up by the police of the 'Vigilantes' in 1957–58, an attempt by the community to administer the 'rough and ready' justice of the streets to what—in some areas—was beginning to threaten families and children. The fear was that 'children would come to regard prostitution as a possible way of life' but the impetus was given added violence by the identification of prostitution with 'the blacks', whose reliance on the girls was—to a large extent—forced by the absence of their own women, and the stigma attached by the stable working-class community to a girl who went with a coloured man. The only resort for unmarried negroes were those white women the local community itself rejected. White adolescents come to share the blanket aversion of their parents for 'the blacks and their women. . . . I bet you five quid you can't walk with me down Cavell Street and point to three houses that aren't brothels. It's the blacks. Send the cunts back from where they came from. . . . They import girls, most of 'em Irish. There hasn't been a pross nicked in two years.'

(i) Conflict

Both the 'conflict' subculture of Cloward and Ohlin, and the 'conflict-oriented' adaptation of Cohen and Short, are based on the institutionalisation of violence in the street warfare ('rumbles') of juvenile delinquent fighting gangs in New York, Chicago and other metropolitan centres. In both Stepney and Poplar, no inter-gang, and barely any inter-group, fighting was reported or observed, though there was a generally disseminated proclivity towards limited forms of toughness and aggression. A 'punch-up' that was witnessed in the Aldgate Wimpy appeared typical of the form taken by most adolescent aggression in the East End, though 'punch-ups' are supposed to be pre-arranged. This particular scuffle took place on a Friday evening about 10.30, began with one male teenager insulting another, blows were exchanged and—as the place was tightly packed with male teenagers and their girls—the fight snowballed so that those who were in the fight and those who were trying to watch became indistinguishable. A young P.C. came into the Wimpy, forced his way through the struggle, had his helmet knocked off but separated the two central protagonists, and ordered them outside. They apparently got away without being charged. This type of scuffle was frequent in this café, there were fights in or around or at the back of the building, usually at weekends following Friday pay-day. But:

> 'They're nothing much. . . . Nothing gets broken, except perhaps somebody's nose. There's no knives or anything more than a bottle, but hardly even that.'

The general view was that 'old-style' battles, between marauding mobs (as distinct from structured gangs) from nearby areas such as Hoxton and local mobs, were very much a thing of the past, of the 40's and early 50's.[6] The 'Teds' never really 'caught on' in Stepney and Poplar, snuffed out by an essentially conservative working-class community which frowned on any real violence as a threat to family life and children. But even at its height, 'old-style' delinquency lacked the gang-structure, the concept of 'turf' and the idealisation of 'heart' which are held to be characteristic of the American street-gang warfare situation.

The Poplar boys were never seen to display even that degree of aggression that took place ritually in Stepney. Lacking in these boys was another characteristic of the American situation, the willingness to 'talk delinquency'. Axiomatic, however, was the absence of any 'real' aggression:

[6] This is not to deny that, more recently, in Islington and Shoreditch, for example, youth workers and police have been worried by the increase in 'tooling up' with guns instead of knives, etc. The case for 'detached work' in such areas, and in Soho—a focal point for buying and selling weapons—is particularly strong. The 'detached worker' would serve as much to give an unbiased picture of what was happening in an area, as for any possible 'preventive' role. At present, it only needs one 'near-group' mobilised by a seriously disturbed youngster with a gun to spark off claims that 'gang warfare' has broken out.

. . . I asked him if a big bunch had ever tried to take this particular café over, since it was the only one of its kind nearby. . . . Lennie said no, there was none of that kind of thing. 'It's only common sense. If a bunch came in now, there's not many of us here at the moment, they could clear us out. But we'd find out where they came from and we'd get all the boys from here, and all the boys from Bow, and we'd go and beat them up tomorrow night. No, there's never been anything like that. Stands to reason. If a negro boy comes in, he's going to feel scared because we're all whites, but we don't take any notice. The other night four negro boys came in but nobody took any notice. If seven or eight of 'em come in, then we might tell 'em to clear out, but they'd never do that. No, about once a month you'll get a real fight between two of the boys here, but nothing like gangs fighting.'

In other words, conflict for 'neighbourhood hegemony' just doesn't apply in Poplar, or Stepney, or—with few exceptions—throughout London. Fights occur, but for more straightforward reasons:

'Bill's birthday party. . . . That ended up in a fight. These two boys turned up in a van and started messing about with Bill's girl, so we threw 'em out. They came back and there's five more of 'em in the back of the van with fucking great hooks from the docks. We beat 'em off throwing bottles at 'em. One of 'em gets his hook in Ray's jersey. Ray just says, "here, get your hook out of my jersey". The bloke takes it out and Ray just hits him in the face with this bottle. . . . Nobody got hurt bad.'

In general, however, the attitude was one of avoiding violence. Pete refused to use a snooker room because 'the yobs' who hung around the place used violence on newcomers:

'. . . They come from round Barking. If you go in there, they just beat you up. . . . That's their enjoyment, like ours is hanging around here and stealing cars. . . . They'd never let me in that gang down there, and I wouldn't want to, anyway. *They're too tough*. They don't even let you get to know them. You speak to them and they just walk past you in the street, then two or three of them'll split off and get you. . . .'

But this kind of vicious hostility was the exception, and clearly regarded as such by the boys themselves. Their own aggression, mostly verbal, followed the lines indicated by Miller in his analysis of aggression in a boys' street-corner group, i.e. narrow in content, target and range of expression, and playing itself out within the confines of the group.

The nearest approximation to conflict-orientated adolescent delinquency was the occasional short-term mobilisation for street forays.[7] The difference was well summarised by the director of a well-organised Stepney youth club who had been to New York:

'. . . I went out to several locations. We have gangs here, there's no denying that, but they're nothing like the ones in New York. They have names, there, like the Comanches. . . . Here, the boys use bike-chains or knives and—occasionally—a kid gets killed by accident. But there they use guns and plan murder in advance, they premeditate that such and such a boy should be liquidated. . . . I give the street-workers there all credit, but they came too late. Here a boy leaves school and is working hard straightaway. There they stay at school until 16 or 17, they're bored, uninterested and don't get into a job when they leave school the way a boy does over here. . . . You can read the statistics any way you like. A twenty per cent rise in juvenile crime could mean just that the kids don't get away with it. When I was a kid, I stole, but I could run faster than any copper. Now the police have cars. . . . It's important to get this in perspective. Thirty years ago, you honestly couldn't walk through Stepney without fear of being molested. . . . Well, I've been here ten to fifteen years and I've never been beaten up yet, even in the worst districts. There's a lot of exaggeration. There's less *real* delinquency than ever before.'

(j) Retreatist

While no evidence at all was found to suggest the existence of an adolescent retreatist subculture, characterised in its ideal-typical form, according to the Cloward-Ohlin criteria, by the consumption of alcohol, drugs, jazz and sex, two subgroups in the populations studied possessed affinities with Merton's category of retreatism, which does not postulate specifically delinquent or criminal behaviour, and which does not entail contracultural self-images of the subgroup as an élite. These two subgroups were the young coloured males who lived or hung around Cable Street and its environs—some of whom were involved in prostitution, gambling, hemp- or marihuana-smoking,

[7] See pp. 198–202.

heavy drinking and violence—and the young adult white 'yobs' or layabouts who shared this milieu, but who are characteristic of any inner urban working-class area, and are not confined to any specific 'quarter'.

(*i*) *The 'blacks'*: Banton, writing on the basis of research in Stepney's coloured quarter of Cable Street between 1950–52,[8] described and analysed the situation of what was then a racial and cultural enclave in terms which still apply to the tensions between white and coloured in west Stepney today, despite the many intervening changes. The biggest change has been the spread of immigrant residence from the immediate Cable Street area to Spitalfields, areas north of the Commercial Road and parts of Mile End and Bow. The Cable Street sector, however, still accommodates those coloured immigrants who are (a) in transit, and (b) lacking in the skills needed for mobility and the ability to cope with life in a complex, technological society. Many of the pressures on this partly residual, partly transitional population are shared by all immigrants to Britain, whether white or coloured. Stepney has been an immigrant area for centuries, and 'antagonism towards immigrants is the rule, not the exception'.[9] Between 1881 and 1901, the number of aliens in the two wards of Whitechapel and St. George's in West Stepney increased by 37 per cent mostly following the immigration of Jews after the pogroms in Russia and Eastern Europe. In 1900, it was estimated that there were 100,000 Jews in East London, nearly all of whom lived in Stepney, and slightly over half being aliens. Prior to this, by about 1880, the last remnants of middle-class respectability had left Stepney with the exodus of the old sea-captains and their families from Wellclose Square, and the merchants from the old Huguenot district around Spitalfields. Stepney was now uniformly working-class, its characteristic industries were becoming established—tailoring in particular—back-yard workshops and 'sweated' garment trades sprang up and increased the shortage of space. Housing conditions attracted philanthropists, and huge blocks of 'model' dwellings went up, such as the Brady Dwellings, barrack-like rewards for the thrifty poor. These charitable activities, although largely beneficial, combined with the construction of the huge Rowton House in 1892

[8] M. Banton, *The Coloured Quarter* (1955).
[9] Banton, op. cit., p. 18.

and the massive Jewish influx to establish Stepney as the home of 'the strangers, the shiftless and the derelict' and it is from this period that Stepney's notoriety for crime and poverty springs, the Press-fostered perpetuation of this reputation being responsible for much harm.[10] Obviously, housing and employment are the most urgent problems for all immigrants to Stepney in particular, or the country as a whole. But the Negro—i.e. West African and West Indian—Cable Street population are unrepresentative of both their own immigrant population as a whole and of all immigrants in general, in that they lack the skills to overcome the handicaps attached to finding employment and housing. The situation is vitiated even further in west Stepney by the critical shortage of housing, and the enormous amount of pre-twentieth century slum property which is both privately owned and almost invariably expensive to rent. Virtually barred from council flats, the 'blacks' inevitable resort is to this deteriorating property. Local white residents link the onset of deterioration with the arrival of the 'blacks' and blame the newcomers for the deterioration, whereas 'they are its result, not its cause'.[11] Also, conventional British attitudes towards coloured people are such that few white women will associate with them; those who do are mostly women who have failed—or been refused the chance—to find a satisfying role in conventional society, and their frequent instability underlies the unhappiness of many mixed marriages. This prohibition by the working-class community of female contact with young coloured males led—in the absence of an equal number of coloured females—to an inevitable market for prostitution. Deprived in the areas of jobs, sex, housing and leisure, this sector of the coloured population—which arrived in this country with high expectations as to earnings and miscegenation—have adopted a retreatist way of life sufficiently desperate to create a sub-group situation of anomie.

The situation is worse for West Africans, West Indians, Maltese and Cypriots than for the other, and quite distinct, coloured groups, such as the Pakistanis, Indians and Arabs. The two groups entertain different aspirations and expectations

---

[10] For a vivid evocation of 'working-class culture' at this period and its squalor and suffering, see Jack London's *The People of the Abyss* and also *Child of the Jago* by Arthur Morison.

[11] Banton, op. cit., p. 71.

towards life and work in Britain, the first group typically immi-
grating with settlement in mind, the second with more limited
economic ambitions: the one is an immigrant group, the other
migrant workers.

> The Pakistanis and Sikhs are examples of non-assimilating or
> *accommodating* as opposed to *adapting* groups. Many of them are
> migrant workers who will return to their homeland when they have
> saved enough money, but those who remain will seek to preserve
> a group life of their own. . . . The West African and West Indian
> immigrants begin with an entirely different outlook. One of the
> factors encouraging them to leave the colonies was their idealisa-
> tion of Britain and their acceptance of our culture—in many
> aspects—as superior to their own. The Negro immigrants see no
> reason for separate practices. They favour amalgamation of
> ethnic stocks. A person's membership of the immigrant grouping
> does not in any way hinder him in his relations with non-
> immigrants.[12]

As Banton asserts, the clear-cut objectives of the accommodating
groups have generated a disciplined approach to jobs and housing,
via a network of contacts based on café-society: 'cohesion will
always be weaker in an adapting group, for the major interests of
the members lie outside the group'.[13] This fragmentation makes
for a greater vulnerability to adverse social pressures. Lacking
the insulation provided by this kind of group-life, and dis-
illusioned with the central impulse underlying immigration—
the tragic misconception, in some cases, that Britain was an El
Dorado—the less skilled among the young adult Negro males
are faced not simply with value-conflict, but with disenchantment
with the conventional value-systems of both their own and the
host society.

Banton estimated[14] that well over two-thirds (c. 70%) of
West Indian and West African males in Stepney were employed
in unskilled or semi-skilled work, while the number employed
was unknown. Yet: 'No coloured man go home unless he rich.
Too much shame. Everyone laugh at him.'[15] For few sectors of

[12] Banton, op. cit., pp. 74–75.
[13] Ibid., p. 233.
[14] Banton, op. cit., p. 132.
[15] J. Lawrie, *The Marriage of Gor* (1960), p. 137; a humane account of ten years'
'respectable' co-habitation in appalling conditions on Cavell Street between a
Gambian and an English woman and their family.

the population is the ends-means disparity more cruelly marked than for the young adult male sector of the Cable Street coloured population: the impregnation of their milieux with prostitution, gambling, hemp-smoking, heavy drinking and violence—the latter a non-correlate for retreatism by Cloward-Ohlin criteria— is a functional outgrowth of their socio-cultural situation. Prostitution flourishes due to the 'blacks' sexual deprivation consequent upon discrimination and socio-cultural apartheid; illegal gambling represents the residue of El Dorado attitudes, subsequent disillusion, and an inability to treat money as sacred; the hemp-smoking minority are strengthened in the habit by the disappointments of immigration; heavy drinking is in part the result of the function of the pub as the blacks' sole means of rendezvous and congregation (much as it used to be for the manual working-classes before World War 2), except for coloured-owned caffs and clubs. Interaction between white and coloured is permissible on a commercial basis. Because of the strength of the resultant makeshift relational system, and because of the placing of blame for failure on external sources,[16] violence is very near the surface—a tendency reinforced by the presence in the area of the female 'misfits' on whom the 'blacks' place such reliance as sexual resource, and white petty criminals who see the 'blacks' as ready-made 'suckers'. A constant factor throughout in this sub-area is the stagnant housing deterioration situation, which attracts the coloured immigrant 'residue' and repels the socially mobile and technically skilled members of the coloured population.

Examples of mutual sponging, room-sharing, disputes over gambling and women leading to unreported petty violence are too numerous to mention. But the volatile situation in which the 'blacks' live also furnishes examples of political extremism and deep-rooted feelings of persecution, springing from treatment in the Press, by the police, by social agencies and labour exchanges, employers, and the white community in general, factors which do not apply in areas attracting the more stable and skilled section of coloured immigrants such as Brixton, where gradual and uneventful assimilation is taking place despite suspicion and initial discriminatory practices by the local white residents:

[16] See J. F. Short, Jr. and A. F. Henry, *Suicide and Homicide* (1955).

Sam worked in a gas-works as a labourer, had done so for a year, had been in England since 1946, and stayed in Stepney because 'my people are here'—he was Nigerian. He was married and had four kids. We talked in the pub, which accommodated 20-25 Negroes (Arabs, Pakistanis, etc., avoided it), one Negress and several middle-aged-seeming white women, 'slags' to the whites. He was extravagantly dressed, wearing a Cossack hat—'From Moscow. I'm a Communist'—and drank strong bottled ale. He refused a cigarette, and asked me what I did. I said I was a writer. 'Man, I don't like publicity,' he yelled. 'Stupid' journalists gave coloured people 'bad publicity'. 'They all work for government and, you know, if a journalist write good things about coloured man, West African or West Indian, the editor, he censor it.' Sam wore a Nigerian Independence badge, and alternated between saying 'the only hope for the world is that all peoples live in peace and understanding' and 'I hate the English. Why don't they go away, go away from Africa and leave us alone, 'cos I tell you, man, five years ago, even five, Africa was asleep, but now she's waking up, she's *awake*.' He shouted that 'English socialists' were 'hypocrites', the rest were 'capitalists' and he'd 'machine-gun them down' if he got power. He identified himself with the working-classes, but 'the English working-class is the stupidest in the world. They are really ignorant, some of them.' His friend tried to calm him down, and asked me: 'Did you get him on to politics?' The rest kept well away. 'Some men have hundred of thousand of pounds they don't know what to do with except drink champagne, and outside in street'—he jabbed at the window—'poor boy hasn't got a penny, nothing to eat. If I in power, I take all money away from rich, give to poor boys.' He eventually calmed himself down by smoking a reefer in the lavatory, but secretly, he knew it was against the law. The 'cat' would have flaunted his marihuana.

Likewise, the Chicago 'cat' and the New York 'retreatist' would have avoided violence, politics and jobs, would have cultivated an elitist philosophy absent in Cable Street, and would have displayed their knowledge of jazz, hustling and drug-lore. But the affinities with retreatism would increase but for the chink in the armour of white discrimination supplied by the pub-owners— who cannot maintain an impersonal commercial relationship as white café-owners and shop-keepers typically do—and the 'blacks' women', who mix despite sanctions from both white and coloured:

'Some people spit at us in the street, black people, his own people. One came in here the other day and shouted 'nigger' at him. His own people. And we hate that word anyway, we hate 'blacks' as well, even though they call themselves that.'

(*ii*) *The 'double failures'*: Sharing the milieux of the 'blacks' in west Stepney, and 'the boys' in Poplar and the rest of Stepney the young adult, frequently ex-institutional 'yobs' are typically out-of-work or in jobs which can barely be described as occupations, such as serving in and sweeping up caffs on a casual basis. They live on the dole, by sponging, the occasional petty 'job' and—in west Stepney—acting as pimp, ponce or 'protector' for a girl. Failures by both conventional and criminal standards, evidence for retreatism lies in their mode of drift and withdrawal from any kind of adult responsibility. A group of 'yobs' in the Poplar caff embodied the fate of the aged 'corner-boy', socially incompetent and increasingly desperate as time brought no tangible reward or achievement:

X at one point looked around at the teenagers in the caff and said: 'Look at these kids, they can't be more than 16 or 17, can they?' He said: 'I'll be 24 next week,' as if he had only just thought of it. They were all 23–24, scruffy, down-and-out, unemployed, without even cigarettes. X invited Y out the following night: he had two 'bints' and no mate to take along. 'We'll get both ends up,' he said, clenching his fists and thrusting them in the air. 'One of 'em's married to a geezer who's in the nick. The other's engaged to a bloke who's in hospital. Fuck 'em, that's what I say.' . . . Y said he liked 'whip rounds' best, where you whip round just before closing-time for money to buy as many crates of beer as you can, take it somewhere and have a party. . . . X had been on probation for five years and 'inside' for a bit when he was 17. He mentioned a friend of his who was scared of singing in the street. 'He said, look out, there's a copper.' I said: 'Fuck that. Fuck the Law.' I was singing and I had a piss in a doorway as well. . . . Y, who had been moaning about life and threatening to throw himself in the canal, said he was looking forward to his 25th birthday, as he could have a party. But he was also worried about how old he was getting. He was recently back from looking for work in Liverpool and Leeds and travelling round the country. . . . He was threatening to beat up his brother-in-law, with whom he was living and who 'kept ordering' him about. X became enthusiastic and said: 'We'll get all the boys and go and punch him up. All the boys.' Y said he wouldn't need anybody else, he could do it himself 'if I get just one word from him to-night.'

They came into the café less and less, and finally disappeared altogether. As the generations slot in behind them, their chances of breaking the pattern, of assuming some vestige of meaningful responsibility, dwindle. Their worst possible fate is the meths. and the bomb-site, or—as their despair grows—a crime of violence. Few groups are more in need of human agency. Equivalent cliques moved in the Maltese caffs on Commercial Road and the café-society of Cable Street. In West Stepney, they mingle more with those engaged in prostitution, drug-use and peddling, cater and act as carriers for seamen and 'tourists' from the West End who come slumming 'to see the vice'. Their participation in petty criminality increases their aversion to and suspicion of the police and any outsider. Content to degenerate in the vapid café-world of Cable Street and Brick Lane, they are more brutalised, and correspondingly more dangerous, than their Poplar counterparts. The Poplar 'yobs', however, were essentially 'local' boys; those in west Stepney had invariably drifted in from other parts of London and the rest of the country.

The definition of retreatism adopted by Cloward and Ohlin is much narrower than that devised by Merton, which is capable of subdivision:

> One prominent type of apathy is the loss of involvement in a previously sought cultural goal, such as occurs when continued striving results in persistent and seemingly unavoidable frustration. The loss of central life-goals leaves the individual in a social vacuum, without focal direction or meaning. But another crucial kind of apathy seems to emerge from conditions of great normative complexity and/or rapid change, when individuals are pulled this way and that by numerous conflicting norms and goals, until the person is literally disoriented and de-moralised, unable to secure a firm commitment to a set of norms that he can feel as self-consistent. . . .[17]

It is suggested that the affinities with retreatism of the 'yobs' is of the former type, those of the 'blacks' with the latter type.

[17] R. M. Williams, Jr., *American Society* (1951), pp. 534-35, quoted by R. K. Merton, *Social Theory and Social Structure* (1957), p. 190.

Either way, the criminality of both groups is associated by male, working-class adolescents in general with downward mobility rather than desirable styles of life. This in part explains the lack of convergence between juvenile and adult crime rates noted in Chapter 6.

(*k*) Integrated/Unintegrated Areas

Central to the theorisation of Cloward and Ohlin is the distinction made by Kobrin between 'integrated' and 'unintegrated' areas as forcing-grounds for subcultural differentiation. While no part of Stepney or Poplar can be described as an 'integrated' area, western Stepney aligns almost exactly with the description given by Cloward and Ohlin of what constitutes an 'unintegrated' area:

> The many forces making for instability in the social organisation of some slum areas include high rates of vertical and geographic mobility; massive housing projects . . . and changing land use. . . . Forces of this kind keep a community off balance, for tentative efforts to develop community organisation are quickly checked. Transiency and instability become the over-riding features of social life. . . . The disorganised slum, populated in part by failures in the conventional world, also contains the outcasts of the criminal world. This is not to say that crime is non-existent in such cases, *but what crime there is tends to be individualistic, unorganised, petty, poorly paid, and unprotected.* This is the haunt of the small-time thief, the grifter, the pimp, the jackroller, the unsophisticated con-man, the pickpocket who is all thumbs, and others who cannot graduate beyond 'heisting' candy stores or 'busting' gas stations. Since they are unorganised and without financial resources, criminals in these areas cannot purchase immunity from protection. . . . Hence they are harassed by the police, and many of them spend the better part of their lives in prison.[18]

West Stepney, except for Wapping, has undergone, since the war, precisely this type of tremendous demographical upheaval, and has been left with a residue of slum housing, ethnic confusion and erratic population turnover. Its pervasive petty criminal elements lack all but the most rudimentary organisation, and there is little stable community life, except where pockets of the traditional Jewish community remain. Experience in many parts of west Stepney diametrically opposed the East End's reputation

[18] Cloward and Ohlin, op. cit., pp. 172–173.

for 'community' and 'hospitality' (which sprang from the old Jewish and Cockney neighbourhoods, now largely dispersed). For example, experience gained in census-taking (1961) in one pocket of Spitalfields tenementland produced the following impressions:

The warren-like tenements were erected in 1889 and are now privately owned by a property company; accounting for over half the households in the tiny census-area. Rents are low, 8s. for a single room, unfurnished and without any amenities save the sharing of cold water and a latrine outside on the balcony. The flats are five storeys high, about 40 rooms to a balcony. There are no multiple households, and many families have three rooms, converted into a single flat by demolition of party-walls. Some interiors are, against all odds, quite affluent. Many have incorporated their own hot-and-cold, but few have a bath and none have sole use of a toilet. Key-money is frequently paid: several couples, mostly old, live together extra-maritally. Many single workmen and very poor, old women live alone, the latter recluse-like and unapproached except by welfare workers from the nearby Toynbee Hall. There is nothing approaching community spirit. There was little interaction between neighbours: 'We hardly see him/her' and 'You'll only catch him/her in early in the morning or after 11 at night,' etc. The typical household situations are (*a*) old man or woman living alone, (*b*) middle-aged or old couple, and (*c*) young couple with at least two children aged under 11. Very few teenagers were encountered. Age-structure is loaded with the old. The needs of several of these old people approach the desperate. . . . The population of 'the buildings' is ethnically varied. The hard core are Irish, with several Maltese, Cypriot and a few Jewish families. There are *no* West Indian or African immigrants, few of English descent. The Jews are mainly first-generation from Poland, East Europe or Russia. The Irish and English display a consistent insularity towards the rest throughout, often mixing up nationalities, e.g. 'They're Italian' or 'Greeks' for Maltese and Cypriots. With few exceptions, the occupational structure is uniformly unskilled and semi-skilled working-class. . . . Dislike of contact with officialdom and resentment of any kind of intrusion is automatic. People took time to overcome their suspicion of the census operation, but by the time for collecting the forms came, they were much friendlier and more hospitable. . . . Some passage-ways are completely blank in that they completely lack any interrelationship between neighbours. Other blocks in the area have more amenities than these tenements—e.g. indoor lavatory—and tenants less residual in the income-scale. They have more Jewish and English, more big families, more neighbourliness and less constriction. One couple with six children in two rooms was the extreme, well-kept and nicely-furnished as it was. . . . This is no 'teeming' slum of the Chicago-in-the-Twenties pattern. Few children played in the rubble, no gangs hung around. People 'kept themselves to themselves', and the huge forecourt was often deserted. The refusal and/or inability to be 'bothered' goes with the overall decrepitude of the property, the squalor of the 'amenities', the grey asphalt forecourt, the padlocked, silent doors. . . .[19]

The concept of the 'integrated' area simply does not apply, despite the existence in Spitalfields of several 'underworld' clubs (e.g., until 1960, the PEN Club on Duval Street) as there is little trace of any interdependence between the 'carriers' of criminal and conventional values. It is difficult to think of a London district, except perhaps Soho—largely non-residential—where such 'integration' exists. Many areas, including Stepney, feasibly contain bases for such integration on a supply-and-demand foundation, e.g. shopkeepers buying stolen goods, cigarettes, etc., as a regular transaction, but there is no overt institutionalisation of these links as in Whyte's 'Cornerville' or certain areas of New York.

Apart from West Stepney, therefore, Stepney and Poplar cannot be described as either 'integrated' or 'unintegrated' areas but simply as traditional working-class areas, combining the 'rough' and the 'respectable', but eschewing the overtly criminal elements. In the 'unintegrated' area of West Stepney, the criminal element is also frequently ostracised but community solidarity is too weakened to combat their influence in any systematic way. In an 'integrated' area, the syndicate itself and the police, however corrupt, would exert control over illegal violence and brutality. As Whyte observed: 'In Cornerville . . . the primary function of the police department is not the enforcement of law but the regulation of illegal activities.'[20] In an 'unintegrated,

[19] Audrey Harvey has done more than anyone to publicise the leprous state of much property, all privately-owned, in the East End, via articles in the *New Statesman* and in her *Tenants in Danger* (1964).

[20] W. F. Whyte, *Street Corner Society* (1955 ed.), Ch. 4, on 'The Social Structure of Racketeering.'

area, police strength is frequently outstripped by the sheer pervasiveness of such activities as prostitution and gambling, and the fragmentation of the community gives individual families no redress against 'the vice':

Mrs. B—— lived on a mean, near-derelict street between Commercial Road and Cable Street. She is married to a Polish builder's scaffolder. They have three boys, aged 3, 2 and 1, and live in one room on the ground-floor of a condemned three-storey block. 'I've never lived in a place as bad as this.' Next door is a brothel, whose working hours are 11–3 in the morning, and whose door-slams keep the children awake at night. Her 3 year-old boy keeps finding contraceptives on the door-step and in the back-yard. He thinks they're balloons, and sucks them. Five coloured people live upstairs, and he had spat at one the day before. 'He shouldn't have done that. Before we came here he never would have. He's picked that kind of thing up round here. Soon he'll be swearing. He fights his brother all the time now. He never used to. If we don't get away from here, I don't know what he's going to grow up like.' The Negro had threatened to hit the boy, had called Mrs. B—— a 'filthy whore' and a 'cunt'. Mrs. B— spelt out the second word, 'c–u–n–t'. They'd been in the room about 15 months. It was about 14' by 12' by 10', was almost entirely filled by the double bed, the three cots and a wardrobe. 'When he hears them outside at night, he (the boy) gets scared and has to come to bed with us. That means we get no sleep.' The room was—incredibly—spotlessly clean. . . . She'd tried keeping the one lavatory which served for both houses clean, but it was impossible: the same with the yard, which was littered with newspapers and food-scraps the day after she'd scrubbed it out. The tenants upstairs threw rubbish out of the window. The doctor had confirmed that her health had suffered from living there: gastro-enteritis, her hair falling out through 'nerves', the doctor himself had told her this. She was mainly afraid of the children picking up disease. . . . A few weeks after they'd moved in, she'd answered a knock at the door. A man had asked if Maria was in. She told him he had the wrong house, and tried to shut the door. He wedged his foot in it, said Maria lived there. She said Maria must have moved, she lived there now. He said all he wanted was a short time, and she'd do. She somehow got the door shut. 'But they take you for just another one of them round here. I sensed it the first few days, people look at you in the street.' There were frequent incidents of violence between clients and the girls. . . . One night, they were awoken at about three in the morning by shouting and singing in the passage. Mr. B—— got up to ask them to quieten down. As he opened the door, a man burst in and hit him in the face with a bottle. Mrs. B—— got out of bed, and the man hit her in the face. The children were screaming. This time, the police were effective, the man got two years. Eventually, the B——'s struck it lucky. Mrs. B—— had said: 'I couldn't stand another winter here.' They moved round the corner to a two-roomed 'flat', but fewer people shared the lavatory, and the rent was the same, three pounds ten a week. . . .' They had, of course, tried all the usual ways of getting a flat, but landlords wouldn't take more than one child, and they'd only been on the Council list for four years. The house, although condemned, was not in a re-development area, so they stood no chance of being re-housed through demolition. They were afraid to move out of the area, as the husband might not have found as good a job.

The case of the B——'s illustrates the disorganisation of the 'unintegrated' slum area. The absence in this 'unintegrated' area of any approximation to an adolescent 'conflict' subculture is, however, of great relevance for the application of the Cloward-Ohlin hypothesis to the English situation.

(*l*) *Age-Level Integration*
Even taking generalised patterns of behaviour as analogous to adolescent contracultural structures, there appears to be little or no integration between those engaged in delinquent and criminal activities at different age-levels. This was to be expected from the Cloward-Ohlin theory, granted the absence in Stepney and Poplar of any 'integration' between legitimate and illegitimate opportunity structures. Delinquent adolescents in their late teens living locally typically avoided the 'unintegrated' adult crime areas of Cable Street and Cannon Street Road, Brick Lane, etc. As with the Poplar boys, their preference was for the exclusively teenage caff, though in Stepney, the great variety of youth clubs available eased the pressure of the adolescents' need for a café-life of their own. The Poplar boys occasionally inter-acted, but in no sense integrated, with the 'yobs' who used the caff, and who eventually 'didn't come in no more'. The boys sympathised, but never identified with them and, where the kind of criminality they represented was associated with 'the

blacks', often displayed antagonism. As already stated, the 'yobs' seemed too inadequate and too redolent of failure to attract the boys. The Poplar boys avoided the notorious Stepney caffs:

> 'What, them on Cable Street? *They're too rough down there.* You get your throat cut down there.' Ray later went down Cable Street one night, and was genuinely disappointed: 'It's dead round there. Hardly any caffs. Nothing going on.'

The air of depression, the apparently boarded-up caffs, the few 'blacks' hanging around, had dissipated any expectation of glamour and excitement. But the Stepney boys, who knew the area better, shared this aversion. After the youth clubs closed, there was the Wimpy and little else, despite the restrictions this imposed:

> En route to the Wimpy, the group swelled to eight. They jostled each other all the way down Aldgate. A policeman stopped them after a bit, but they knew him, he came down to the club now and again, 'he's the only decent copper round here,' said Peter. 'That's because he's a City copper. The East London cops think they own the place.' The complaint was that they told the boys to move on for no apparent reason. At Gardiner's Corner, Peter pointed to two men, lounging in a shop doorway. 'Plain-clothes,' he said. 'You can smell 'em.' Apparently, they always wore the same clothes, blue sports shirt and sturdy black shoes. 'You can tell 'em a mile off.' And, in fact, as we hung around the Wimpy doorway, one of them came up: 'Police. Get inside or move away, we can't have you blocking the pavement.' The boys moved inside with studied contempt. On the pavement they could watch the girls, spot the cars and compare the scooters parked outside. Inside they had to sit, but they refused to buy a tea, all drinks being 1/- after 10 in the Wimpy, which, they asserted, was the only place they could go after 10. They never went in a workman's caff just up the road, 'it's never open when we can go in.' They went right to the back of the Wimpy and sat down, not one of them making a purchase. 'I'm not paying a shilling for a tea,' summarised Peter. . . . A stone's throw away were the all-night caffs on the Commercial Road and, a little further away, the Cable Street caffs. But they insisted there was absolutely nowhere else to go except the Wimpy. *They never 'went near' the Commercial Road or Cable Street caffs.*

The impregnation of west Stepney with a tremendous variety

of youth clubs means that delinquent male adolescents have a great deal of contact with conventional-world adults, who are frequently far from the image of the middle-class 'do-gooder', and are experienced, adult, working-class and local. This state of affairs is absent in other high delinquency areas, e.g. the Elephant and Castle in Southwark, where clubs are uniformly church or LCC-run, and where the 'unattached' resort by default to the few commercial caffs which are open at night, in one case a front for a brothel and gambling. The situation in Stepney ensures that even consistently delinquent boys have more contact with adults representing the values of the larger society, rather than the adult criminal world. Adolescents in the main Spitalfields Jewish club avoid even the Wimpy, as it is not kosher. Even in the Poplar caff, in an area which lacked the youth-club ethos, adult criminal role models were hardly in evidence, as the self-image of the boys as 'the Poplar hooligans' testifies. Also, as has previously been stated, criminals—in common with teachers, youth workers and policemen—are adults. This matters, when most adolescent delinquents are teenagers first, delinquents second.

(*m*) *Subcultural Integration*
As the patterns of behaviour—here used as analogous to delinquent subcultures—are aligned with age-levels, the same analysis applies as for age-level integration. This has had the beneficial effect so far of blocking adolescents from systematic drug-use.

Summary: Once West Stepney is clearly identified as an 'unintegrated' area, and the rest of the two boroughs as neither 'integrated' nor 'unintegrated', the theorisation of Cloward and Ohlin is negatively validated. The absence of a male adolescent 'conflict' contraculture is understandable in terms of the pressure of an adequate legitimate opportunity structure and a poverty-stricken illegitimate opportunity structure associated with downward mobility and ethnic 'out-groups'. Only for the young adult single coloured males who form the Cable Street area residuum is the legitimate opportunity structure clearly inadequate, but their numbers are too small for the emergence of any full-blown retreatist subculture.

(*n*) *Status Frustration*

The foregoing attempt at descriptive analysis leaves many questions unasked, as well as unanswered. The main question from both the Cohen and the Cloward-Ohlin viewpoints is: what response(s) does the male, working-class adolescent give to being accounted a failure—in middle-class terms—in the middle-class contexts of the school and the job-market? A corollary question is: irrespective of response, is the working-class adolescent at any time a victim of 'status frustration'? Answers are enormously difficult to provide, mainly because of the well-known circularity by which the answer is given in terms of the very behaviour one is seeking to explain, e.g. in this case, that the delinquent boy must experience status frustration since the delinquent group/gang provides him with an alternative source of status, thus enabling him to cope with his 'problem of adjustment'. But what criteria are available to assess whether or not the working-class boy typically meets with a 'problem of adjustment' at all? The following criteria leave much to be desired, but were used in a rough way in empirical research:

Evidence (past or present) for:

No 'problem of adjustment'	Experience of 'problem of adjustment'
1. Satisfaction with type of job.	Dissatisfaction with type of job.
2. Tolerance/passive avoidance of middle-class people and institutions.	Active resentment/antagonism to same.
3. No self-image as 'failure'.	Feeling of 'having failed'.
4. No desire for change of membership-group.	Thwarted desire for such a change.
5. Insulation from middle-class values.	Some internalisation of middle-class values.

Criteria 4 and 5 in particular are not presented as scientifically viable, but simply as indications of information sought.

With some exceptions, observation pointed on all criteria to the absence of any 'problem of adjustment' of the kind envisaged by Cohen in the lives of both the Poplar boys and those adolescents encountered in Stepney. There was an almost monolithic conformity to the traditional working-class value-system, and little discontent with working-class status, especially in the occupational sphere. This is not to say there were no economic dissatisfactions, but these are not peculiar to working-class adolescents: they permeate the working-class at all age-and skill-levels. The Poplar group showed—with the exception of Pete—no frustration over social status. Their self-image was not that of the 'failure' any more than it was that of a 'success': they did not think in these terms. The Poplar boys all had jobs: timber-shifter, lagger's mate, semi-skilled operatives, labourer; they earned roughly £8 a week. The highest status they could reasonably attain was chargehand or foreman. They 'chucked in' their jobs frequently, changing them for others bringing in fractionally higher wages or involving marginally different working conditions. Pete chucked in one job where he earned £8 for a 5½ day week for one where he earned £10 for a 7 day week, the first in a scrap-yard, the second as a lagger's mate. 'It's lousy, but better than before.' They were inactive politically, but traditionally claimed to be 'solid Labour'. They'd all left school at the age of 15—secondary modern—'to earn some money. . . . Everything depends on money round here.' They thought the school system was 'lousy' but wouldn't want to have been 'upper-class' and gone to college. In the absence of distinctive job-content, money is the sole differentiating criterion. They have access to a very narrow range of occupations, and work the changes between them without much sense of loss or gain. But most of them had a relative in the docks, who could get them into the 'closed shop' of dockland when they were 21. The boys were generally confident that adult status would bring high wages. Asked if any of the bunch had a car, Lennie replied: 'Yeah, several of our mates have got one. Ford V8, cars like that. I'll probably get one in a couple of years' time, when the money starts coming in.' (i.e. £11–12 a week at 18). Unless this group was completely unrepresentative, then a large stratum of working-class adolescents are still content to be 'workmanlike'.

The two exceptions in the Poplar group to the above pattern of status acceptance were Pete and Tony. Pete aspired to be something more than an expendable cog in a static and routinised industrial machine:

He was 16½ and worked on the tugs, didn't like it much, but wasn't going to work in a factory. 'That's all there is around here, factories. I tried for the Merchant Navy but they turned me down. Too many jobs. Seven.' The Youth Employment was no good, they 'never gave you anything'. He'd leave Poplar if he had the money. He was one of a family of nine and was very despondent about money and life in general. 'I have to find two pound ten every week for my mother. I can't afford to lose my job.' Nevertheless, he changed his job at least twice in six months to bring his total to ten jobs in eighteen months since leaving secondary modern. He added: 'But what can I do? I can't spell or read or write. What's life anyway? You go to school at five, you leave at fifteen, get a job, leave at sixty-five and then die. That's life. What is it that teenagers are supposed to do.' Politics meant nothing to him. He wanted, if anything, to own his own business, a lorry of his own for haulage, but at that moment he was too young to drive. He viewed life as a dead end, like a job without prospects that you can't throw up. It was not only lack of money that depressed him: it was mainly the powerlessness and the routine degradation of the jobs to which he had access. At one point he was offered a job 'stacking sacks in a factory. They can keep *that*.' Pete 'chucked up' his job on the tugs, however, simply became 'fed up with it,' and got more money—£9 a week—working for a scrap-iron firm, as lorry-driver's mate. I asked him if there were any prospects at all in what he was doing. 'Prospects?' he said. 'What prospects? Don't make me laugh. How am I going to get a job with prospects?' He regarded even this kind of job as a bulwark against a delinquent career: 'If I ever run out of money again, I'm going to go out and do a job for some,' and 'I've stopped nickin' now, but if I'm ever out of a job again I'm going straight back to it.' He thought he might follow his father into the docks at the age of 21, but was still bitter about having been turned down for the other occupational escape-route for East End boys, the Merchant Navy.

If Pete stood apart from the group because of his sceptical appraisal of his own 'life-chances', Tony was never accepted as one of 'the boys' because of his decisively better 'life-chances'. Tony was that archetype, the grammar school boy in a 'black' secondary modern school area. About car-borrowing, Pete said:

'No, he wouldn't come in on anything like that. He does some things, but he's got an apprenticeship. *He's got something to lose.*'

Informal Observation

Tony had a 5-year apprenticeship as a technician lined up for
him when he left school in a few months at 16½. 'It's only three
quid a week till you're 21, but after that you get 15. I've got
a cousin, he's a chief draughtsman for——, he gets 35 quid a
week.' Tony liked his school, and the teachers, but was appre-
hensive about staying on, as he'd be too old for an apprenticeship after 17, and anyway he needed to be earning something.
Lennie chipped in about his old school:

'They have an annual report. You know what was in the annual
report last year? Nine pregnancies. That's the kind of school
ours is.'

The group had an ambiguous attitude towards Tony, criticising
him about behaviour which passed unnoticed in others. If he
played badly on the pin-table, he was taunted, if only mildly:
'What you playin' at?', 'You never were any good at this, were
you?' Tony said 'Fuck' more often than the others in a weird
attempt to integrate, but they remained inconsistently friendly.
Eventually he stopped coming in. Asked where he was 'these
days', Lennie said:

'Don't know. Don't care about him. His father doesn't like him
coming in here, or something. Oh, he comes in now and again,
but we're not all that bothered.'

Attitudes in Stepney were broadly similar, though the adolescents there were encountered in youth-clubs as opposed to caffs
and pubs, and no group's views were tapped over time. A feature
of Stepney is its abundance of youth clubs of great variety and
its possession of more grammar schools than are needed by
available population, for much the same reasons that it is over-
crowded with churches. Stepney grammar schools are largely
filled by children commuting in from Essex. In some, local
pupils are a minority. In one girls' grammar school, the local
girls were a small, ostracised out-group. The large number of
youth clubs—stratified into Jewish and non-Jewish, 'respectable'
and 'rough' working-class—often attracted many users from
other boroughs. Some clubs catered for the delinquent,
'unattached' boy who in other areas would typically have resorted
to the caff. One such club was liked because 'there's no rules
here'; but in fact a rough-and-ready discipline was maintained

by adult helpers who had used the club in their teens and lived locally. These clubs were especially valued for dances in an area without dance-halls, the nearest being the Poplar 'Civic'. The process of selection in most church and LCC-run youth clubs left the 'rough' residue for this kind of club, which did not attempt to emulate their—at best—smooth organisation and well-run 'activities'. Throughout, only one example of vocal resentment about education and jobs was elicited (in a club where the helpers commented on the 'respectability' of the kids):

> 'I got an apprenticeship. What's that? At 19, I earn eight quid. . . . You get a second-class education and you get a second-class job with it. A pal of mine left school the other week and got a job as a lagger. A lagger. You can't get any lower than a lagger.'

Things were fixed against them in the East End, 'we can't possibly get a better job.' This isolated example of vehemence against the social structure came, significantly, from a boy in a skilled job, atypical because he articulated dissatisfaction with the type of job to which he had access, rather than with simply the job he had at the time. He vocalised the kind of resentment which was constantly looked for, but rarely found, in both boroughs.

Status-frustration, as portrayed by Cohen, appeared to be found in inverse, rather than direct, correlation with 'subcultural' delinquency. Discontent with role allotment, and resentment at structural blockage to upward mobility, seemed to be associated with lower-stream grammar and technical school, and upper echelon 'A' stream secondary modern school, boys—rather than the products of the typical 'black' secondary modern school. It must be emphasised that Cohen's theorisation stressed the occurrence of status-frustration at an earlier stage than late adolescence, and only research at the pre-school leaving stage in secondary moderns would supply any valid data on this point. Also, where status-frustration *did* occur in a lower unskilled and semi-skilled working-class context, it produced a degree of desperation which found some outlet—but no 'gang' status 'solution'—in delinquency. But the norm in this lower-class context appeared to be one of status acceptance. In this context, the 'renegade'—in Simmel's[21] sense—was not the delinquent boy

---

[21] G. Simmel, *Conflict* (1955), tr. K. H. Wolff, pp. 47–48.

(unless the delinquency took violent form) but the 'college' boy, who sought a change of reference-group, either as skilled technical or white-collar salariat worker. The East End may be too atypical in this connection for any generalisation to be made on the basis of experience there. Its dockland especially has institutionalised the 'cult' of manual work, and—outside the Jewish population—all the cultural pressures are against the upwardly mobile child. The absence of any real pressure for upward mobility is in part explained by the lack of any tangible incentive to make any but the biggest upward climb. Full juvenile and adult employment are probably enough to make for status acceptance, in an area where wages are as high in many manual jobs as in most routine white-collar jobs, especially those involving academic qualifications, such as teacher, youth worker, probation officer—the middle-class representatives with whom the working-class boy comes into most frequent contact. In the docks and the markets, wages are appreciably higher—though much more erratic—than in office or low-prestige academic jobs. But Stepney and Poplar are not appreciably more conservative and hide-bound in class and occupational beliefs and values than are traditional working-class areas in many cities. The constrictions of the working-class value-system are still powerful enough to render technically low-status jobs acceptable. The working-class boys encountered typically measured themselves not against 'all comers', but against their own class-bound peer-group. The upwardly mobile working-class 'college'[22] boy is the 'renegade', and the delinquent gang is rendered unnecessary as a defence mechanism against status-frustration. This situation appears to have barely changed so far, but feasibly—as we expand our educational elites, recruit more from the lower working classes for our academically qualified technicians and administrators, and as the job-market for unskilled and semi-skilled labour contracts—the conservatism of the working-class value-system will weaken. 'The boys' still think in terms of 'Them' and 'Us' rather than in terms of 'Success' and 'Failure': the first implies a sense of group-affiliation and class solidarity; the second connotes the stress and strain of individual achievement: the first emphasises collective goals, fought for and won by union bargaining and strength; the second

[22] In this context, the grammar-school boy.

implies individual goals, to which access is controlled by exterior criteria. The more the situation changes from the first to the second configuration, the more prone working-class male adolescents will be to that specific 'problem of adjustment' which Cohen postulated as the core incentive to gang delinquency.

(*o*) *Alienation*

The concept of 'alienation' plays as central a role in the sub-cultural theorisation of Cloward and Ohlin as 'status-frustration' does in that of Cohen, and the largely negative findings for the latter apply even more forcibly for the former. There was barely any evidence to suggest that delinquent adolescents achieved any degree of alienation in the Cloward-Ohlin sense, i.e. 'withdrawal of attributions of legitimacy for conventional norms'. If the findings on 'status-frustration' were substantially correct, this is hardly a surprising conclusion: 'status-frustration' or profound disenchantment with available legitimate opportunities, is the stage in the delinquent subcultural sequence prior to the possible emergence of the alienated response. Alienation in this context means much more than a boy 'not liking' his job, or feeling at odds with the machine he operates. It means rejection of the normative system by which he was allotted the job, came to operate the machine, in the first place. Yet the jobs of the Poplar boys and—notoriously—of a disproportionate number of male delinquents, including the most recalcitrant, were of low status even by working-class standards. These boys were not impervious to the working-class image of 'the good job', the autonomy of the craftsman, the physical toughness of the stevedore, the offbeat glamour and on-shore independence of the Merchant seaman, the high wages and security awaiting the apprentice. Enough of their peers occupy these jobs for the contrast to be ever-present. To deny on their behalf any real degree of status-frustration and alienation is not to present a picture of boys who are happy to be laggers—'the lowest of the low'—van-boys, labourers, etc. What has been achieved, rather, is an opting-out of the joint middle- and skilled working-class value-system whereby work is extolled as a central life-issue, and whereby the male adolescent of semi- and unskilled origin is enjoined to either 'better himself' or 'accept his station in life'. To insulate themselves against the harsh implications of this creed, the adolescent in a 'dead-end' job, in a 'dead' neighbour-hood, extricates himself from the belief in work as of any impor-tance beyond the simple provision of income, and deflects what aspirations he has left into areas of what has been termed 'non-work' (rather than leisure).

This process has been best described as one of 'dissociation', as distinct from 'status-frustration' or 'alienation':

> Satisfaction from work and the significance attached to it will depend not only on the nature of the work, but also on the expectations which the individual brings to his job. These in turn will be the result of complex processes of selection and socialisa-tion, which begin at 11 + with entry to the grammar or modern school, each of which carries its stream of children on to broad groups of occupations. . . . For the less able child in the lower forms of the modern school, the dominant picture that emerges is one of school as a source of boredom and frustration.[23] In many schools the imposition of dull, mechanical tasks, which lack any apparent significance or relevance to the life of the child, effectively train him to accept the routine demands of industry. The transition from school to work involves little more than a change of routine.[24] Many expect little from work and are satisfied with what they find, even though the work is repetitive and makes few demands. The secondary modern boy leaving school at 15 has received early training in dissociating himself from the demands which 'they' make upon him. *He simply doesn't care.* It is not surprising that psychologists have discovered that many are content to carry out routine tasks. Dissatisfaction is a measure of the gap between aspiration and achievement. *For many, no such gap exists—their expectations and aspirations are centred on the world outside the factory.*[25]

In school, the problem is not one of structured protest, defiance and rebellion against middle-class norms, but of pupil inertia, boredom and passivity, with periodic outbursts of what Webb termed 'spontaneity, irrepressibility and rule-breaking' as a reaction against the shackling of their individualism by the school as a legitimised agency of control. In this connection,

[23] See M. P. Carter, *Home, School and Work* (1962).
[24] See also Webb, 'Sociology of a School,' *Brit. J. Sociol.*, Vol. 13, No. 3, Sept. 1962.
[25] See S. Cotgrove and S. Parker, 'Work and Non-Work', *New Society*, Vol. 41, 11/7/1963, pp. 18–19.

the apology offered by the father of a Stepney boy who refused to be interviewed is of interest. The boy had previously reluctantly agreed to be interviewed, but on the date, had gone out to the pictures with his wife. The father simply offered 'They don't take to people with education' as a reason, a classic instance of dissociation, of evasion and withdrawal, as opposed to outright annoyance and anger at being pestered.

Cotgrove and Parker, in reviewing recent studies in industrial sociology, go a long way towards establishing a frame of reference for the analysis of the work situation as a main determinant of attitudes and values in areas of non-work. They complain that

> the sociologist, if he has looked outside the factory, has searched mainly for clues which would throw light on industrial behaviour. . . . The great weakness of such studies is their failure to sort out the components of the working-class situation and relate them to working-class culture, leisure and family life. . . . Short term hedonism, belief in fate, and the distinction between 'them' who decide and 'us' who passively carry out instructions . . . may well stem from the typical factory work situation, characterised by a lack of autonomy and involvement.[26]

'Extreme' occupations make the clearest impact on areas of non-work. The miner, for example, in particular the face worker,

> is deeply involved in his work and enjoys relative autonomy at the coal face. But it is dangerous and damaging work, demanding the closest co-operation . . . which makes its indelible imprint on life after work—the forgetfulness of alcohol in the long round of pub visits on Saturday and Sunday, wives left at home, and the deep significance of the trade union. . . .

The 'organisation man' is affected in a fashion equally commensurate with the demands and prospects of his occupation, which encourages the long view, the promise of deferred gratification, the blurring of the distinction between work and leisure.

> Yet although the effect of work on non-work activities is so marked . . . for the great mass of industrial workers, and for many white-collar workers too, *work is not a significant area of life*. . . . The activities most valued are found chiefly outside work.

[26] Cited here are: N. Dennis, F. Henriques and C. Slaughter, *Coal is our Life* (1956); C. Sigal, *Weekend in Dinlock* (1960); J. Tunstall, *The Fishermen* (1962).

The factory worker is seldom work-centred. Work for him is not something on which he centres his interests, his hopes and aspirations, nor even his worries.

Baldamus has shown[27] 'that the mental and skill demands made by the work task are of major importance' as determinants of 'involvement in work or dissociation from it'. The secondary modern 'drop-out', destined at 15 for the shallow range of unskilled and semi-skilled jobs, is already schooled to dissociation by the educational process.

> Those for whom work lacks intrinsic interest are likely to look elsewhere for satisfaction and achievement and to see work simply as a source of income. . . . In nine-to-five jobs, no obligations need encroach on leisure time. . . . Some, for whom work is not an area for free and meaningful action, turn to leisure as compensation. . . . Leisure . . . may be sought as an escape from the monotony of work, given over to such feverish pleasures as speedway and jiving. Withdrawal to home-centredness offers compensations of a different kind. Here, a man is boss of his own small world, and can engage in meaningful tasks of his own choosing. . . .

'The influence of work, however, is by no means confined to leisure activities. It may shape in a variety of ways political attitudes, family patterns, and even the 'world view' of the worker.' Lockwood[28] found the crucial pressures underlying the 'class consciousness' of the clerk, and his attitude towards unionisation, stemmed from the work situation—with its paternalistic relationship and sense of identity with the employer—rather than from market determined income. Cotgrove and Parker conclude that

> if, in fact, many of the components of working class attitudes and values spring from their position in the authority structure of industry or from the nature of the tasks they carry out, rather than from poverty and insecurity,[29] then affluence alone will not bring about the changes we might otherwise predict. The fact that work is not a central life interest for most has important

[27] W. Baldamus, 'Types of Work and Motivation', *Brit. J. Sociol.*, March 1951.
[28] D. Lockwood, *The Blackcoated Worker* (1958).
[29] E.g., if poverty, misery, insecurity and sheer generalised deprivation were the mainsprings of crime and delinquency, then the old age pensioners would be the most crime-ridden sector.

implications. If we choose to concentrate on non-work satisfactions, we shall need to know much more about the extent to which work moulds leisure activities, and how far satisfying leisure can, in fact, compensate for alienating work. . . . What we can certainly say is that *work sets limits on the kind of leisure which are possible* and seem to be desirable, and profoundly influences non-work activities, beliefs and attitudes.

For 'the boys' in Stepney and Poplar, dissociation at work seemed to be coupled with dissociation in leisure. Granted the abundance of youth work in Stepney, the cause for surprise is not that this pattern has been broken down slightly, but that it has resisted such a variety of middle-class oriented blandishments. But it cannot be asserted that dissociation extends to the 'world view' of these adolescents, and it is this 'world-view' that affords least evidence of alienation in the Cloward-Ohlin sense. For example, the Poplar group showed firm loyalty to the monarchy, the government, etc. They disagreed with the way white Americans treated Negroes. Hatred of 'coppers'—'the boys'' sworn enemy—was not a manifestation of 'withdrawal of attributions of legitimacy from conventional norms', but rather a particularistic aversion to the kind of control enforced by the police. This was combined with an attitude verging on what Sykes and Matza termed 'techniques of neutralisation'—e.g. 'Coppers are a lot of cunts. They closed everything down, all the caffs. They stop us doing anything, always moving us along', etc.—i.e. 'accusing the accusers', though there is undoubted truth in their charge of differential victimisation. Police justification for this would be valid, however, as the groupings they break up and 'move on' are often ripe for trouble-making: removal of the causes which led the groups to form and 'hang about' in this way is not the police's concern. Yet hatred of the police is often suspended. The friendly cop is a rarity, but is enormously respected. Also, on one occasion, Ray listened in to a police car bulletin. He expressed no resentment, just excitement. The police, normally repressive, had for once *been* a source of excitement. 'Plain-clothes', however, are quite beyond the pale.

'Dissociation' for 'the boys' is generally from middle-class dominated institutions, rather than from the total non-working-class society. One of a group of 'ton-kids' who used the caff occasionally expressed this almost too articulately:

'We go fast, but we watch it. We wait for straight stretches of road most of the time. *There's none of this defiance of society.* That's all in the newspapers and the newspapers are all wrong. They're just sensationalising to sell more newspapers. . . .'

Even about the Remand Home, the group showed clear preference for conniving dissociation from its aims rather than alienation from its norms:

'It's better "inside" than out here. Prison's alright. And places like Stamford House, that's just a holiday camp. You go there and behave yourself for a fortnight and they make you a prefect. Then you get more time to watch the telly, you don't have to do jobs, things like that.'

Interaction between middle-class 'helpers' and working-class 'delinquents' in youth-clubs provides many instances of confrontation producing friction, but antagonism resulted in dissociation rather than open conflict on the part of the adolescent. Overt hostility is rarely the consequence of such interaction, even where middle-class intrusion is resented. By analogy, the 'inverted snobbery' peculiar to the English working-class is the hall-mark of dissociation and its maintenance is an antidote to feelings of alienation.

(p) *Anomie*

Analysis so far has concentrated on what might be termed the consistently delinquent 'corner boy'—Cohen's clear-cut distinction between the 'corner' and the 'delinquent' boy appearing to be inappropriate at this juncture—and not on the working-class 'college' boy, the aspirant highly skilled manual and technical workers, or the conforming 'corner boy'. Also excluded are delinquent boys bent on pursuing a nascent professional criminal career—often on the basis of almost unbroken institutionalisation —and 'lone' offenders who commit delinquencies with no traceable pattern, e.g. those for whom delinquency is symptomatic of mental illness. It is still thought that the group delinquent 'corner boy' pattern accounts for the bulk of the major adolescent offences, i.e. the diversified activities of break-ins, car-borrowing, simple larcenies and theft from machines, rowdyism, receiving, weapon-carrying and—more atypically—vandalism and violence against the person. Yet these adolescents did not appear to be subject—or to have been subjected in the past—to any critical degree of status frustration or alienation. Interaction within middle-class institutions, and the experience of 'failure' in the context of both middle-class and upper working-class contexts, appeared to have evoked the response of dissociation from the ethic that work, and occupational status, were of crucial importance as a focal area for 'ego-involvement'. As a result, their reference- and membership-groups were pretty well aligned. This is not to deny that they were subject to a mild form of economic anomie, but this is not peculiar to the male working-class adolescent sector. It is built into the consumer economy as incentive for all classes and all age-levels.[30] But the strain towards anomie is not generated solely by frustrations encountered in monetary and occupational spheres. As Merton has repeatedly stressed:

> ... the general theory of social structure and anomie is *not* confined to the specific goal of monetary success and of social restrictions upon access to it. . . . In terms of the general conception, *any* cultural goals which receive extreme and only negligibly qualified emphasis in the culture of a group will serve to attenuate the emphasis on institutionalised practices and make for anomie.[31]

Dissociation from the goal of occupational achievement—which feasibly occurs long before entry into the job-market—forestalls Cohen's issue of status-frustration: the 'problem of adjustment', consequent upon internalisation of middle-class values to at least some extent, never occurs. There is little merging: working-class and middle-class value-systems meet in head-on clash. As Merton, again, has stated:

> ... the theory (of anomie) . . . sees the conflict between culturally defined goals and institutional norms as one *source* of anomie; it does not *equate* value-conflict and anomie. Quite the contrary: conflict between the norms held by distinct subgroups in a society of course often results *in an increased adherence to the norms prevailing in each subgroup*. It is the conflict between culturally accepted values and the socially structured difficulties of living up to these values which exerts pressure towards deviant behaviour and disruption of the normative system.[32]

[30] Cf. the discussion by T. H. Marshall, *Sociology at the Crossroads* (1963) pp. 317-318.
[31] R. K. Merton, *Social Theory and Social Structure* (1957), p. 181.
[32] Merton, op. cit., pp. 190–191.

By acceptance of low job aspirations, the 'corner boy' is released from the pressures of upward mobility, and his view of the legitimacy of 'lower class culture' is endorsed. But dissociation—as has already been stated—means withdrawal of interest in work except as a source of income, and this has concomitant implications for his behaviour, with others similarly circumstanced, in areas of 'non-work'. Feasibly, the more debasing his job-content and the more dissociated he feels from work, the more the lower working-class 'corner boy' tries to recoup in leisure something of the freedom, achievement, autonomy and excitement he is denied in work. In other words, Cohen's concept of 'status frustration' might possibly apply in this country if 'status' is defined in the Weberian sense of 'style of life' and consumer behaviour, rather than in the narrower sense of occupational prestige and aspirations to middle-class orientated achievement.

(q) 'Subterranean' Values and Leisure Goals

Sykes and Matza, by viewing 'adolescents in general and delinquents in particular as the last leisure class',[33] have attacked the conception that the values underlying the delinquent's behaviour constitute a deviant normative system. They assert that: 'A number of supposedly delinquent values are closely akin to those embodied in the leisure activities of the dominant society'. They hold that: (a) the values behind much juvenile delinquency are far less deviant than commonly portrayed, and (b) the faulty picture is due to gross over-simplification of the middle-class value-system.[34] Three major themes have emerged from the variety of classic accounts of delinquent behaviour and values, although consensus is limited to substance, and not interpretation: (i) delinquents are typically immersed in a restless search for excitement, thrills or 'kicks'; (ii) delinquents commonly exhibit a disdain for 'getting on' in the realm of work; (iii) delinquents characteristically accept aggressive toughness as a proof of masculinity.

[33] D. Matza and G. Sykes, 'Delinquency and Subterranean Values', *Amer. Sociol. Rev.*, Vol. 26, No. 5, Oct. 1961, pp. 712–719.
[34] In defending Cohen in particular against the charge that he 'grossly over-simplifies' the middle-class value-system, and 'reduces' the value-system of the whole society to that of the middle class, it can be asserted that this is precisely what the school sets out to achieve. Hence the strength of the postulated reaction against the value-system symbolised by the school context.

(i) is not accommodated by legitimate outlets such as organised recreation, for the very fact that an activity involves breaking the law is precisely the source of excitement. In courting danger, provoking authority, etc., 'the delinquent is not simply enduring hazards: *he is also creating hazards in a deliberate attempt to manufacture excitement'*. The excitement that stems from danger and law-violation, e.g. especially in 'chicken runs' and 'rumbles', is not a by-product, but a—possibly the—motivating force.

(ii) places the delinquent firmly in the category of the unemployed, the casual worker, or the boy in the 'dead-end' job. Even where 'occupational goals involving the steady job or cautious advancement' are available, 'it takes deep faith—and naïveté—to believe that hard work at the lower end of the occupational hierarchy is a sure path to worldly success'. (In the words of a later-day 'courtesan', Mandy Rice-Davies, who began with a low-status background: 'Nobody ever made a bomb by plodding along in a dull job.' (paraphrase)).

(iii) is commonly interpreted as an index of the delinquent's alienation from the larger society, his aggression—whether verbal or physical—seen as an outlet for basic hostility, hatred, and the urge to injure and destroy. This may be so for atypical big-city 'structured' gangs. More typically, it expresses the delinquent's familiarity with the ethic that manhood is reached via an ability to 'take it' and 'hand it out'.

Far from taking this configuration of values as indicative of the delinquent's deviation from the dominant society, Sykes and Matza note its affinities with the code of Veblen's 'gentleman of leisure'. The emphasis on daring; rejection of the prosaic discipline of work; the flair for conspicuous consumption; the respect accorded to manhood demonstrated by force; all find a prototype in Veblen's leisured elite. Only the *mode* of expression—delinquency—is unfamiliar. *'The values are obscured by their context.'* But the context alone is not sufficient to account for the attribution of deviance to the delinquent's values. 'In our haste to create a standard from which deviance can be measured, we have reduced the value-system of the whole society to that of the middle class', and our portrayal of that value-system is grossly oversimplified. By an over-emphasis on the individualistic pursuit of work-goals, the Protestant Ethic and the deferred gratification pattern, and by a similar inflation of the ethic of reciprocity, belief in luck and short-run hedonism, we have polarised middle-class and working-class value-systems. Sykes and Matza compare these value-system portrayals to the now outmoded racial group portrayals, i.e. they amount to 'a distinct grouping of specific values unique to the social class in which they are found', instead of basing analysis on the 'distribution of frequencies', i.e.: 'Most values . . . appear in most social classes; the social classes differ, however, in the frequency with which the values appear'.

In any event, and whatever degree of distinctiveness is held to obtain between the value-systems of the social classes, Sykes and Matza argue that *all* classes accommodate certain 'subterranean values'—values which are in conflict or competition with other deeply held values, but which are still recognised and accepted by many.[35] 'These contradictions in values . . . may exist in a single individual and give rise to profound feelings of ambivalence in many areas of life.' They are akin to private as opposed to public morality, but they are not—*per se*—deviant.

Delinquent values, therefore, have their counterparts in the dominant society, most crucially in the upper and middle class sectors. But their expression is muted, confined to certain circumstances, such as holidays, sport, recreations, private conversation. Members of the middle class—and of all classes—seek excitement in gambling, parties, night-clubbing etc. 'Most societies provide room for . . . a sort of periodic anomie, in which thrill-seeking is allowed to emerge.' Indeed, 'the search for adventure, excitement . . . is a subterranean value that now often exists side by side with the values of security, routinisation, etc. It is not a deviant value . . . but must be held in abeyance until the proper circumstances for it arrive . . . In many cases, the delinquent suffers from bad timing.' Likewise, it can hardly be claimed that the dominant society is fully and unquestioningly

[35] Sykes and Matza fail to note that Cohen advanced much the same point, but regarded it as less crucial for an understanding of the middle-class value-system: 'The delinquent is the rogue male. His conduct may be viewed not only negatively . . .; positively it may be viewed as the exploitation of modes of behaviour which are traditionally symbolic of untrammelled masculinity, which are renounced by middle-class culture because incompatible with its ends, but which are not without . . . glamour and romance . . . They find their way into the respectable culture . . . only in disciplined and attenuated forms. . . . *They are not, however, allowed to interfere with the serious business of life.* The delinquent . . . is freer to divert these *subterranean currents* of our cultural tradition to his own use.' Cohen, op. cit., p. 140.

committed to hard work. The notion of 'pull' and 'contacts', the idea of the 'soft' job—for the working-class in England, the 'good skive'—are widespread. Riesman's 'inside-dopester', Whyte's 'organisation man' and Mills' 'fixer' are all concepts 'undermining the Weberian sociologists' affirmation of *the* work values of society'. In his disdain for the monotony of manual labour and his desire for 'easy' money, 'the delinquent is . . . in step with his time'. As for aggression, the dominant society exhibits a widespread taste for violence; books, magazines, films and TV jointly peddle fantasies of violence, from James Bond to 'Psycho', as well as acting as vehicles for the dissemination of criminal techniques. The actual use of aggression and violence in war and law enforcement provide further endorsement of the acceptance of aggression and violence on the part of the dominant social order. The equation between physical toughness and virility is also widely accepted, though the use of aggression is surrounded by many prohibitions.

In brief, Sykes and Matza argue that, far from standing as an alien in the body of society, the delinquent may represent instead a dangerous reflection or caricature. By picking up and emphasising the subterranean part of the dominant value system, the delinquent serves to reinforce the overtly law-abiding in their tenure of its more respectable and publicly proclaimed values. 'These values bind the delinquent to the society whose laws he violates', and this sharing facilitates his 'reformation' with the coming of adult status. 'To the objection that much juvenile behaviour other than simply delinquent behaviour would then be analysed as an extension of the adult world rather than as a product of a distinctly adolescent subculture', Matza and Sykes reply that this is 'precisely their thesis'.

In approaching the relationship between delinquency and social class, however, the argument of Sykes and Matza comes to verge on the perverse. Because they have answered the question: 'What makes delinquency attractive in the first place?' exclusively in terms of leisure values, i.e. the values of what they term a 'leisure class', and because they assert these values apply to adolescents at all class levels, they are led to assert that delinquency is more or less evenly distributed throughout the social class structure. This argument is not only based largely on absence of evidence: it runs counter to the massive amount of evidence that exists. It is not enough to insist that the non-delinquent is a rarity. This is by now a criminological truism. Most evidence supports the view that group delinquency is more frequent, persistent, diversified and less amenable to control among male, working-class, urban adolescents than in any other sector. Moreover, this view is consistent with the theorisation of Matza and Sykes, provided that the concept of *differential access to leisure goals* is utilised, along with theorisation on the differential *distribution* and *functions* of leisure among adolescents.

Temporarily leaving out of consideration a small, moneyed, upper class élite, the distribution of leisure in adolescence by social class is clearly determined by educational allotment. At school, the non-secondary modern boy is subject to a rigorous academic time-table, home-work, and frequently school-sponsored commitments in sport and voluntary associations. Increasingly, this pattern of obligations—which eats into non-school activities —is unbroken till the age of 18, with the transition from school to higher education or training. The early leaver at 16 typically moves into a white-collar job, where he pursues an achievement-oriented career, frequently involving part-time or further education. Hence, the non-secondary modern school-boy is institutionally restrained from the most basic delinquency-producing situation of all: an abundance of 'free' time. The same applies on a lesser scale to a sizeable minority of upper stream secondary modern boys, who obtain apprenticeship, lower-grade white-collar jobs, or trainee skilled occupations, which involve either day release or evening classes. But for the substantial majority of secondary modern boys, both at and after school, few commitments encroach on leisure time.

Paradoxically, these adolescents—who have most leisure— also *need* it most, and ask more of it. Matza and Sykes have stated that all adolescents are alike in that 'they move in a limbo between earlier parental domination and future integration with the social structure through the bonds of work and marriage'. But for the grammar, technical and skilled working-class boy, it is not so much a limbo as a period of structured training for future role performance. Society has invested much more heavily in this type of adolescent than in the average secondary modern 'drop out' destined for the narrow ranges of numerous and interchangeable semi- and unskilled manual jobs. The strong likelihood of dissociation from this latter type of work has already been discussed, as have the consequences of dissociation for involvement in areas of non-work. Home-centredness is clearly unthinkable for most working-class male adolescents before their own marriage: numerous studies have pointed to the early age at which the working-class adolescent—quite distinctly from the middle-class boy—disentangles himself from parental domination. Similarly, the nature of his work appears to disincline him towards political and community activity. The only non-work area to which he is unequivocally attracted is straightforward, uncluttered leisure. Yet dissociation from the work situation, and from middle-class dominated authority contexts, has its corollary in leisure: the rejection of the youth club, except for those few which exert little discipline, do not insist on regular attendance, and do not intrude on the group's or the individual's autonomy. Hence the emphasis on commercial milieux, the caff, the cinema, the dance-hall. For work-oriented adolescents, no such prohibitions apply. School- and job-satisfaction often leave them self-sufficient in leisure: mere idleness, sheer relaxation, is enough. But the youth club, with its 'activities' and 'constructive' frame of reference, accommodates them if they feel the need for direction in leisure. Also, academically-oriented education has equipped them for individualistic leisure pursuits, such as reading, hobbies, etc. It is the 'corner boy'—who has most leisure, and lays most stress on it as the area for self-realisation—who has least resources at his disposal to use it positively.

It is in this situation that the adolescent 'corner boy' encounters blockage of access to certain leisure goals common to all adolescents. The concept of this group as a discriminated-against 'leisure class' involves little tampering with the formula proposed by Matza and Sykes. Leisure goals as a term is meant to subsume both 'subterranean values'—the search for excitement, the pursuit of aggression[36]—and certain leisure aspirations and expectations reflected in and perpetuated by 'teenage' culture—sophistication (clothes, wit), smartness, 'exploit', 'kicks'. Achievement in some or all of these areas might be said to constitute

---

[36] For Sykes and Matza, 'disdain for work' entailed apotheosis of 'the big score': this was jettisoned in an English context.

'success' in leisure for adolescents. 'Teenage culture' stresses the possession of these attributes and the pursuit of these collective goals. It also lays special emphasis on certain artefacts and institutions: the fast car or motor-bike, the 'regular' girl, record-players, parties, etc. Rising expectations of leisure over the last decade have brought goals formerly within the reach of a minority into the purview of all: the holiday abroad, trips to the country, all-night 'raves', the kick of speed.[37] The genuinely leisured, upper-class adolescent has full access to these goals, as have most students. By contrast, the 'corner boy' is relatively deprived in access to arenas for this kind of 'exploit'. Law-breaking is the only area of excitement to which he has absolutely untrammelled access. 'Anything you get enjoyment from round here, you're breaking the law' and 'We did it for a bit of a giggle' or 'Just for laughs': these disavowals of malice are more than techniques of neutralisation: they are euphemisms for the absence of legitimate opportunities to realise leisure goals.

Observation in Stepney and Poplar gave some support for this view. A focal issue for the Poplar boys was what they termed the 'deadness' of the area, 'nothing going on', their aversion to the one institution—the youth club—which might have contained their 'periodic outbursts of anomie' (Matza and Sykes). Those with bikes had a valid outlet:

> 'We go fast, but we watch it. . . . There's none of this defiance of society. . . . *The bikes for us are mainly a chance*. We can get to places on the bikes we'd never get a sniff at without. We go to the Isle of Wight, Maidstone and so on. We can take the girls out on them. . . . There's a few nuts but not many. We never drink beer and I hardly smoke. We take good care when we're driving, even if we do go fast.'

Some did express the conventional 'ton-kid' persona, 'We go on "burn ups", playing "chicken" with each other . . . For the kick, the speed, *you* know', but the dominant attitude inclined to the former. The caff was virtually the only milieu for those without bikes (none had scooters, though Bill eventually bought a car for £20): apart from the cinema and dancing at the 'Civic',

---

[37] The Teddy Boy Movement can be seen, in part, as a response to the biggest single rise in adolescent leisure expectations of the last decade, i.e., the arrival of 'rock' and the full flowering of commercial 'teenage' culture; cf. Fyvel, op. cit., p. 70.

it was their only legitimate arena for excitement. Their behaviour in the caff was characterised by a milling restlessness, punctuated by long bouts on the pinball machine, the jukebox, etc. Strain was generated by the sheer absence of tension, the feeling that something ought to be 'going on'. Outside the area, they looked for the same framework: 'We go up the West End sometimes, go in those amusement arcades', and once came back tattooed, skull-and-crossbones, etc. on the forearm. Only work, sleep, the cinema and 'courting' took them outside the caff. They were interested in no music except pop, no sport, no reading except the *Mirror* every day and comics. They themselves viewed delinquency as a pretext 'for laughs'. a diversion from the long periods of boredom, constriction and inertia of the caff, whose ethos was in 'negative polarity' to the constructive, busy 'activities' of the model youth club.

It is not suggested that these boys constitute a 'leisure class', only that the analogy itself is suggestive. In the absence of work-orientation and job-satisfaction, and lacking the compensations accruing from alternative areas of non-work, such as home-centredness, political activity and community service,[38] the 'corner boy' attaches unusual importance to 'leisure'. There is no reason to suppose that the delinquent 'corner boy' does not share the more general, technically classless 'teenage culture', a culture whose active pursuit depends on freedom from the restraints of adult responsibility, but which reflects the 'subterranean values' of the conventional adult world. There is some reason to suppose, however, that the working-class 'corner boy' both lays greater stress on its leisure goals, and has far less legitimate access to them, than male adolescents differently placed in the social structure. This discrepancy is thought to be enough to provide immediate impetus to a great deal of group delinquency, limited in ferocity but diversified in content. The underlying sources, however, remain culture-conflict along class lines, school failure and subsequent dissociation from work-goals, and consequent non-involvement in desirable areas of non-work. This sequence appears crucial for the short-lived but intense emphasis on a particular set of leisure goals.

[38] Some boys achieve this, e.g., the Poplar 'Teenage Friendship Society' formed to provide help for the old age pensioners.

(v) 'Sexual Deprivation'

It has recently been suggested that Borstal boys have experienced less success than is normal for their peers in establishing hetero-sexual relationships, and that this contributes to recalcitrant delinquency, whether of a subcultural or individualistic kind.[39] It is more likely, however, that subcultural delinquency is a cause, rather than a result, of the inability to form a stable relationship with girls, although the continuing absence of such a relationship serves to perpetuate the delinquent response. Cohen has stressed that, in adulthood, the male's occupational achieve-ments form the principal criterion of status for both husband and wife, and the chief moral responsibility for this achievement rests on the man. 'It follows that the man's success in the adult role is, as compared with the woman's, less dependent on whom he marries and more dependent upon his own achievements. *The woman has more to gain by "marrying up" and more to lose by "marrying down".*'[40] For the adult male, status is ultimately determined by his own occupational success; for the woman, the functional equivalent is marriage to an occupationally successful male.

The more this axiom holds broadly true, irrespective of ethnic and social class subgroup variations, the more disadvantaged is the delinquent boy in his search for regular female company. That he wants such company can hardly be disputed, even if only for motives of sexual 'exploit' as distinct from the need for a stable, demanding relationship. Nor can it be disputed that, save for a minority, the delinquent's girl is a force for conforming behaviour, as opposed to acting as provocateur for delinquent activity. Hence the rigorous separation by delinquents of their 'courting' performance from the life of the peer group. 'Sex' might be a main collective leisure goal for male adolescents, but any relationship is typically maintained apart from the group, even though it might be sought for in group contexts—the dance-hall, the cinema, the walk-round. It is thought that, while the delinquent boy has dissociated himself from occupational achievement, the majority of working-class girls adhere to the necessity for marrying an occupationally successful male, albeit one who can give them 'a good time'. As early marriage becomes

[39] T. C. N. Gibbens, *Psychiatric Studies of Borstal Lads* (1963). See Ch. 6 and p. 107.
[40] Cohen, op. cit., p. 141.

increasingly the norm for female adolescents, an encouraging factor is that the disparity between the need for achievement and the delinquent reality is frequently resolved by a marriage of necessity, and enforced work-orientation and withdrawal into home-centredness and family-building. Where the delinquent either opts out of this solution, or rejects it in advance, he is correspondingly less of a proposition for the conformist-minded female, and resorts to the minority who are sexually accessible and/or promiscuous, but who can exert less control on the delinquent boy's future adjustment to adult responsibilities. Demographically, as well as structurally, the delinquent boy is more likely to have to resort to the promiscuous, or the younger and more inexperienced girl: simply numerically, there are fewer girls than boys available, and girls tend to marry older males. In Stepney and Poplar, in the 14–17 age-group, there are 4,964 males to 4,594 females. This figure in itself is meaningless, as no society has yet achieved a one-to-one male-female correlation. The figures for Stepney and Poplar for the 15–19 and 20–24 age-groups[41] are, however:

	15–19	*20–24*
Single	5, 614 males	3,945 males
	5,076 females	2,620 females
Married	107 males	1,777 males
	480 females	3,051 females

Even between 15 and 19, there are roughly 112 single males for every 100 unmarried females; between 20 and 24, however, there are roughly 3 single males for every 2 single women. While this discrepancy is swollen by the large influx of young adult, single, male immigrants, a minority of young adult delinquents are still likely to be deprived of that stable, marriage-oriented relationship which appears a crucial element in keeping others out of the courts after late adolescence.

The attitude of the Poplar boys was that, although they did not 'want' to get married 'for a long while', they felt that the dangers of non-marriage exceeded the restraints and responsibilities of the event itself. Hence they thought that marriage was best 'while you're young' as 'You have to before long or you get

[41] Census 1961, London, pp. 15, 17, 21.

like blokes who've waited too long, they just sit around moping.' Hence you 'have to' get married, whether you want to or not: the alternatives are too depressing. When Pete found a 'regular' girl, he became noticeably brighter, better-dressed, and strenuously played down the fact that he was going out with a girl: 'She's a nuisance, but going round with her's better than sitting around the caff'; on marriage, he said: 'I'd sooner take the kids for a walk than sit around stinking caffs all day.' While a great deal of cheerful obscenity was attached to 'courting', it brought out a kind of suppressed respectability in the boys, for as long as the date lasted. The more serious the relationship, the more the boy was kept away from trouble, out of the caff. This was expected and encouraged: the only losers were the boys who never made it.

(s) Conclusion

Informal observation among delinquent boys in mid- to late-adolescence supported the theorisation of Cloward and Ohlin that severe deprivation of access to the legitimate opportunity structure is a necessary basis for the emergence of delinquent contracultures, another determinant being the presence or absence of access to the illegitimate opportunity structure. Crucial in Stepney and Poplar was the existence of an adequate, if limited, legitimate opportunity structure, coupled with that of a petty and disorganised illegitimate opportunity structure, associated with downward mobility and ethnic out-groups. Neither is it thought that reactions to 'failure' in the context of middle-class dominated institutions are responsible for generating a sufficient degree of 'status-frustration' to produce a contra-cultural response. However, no attempt was made to assess these reactions in the principal such context, the school. Inferences were based on expressions concerning job-satisfaction, and occupational expectations and aspirations, subsequent to school-leaving. While a generalised pattern of delinquency resembling an extension through adolescence of Cohen's 'parent male sub-culture' was prevalent, the absence of any real degree of malice and negativism seemed to preclude a contracultural interpretation, although—again—study within the context of those schools containing the most deprived children would probably have yielded different behaviour patterns. Certain forms of acquisitive delinquency indulged in by male adolescents, e.g. miscellaneous larcenies, 'fiddling', etc., have their counterparts in the adult world at most class and age-levels, and merely serve to emphasise the subjection of the population as a whole to a condition of 'mild economic anomie'. Likewise, certain forms of violence committed by working-class male adolescents are paralleled in the lower sectors of the adult working class. Those forms of delinquent behaviour peculiar to male adolescents, however, the 'pointless' break-ins, take-and-drive-away, group rowdyism, are thought to originate in the process of dissociation from school and work areas, and a consequent over-emphasis on, combined with relative lack of legitimate access to, certain leisure goals common to the dominant society. Hence the existence of a delinquent subculture, as distinct from a delinquent contraculture, i.e. commonly situated delinquents hold to a set of norms and share a set of values and beliefs hardly markedly different from those characteristic of other sub-groups in the population, as distinct from holding to and embracing a 'contra' normative system hostile to, and formed by reaction against, that of the dominant, 'middle-class' society.

The principal qualifications to the above lie in the basic approach. Contacts throughout the seven months of observation numbered no more than 50, and of these, only about 10—those centering round the Poplar group—were pursued throughout the time spent in the areas. The rest consisted of on-the-spot conversations. Other contacts were made with youth workers, social workers and teachers in the areas, but observation consisted mainly of simply seeing what went on. Observation was rigorously limited to Stepney and Poplar, and an attempt was made to cover all parts of the borough, except possibly the Isle of Dogs. While it is by no means implied that the picture given applies to other parts of inner London or its vast suburbs, it is thought that most delinquency of a subcultural nature elsewhere in London represents either a dilution or an intensification of the above pattern, rather than a radical departure from it. That is, the basis for contracultures exists in the very possibilities for such intensification.

8

SUMMARY AND CONCLUSIONS

I SUMMARY

The use of the concept of the delinquent subculture by Cohen and—adapted—by Cloward and Ohlin is not wholly satisfactory since 'subculture' is too readily applied as a blanket term to any set of sub-group norms, values and beliefs that deviate from an 'ideal-type' dominant middle-class normative system. The distinction by Yinger between 'subculture' and 'contraculture' is thought to clarify the issue, though Yinger's assumption that 'contraculture' subsumes delinquent subculture is in advance of empirical validation. (Confusion re 'subculture' simply reflects the traditional confusion over—and multiple definitions of—'culture') (Chapter 1). Yet neither subculture nor contraculture necessarily apply only to the value-systems of gang delinquents, nor is the gang framework a sufficient proof of a contracultural value-system: this point is illustrated by reference to two empirical studies which embody this issue (Chapter 2).

The two major approaches to delinquent subcultural theorisation—those by Cohen (and Short) and by Cloward and Ohlin—have tended to be regarded as either mutually exclusive (as by Cloward and Ohlin themselves) or as essentially homogeneous (as by some empirical investigators, notably Clark and Wenninger.) Examination of their hypotheses in detail suggests that the points of difference which emerge in the exposition of their theories are due more to differential concentration on certain aspects of the 'five classes of questions' inherent in this theorisation, rather than to substantive differences. Moreover, after the differences due to differential exposition have been eliminated, the apparently substantive differences remaining are seen to flow from Cloward and Ohlin's over-simplification of the Cohen-Short position on two variables: first, middle-class orientation; and second, the 'parent subculture'. These differences can feasibly be reconciled by the introduction of community-type and age-level variables, as utilised in part by Clark and Wenninger and Reiss and Rhodes, and despite the discarding of the latter by Cloward and Ohlin. These innovations would possibly accommodate also their disagreements over types of subcultural *process*. (Chapter 3).

The welter of critiques on the above subcultural theorisation can be classified into four main types: 'limiting', 'extensive', 'applied' and 'basic'. With the exception of one 'applied' study of values in gang delinquency, all critiques so far can be shown either to have internal inconsistencies, to have been anticipated by subcultural theorisation, to be compatible with the major hypotheses, or to enrich them. Despite this, subcultural theorisation is far from validation, and can likely survive only at the expense of considerable modification. Herein lies its promise, but the danger is that it will be applied recklessly to disparate phenomena. What is needed is a firm sense of the limitations of subcultural theorisation on delinquency. (Chapter 4). Such an example of recklessness might be the attempt to apply subcultural theorisation to the English scene, where delinquency in general is hardly a major social problem, where gang delinquency on the American model is non-existent, and where lack of research makes for difficulties not experienced by American investigators. What data exist, however, suggest the reality of subculture, if not contraculture, in large urban and metropolitan areas. The real research question emerges as being whether or not, or to what degree, the male working-class 'failure' is faced with a 'problem of adjustment' at all. (Chapter 5).

Statistical data on crime commission and delinquent residence (ages 8–25) in two East London boroughs, Stepney and Poplar, were used to test two limited propositions inferred from the theorisation of Cohen and of Cloward and Ohlin, on age-level differences and on between-area differences. A fairly distinct offence structure broadly characterised three age-levels: pre- to mid-adolescence, mid- to late-adolescence, early adulthood. Only the early adult offences differed between the boroughs; through adolescence, the regularities of delinquent behaviour appeared more striking than the between-borough differences, though a more distinct semi-'conflict' pattern emerged in Poplar than in Stepney. The data support Cohen's emphasis on age-level differences, and his concept of the 'parent male' subculture seems most relevant to the illegal behaviour involved. But the character of the West Stepney 'criminal' area makes comparative judgment difficult about the proposition inferred from Cloward and Ohlin. More generally, the data confirmed the absence of gang delinquency, although the group factor—declining in importance with age—is still important in late adolescence; also, accomplice rates varied very much by offence. Recidivism rates for all ages were shown to be heavier for the two boroughs than for the MPD generally. Lack of convergence between the delinquency rates for different age-levels by 'natural' area led to the conclusion that either age-specific delinquency and adult crime derived from distinct aetiologies, or the nature of habitual adult crime in the East End acted more as a repellent than a stimulus to young offenders. It was hypothesised that working-class adolescents associated adult criminality with downward mobility, rather than the reverse. Also (while about one-eighth of delinquents not in school had been unemployed for more than three months) the full-employment situation, in London and the South-East, probably crucially influences the mode of delinquent response. Hence, the pattern of delinquency is of a very different order to that emphasised by American sources. This pattern of offences peculiar to mid- to late-adolescents did not seem to be much affected by the presence in Stepney—but not in Poplar—of what the police term a 'criminal class'. (Chapter 6).

This picture was confirmed by informal observation in the boroughs, in particular with one group in Poplar, whose offences fitted the pattern shown by the crime data: petty break-ins, take-and-drive-away, minor rowdyism, various larceny offences. While their expressed norms, values and beliefs hardly differed markedly from those of the adult lower working-class, which are essentially conservative, their differential concentration on these norms, etc. in a specifically 'leisured' context warrants the use of the subculture concept, though not that of contraculture. Their illegal behaviour seemed to be due not to 'alienation' or 'status frustration', but to a process of dissociation from middle-class dominated contexts of school, work and recreation. This disenchantment provoked an over-emphasis on purely 'leisure' goals—sedulously fostered by commercial 'teenage' culture—rather than on other non-work areas. In a situation where he both needs to attain such goals, and cannot readily do so legitimately, the working-class boy is especially prone to illegal behaviour as a means of 'manufacturing' their ethos. Yet the working-class boy who has undergone this process, who has been hampered in school by his attachment to working-class values, reacts to 'failure' not by frustration, reaction-formation etc., but by the re-affirmation of the working-class value-system. Its social constraints still broadly apply, and the normative early marriage—with its family responsibilities, need for a steady job, need to 'get by' if not 'get on'—rob the leisure context of its attraction: alternative solutions have been provided. The need for 'exploit' is killed. This pattern of delinquency is to be distinguished from adolescent offences which characterise offenders of all age-levels generally, whose recent increases have been due, hypothetically, to an increasingly emphasised 'mild economic anomie'. It is also to distinguish it from delinquency springing from gross personal pathologies. It is thought that the pattern outlined above accounts for a serious proportion of group juvenile delinquency, and any general increase in 'dissociation' from the realms of school and work, and exacerbation of leisure goals as a consequence, will result in more delinquency of an 'exploit' variety. There is clearly room along this leisure dimension for goal-restriction severe enough and visible enough to generate contracultural, as distinct from subcultural, modes of adaptation. This may have already occurred in areas less traditionally working-class than the areas studied.

We are now in a better position to answer the question raised in Chapter 5; does the English 'corner boy', accounted a failure in school and work by middle-class standards, typically encounter any 'problem of adjustment' at all? From the evidence presented it appears that he may do, but not of the kind depicted by Cohen as facing his American counterpart. The English 'corner boy' successfully traverses the humiliations of school and job allocation by his re-affirmation of traditional working-class values. This is much what Cohen meant by saying that he 'revises his aspirations downwards'. But in one sphere, that of leisure proper, the old values have lost their potency, and it is to this sphere that the 'corner boy' displaces his search for achievement from the areas of school and work, and from other non-work areas. Beer and skittles, the darts match, the working men's club and the union have little significance for him. In leisure, therefore, the old solutions no longer apply; for the 'corner boy' with 'time on his hands' and 'nothing to lose', the palliated delinquent sub-culture is an attractive and functional solution to a most intensely-felt problem. This is not to say that non-delinquent working-class and middle-class youth face no 'problems of adjustment' in leisure: however, to echo Cohen's emphasis on the different distribution of problems throughout the social class structure, the working-class 'corner boy' is the only one to depend exclusively on leisure as the framework for 'exploit'.

II CONCLUSIONS

On the working basis that dissociation—not alienation—is the normative response of working-class male adolescents to semi- and unskilled work (and to no work at all), and that this is the primary source of much of the delinquency *peculiar* to male adolescents—the analysis should take into account possible pre-ventive measures in three areas: work, school and leisure. Research should also be directed at the efficacy of various 'intervening variables' which operate to keep the delinquency-prone youth from delinquency, assuming that all working-class boys whose 'life chances' push them inexorably towards semi- and unskilled work are in a delinquency-promoting life situation. This is to reverse the conventional procedure, which is to assume that all adolescents are in a conformity-promoting life-situation, and which directs research towards 'intervening variables' which operate to make a boy delinquency-prone. The vast bulk of research in criminology has been directed along these lines in the search for factors which divert the boy from conformity to deviance: 'broken homes', maternal/paternal deprivation, family fragmentation, character-structure: even much sociological theory has implied that it is only when a crime-oriented 'lower class culture' wins out against the conformist conventional culture that a boy adopts deviant behaviour-patterns. However, if it is assumed that the working-class boy *starts out* in a delin-quency-prone life-situation, these variables are seen as *aggravating* rather than as intervening factors, and the researcher is freed to look for variables which keep the working-class boy *from* delinquency: 'college-boy' performance at school; stable middle-class-orientated or 'respectable' stable working-class family background; promise of skilled employment; political activity; community activity; home-centredness; stable courtship; legitimate leisure opportunities, etc. It is obvious that this approach involves research no less difficult than the usual approach: but at least its frame of reference appears more realistic. Instead of regarding the working-class delinquent as a deviant in a conformity-promoting society, it is possible to regard the working-class boy as born into a pre-ordained delinquency-promoting situation. Our task can only then be to change that situation, so that the bulk of working-class youth is freed from pressures to deviancy and heavy personal costs.

Of the three areas mentioned as in need of re-organisation, leisure is the most amenable and the most attractive proposition, but it is here argued that—as indicated in the previous chapter —the 'leisure' problem is at root a work and education problem. Were it not for our educational system's failure to engage the interests and energies of the average and below-average working-class boy, with its subsequent corollaries of dissociation from areas of work and school, his leisure problem would be far less acute. It is instructive here to contrast the dissociation-alienation reaction polarities between British and American youth, taking as a reference point a start made by Turner's distinction between *modes* of ascent through education.[1] Turner maintains that in any industrial society, the *mode* of upward mobility via education is just as crucially important as the *extent* of upward mobility. In Britain, elite status is *given* by existing elites on the basis of ability-linked qualities; in America, elite status is *won* by ability-linked achievement: the first Turner terms 'sponsored', the second 'contest' mobility. Here, one strand of Turner's argument stands out: that in the 'sponsored' system, final selection decisions are made as early as possible in the educational cycle, so that the process of acculturation can get under way; in the 'contest' system, final selection decisions are delayed as long as possible

---

[1] R. H. Turner, 'Modes of Ascent Through Education: "Sponsored" and "Contest" Mobility'. Ch. 12 in Floud, Halsey and Anderson, *Education, Economy and Society* (1961).

so that equality of opportunity is ensured. The central problem for the British system is thus refinement of the criteria for *selection*; for the American system, the development of incentives for *motivation*. In both, a core issue is the 'drop-out' (America) or the 'early leaver' (Britain), but here there are crucial differences in definition: the American 'drop-out' is any boy who refuses to finish high school and so qualify for college entrance; the British 'early leaver' is a boy who has already been pre-selected for higher education in the grammar school, but fails or refuses to stay the course. The point at issue here is that for the British boy, the educational contest is over by the age of 11 or, inferentially, by the age of 7–8 when 'streaming' begins;[2] for the American boy, the contest is technically open until the age of 17. Either way, the costs of failure are severe, but they differ in the reactions they evoke. For the British boy, dissociation is engendered and strengthened by the earliness at which selection (and rejection) takes place: the result is a certain fatalism towards the roles in school and work to which he has been allocated,[3] and an overt stress on fulfilment through leisure comes early. For the American boy, alienation is engendered and strengthened by the lateness with which final decisions are made, but rejection or inability to conform to ultimate criteria is anticipated, and an overt stress on protest comes early. Moreover, the American system lends itself more readily to the entertainment of unrealistic ambitions late into adolescence, so that rejection (in effect) comes all the more cruelly: the British adolescent has had no time and no incentives to nurture such ambitions. It is no surprise to find that the ambitions of British secondary modern pupils are not only firmly geared to their actual life-chances (Veness),[4] but are also much less prone to 'fantasy' aspirations than their American counterparts (M. D. Wilson).

[2] A point confirmed in J. W. B. Douglas, *The Home and the School* (1964).

[3] So much so that, in anticipation of rejection at 11 +, the bulk of working-class boys in turn reject the 11 + ethic, *preferring* the secondary modern to the grammar school and opting out of the academic rat-race prior to selection procedures. This is truly subversive of meritocracy, and represents a refusal to be motivated to strive . . . etc. Unfortunately, this involves not only immense wastage of ability, but a premature cynicism about the role of education in their personal and social development which limits their scope for, and awareness of, *choice* in every sphere of life, not simply the occupational.

[4] T. Veness, *The School-leavers* (1962); Mary D. Wilson, The Vocational Preferences of Secondary Modern School-children,' *Brit. J. Educ. Psych.*, Vol. 23, 1953, pp. 97–113.

Hence, the working-class male adolescent's leisure problems originate in the school- and work-situations to which he is destined by socioeconomic role allocation. These connections are concealed, since his reactions to work-school are not in general of an alienation–status–frustration variety, but the relatively toned-down response of dissociation. Moreover, this propensity for dissociation from the semi- and unskilled job will feasibly worsen as the prospects for semi- and unskilled labour deteriorate. The process is well under way already, and automation will further erode the market- and work-situation of these levels of occupation, at the same time as it increases the visibility of the occupational rewards for skill and educational/technical qualifications.[5] If the situation of the semi- and unskilled young worker is not to deteriorate much further, radical re-organisation of the areas of school and work are basic, and must go further than 'revolutions' we have failed to at worst initiate and at best fulfil in the past.

(a) Work and Education

At present, much secondary modern education serves simply— and functionally—as a massive irritant on those to whom it imparts the meagre skills and discipline needed for recruitment as the unskilled and semi-skilled personnel of the future. In the U.K., prospects for even the manual working-class elite revolve around an outdated apprenticeship system and limited provision for further education. For those at the bottom of the heap', c. 25–30 per cent. of the age-group, there is only the 'dead-end' to which they become early resigned, and from which they early dissociate themselves. It is futile to say the opportunities exist for all when only a minority can be catered for: as long as 'dead-end' jobs persist, there will be a large minority who are not only beckoned into them, but who inevitably will have to take them. Their only recompense is being bought off for a few years by wages which are relatively high for adolescence. (This advantage soon disappears in adulthood). The problem here is partly one of 'social definition':[6] in the U.S.A. it is actually being implied

[5] At present, union strength and collective bargaining have gained some equivalence between much manual and white collar work in terms of income, if not in terms of status, security, 'fringe' benefits, etc., but see R. M. Titmuss, *Income Distribution and Social Change* (1962).

[6] R. A. Cloward, *Social Problems, Social Definitions and Social Opportunities*, pp. 47–48 (April 1963, *unpubl.*).

that, but for 'drop-outs', there would be no 'dead-end' jobs. 'Judging from the near-panic that drop-outs are creating in some circles, one might easily suppose that a precipitous rise in the rate of drop-outs had preceded the concern. Actually, the reverse appears to be true: that Americans of all classes and ethnic affiliations are more education-minded than ever before. As a consequence, rates of drop-out have been declining compared with earlier decades.

Why then the acute anxiety about drop-outs now rather than some years earlier? The answer is to be found in the economic structure. The school system has never adequately engaged and educated children from families at the bottom of our class structure. *In earlier years, this tendency aroused little concern because alienated adolescents could leave school and be absorbed into a vast unskilled and semi-skilled labour-force.* These manual labouring positions had to be filled; someone must always do the less pleasant work of the society. The school system helped to make the prospect of these less pleasant jobs more pleasant by *making education itself an irritant* for children from culturally different and academically unsophisticated families. Under the circumstances, only the most serious advocates of egalitarianism were likely to detect and decry the way in which the society was, through its educational enterprise, sifting and sorting children into manual and non-manual positions according to their social class rather than their basic endowment.[7]

Now automation has changed the picture; the need for manual labour has shrunk and will shrink much more. But educational practices remain much the same. No massive, genuine effort is made to engage the low-income child academically, and so he continues to drop-out: except that now he cannot be absorbed into the labour force. Hence the sudden tendency to define drop-outs as a 'social problem'.

But even if rates of drop-out were to diminish rapidly, we would not be appreciably better off: we would simply have a more sophisticated body of unemployed. For educated or not, we are faced with an occupational structure which is shrinking

[7] It is interesting that even Cloward here pinpoints wrongful *selection*, as distinct from vastly unequal status and rewards from manual/non-manual and unskilled/skilled employment; i.e. the U.S.A.'s basic unemployment problem blinds him to the deficiences of a full employment situation where job holding is vitiated by lack of status, autonomy, privileges, prospects, etc.

relative to the men it must absorb. Thus the streets of our urban slums are slowly filling with young men *who have no prospect of finding manhood through work*: who are coming of age in a society which neither wants them nor needs them.'

The relevance of this analysis to the English situation cannot be stressed too highly. Even in the present *status quo*, the young male unskilled and semi-skilled worker gets a raw deal: if automation is allowed to constitute the prospect of under- and unemployment in this sector, without adequate provision being made to revolutionise the school and further education systems, the raw deal will worsen into no deal at all. If the sizeable rump of non-skilled young male workers become convinced of their own expendability, their reaction in terms of delinquency could well be explosive, and assume fully-fledged contracultural proportions. (Other reactions are possible: high rates of mental illness, for example: crucial here are their definitions of the source of their frustrations). The least likely reaction is the most applicable to their needs: political activism (except for quasi-fascist irrationalism.) If the non-skilled young are to be denied the chance of engaging in building a technological society, as well as benefiting from its performance, the price they exact will be high.

Attempts to 'buy off' their discontent (bigger and better youth clubs) will not work; nor, if they offend by this refusal, will bigger and better borstals. Their root need is to engage in —and be rewarded adequately by—the society in which they live. They are at present humiliated by the subordinate role: likely they will soon be denied any role at all. The paramount need is for a revolution in comprehensive and further education paralleling that envisaged for the universities, and that already silently being effected in many branches of primary education. But for such a revolution to work, for it to engage the interests and energies of lower working-class boys, a restructuring of post-educational work-incentive is basic. Past and present attempts to invigorate secondary education have been and are being undermined by the antiquated structure of manual work. Continuing links between school and work until the early twenties, ways back in as well as ways to new skills and qualifications, are essential. The Crowther[8] and Newsom[9] Reports could be said to

[8] *15-18*, 2 vols., C.A.C.E., 1959.
[9] *Half Our Future*, C.A.C.E., 1964.

provide the blueprint for this kind of future: and in many respects, they do so. The Newsom Report, with its emphasis on the need to impart as much scope for *choice* as possible, both into the syllabus, and into the way the subjects are taught, at secondary moderns, is—in essence—a revolutionary document, which promises to a fully comprehensive system more than would be possible within an unreformed tripartite structure. In its recommendations for overcoming the problems of 'slum' schools, it goes far beyond mere re-building schemes. By its emphasis on 'pupil-centred' teaching, as distinct from the traditional subject-tied approach, it demonstrates how 'formal' education can be related to the personal and social development of children who have previously rejected 'school' or deemed it irrelevant to their lives. By raising the school-leaving age to 16 for all from 1971 on, it also commits the schools to a radical re-thinking of their teaching content and methods, since 'more of the same' would patently be a disaster, and merely raise the peak delinquency age from 14 to 15: school-leaving minus one.

In so far as Newsom's proposals succeed, however, pressure will be exerted on that section of the educational structure which is extremely ill-equipped to meet it: the further education sector. At present, according to the Henniker-Heaton Report[10] on day-release, only 28 per cent of boys aged 15–17 and not in full-time education were granted day-release. Provisional figures from a survey in Bethnal Green show a similar figure of 26 per cent, with another 19 per cent who have experienced some form of evening-only education.[11] Of 148 boys in this sample (aged 15–20) who had been to secondary modern schools, including a few who had been to comprehensives, 55 per cent had had no education since leaving school at 15. Moreover, these figures take no account of courses discontinued, failure rates, and non-attendance, especially severe in evening-only classes. Also, day-release courses are in general narrowly vocational in content, the willingness of the employer to consent to release varies enormously by industry, and type and size of firm, and— under the present voluntary system—incentives to take advantage of day-release facilities are in general limited to the apprentice

[10] *Day Release*, Ministry of Labour, 1964.
[11] To be published by the Institute of Community Studies. Figures quoted by kind permission of Peter Willmott.

or 'trainee', who is already *relatively* well catered for. The irony is that compulsion to undergo full-time education to the age of 16 has been introduced for those who would not have stayed on voluntarily: yet should the assumptions on which this measure is based turn out to be correct, and a vastly increased number of adolescents begin to entertain higher educational and occupational aspirations, no provision has been made to extend the framework of compulsion to part-time further education beyond the age of 16 to meet the demands that they will make. Moreover, since it seems desirable to adhere to Crowther's recommendations for a three-stage implementation of compulsory part-time further education for all—which allows for a five-year regional experiment and a phased extension to the rest of the country taking at least 4 years, all subsequent to the raising of the school-leaving age to 16—such a system appears uattainable before the 1980's, when the needs of Newsom demand that it should arrive by the mid-1970's. The only answer seems to be to begin the regional experiment in further education for all before, not after, the raising of the school-leaving age. Otherwise, for the first and most crucial decade of the Newsom reorganisation, the further education system will be inadequate in face of the expectations generated. The forces making for 'anomie' in such a context would be enormous: and the promise of the Newsom proposals would be needlessly threatened.

No claim is made for comprehensive and further education for all as automatic delinquency preventives, though—on the basis of this analysis—their establishment is a pre-requisite for any halt to rising delinquency rates. They are not recommended for therapeutic, but for the structural, reasons. Automation must bring redundancy in all routine work, so that adaptability and flexibility of skills must be integral to the socialisation of any adolescent in an urban, industrial society. Without automation, or with its postponement, economic stagnation and far worse problems than adolescent under-employment would be inevitable. In planning for automation, therefore, the question is not whether we should have a further education system within the framework of compulsion or not, but when it should arrive and what form it should take. Ideally, the comprehensive framework would be kept intact for all till the age of 18 by the evolution of an institutional form to accommodate sixth forms, technical colleges and all forms of part-time further education. Otherwise, stratification along meritocratic lines will develop as the system grows piecemeal. There should be no 'siphoning off' of early leavers to institutionally separate County Colleges. Also ideally, a regional experiment along these lines should be started by the late 1960's, in order to anticipate both automation and the age-group expansion of the 1970's, and to give the Newsom re-organisation as much support as possible in the further education field. Without these possibilities, the current secondary modern child's conception of the nature of school and work as marginally important only is unlikely to change very much.

(b) Leisure

Little can be done here to affect the situation radically, but even in the present context, much more provision could be made for the boys whose aversion to the present Youth Service sends them 'on the town'—which has correspondingly little to offer, but offers it without overtones of charity-authoritarianism. Such experiments as the Canteens, self-run clubs of the Leicester Youth Ventures kind, spontaneous provision for teenagers made by Tenants' Associations,[12] have proved viable, if hampered and often killed by lack of funds. (The duplicity to which many such schemes are reduced in the quest for money from orthodox fund-giving bodies is itself an area for study.) The desire for a visibly respectable end-product still vitiates the bulk of youth-service fund disposal. The point is not yet taken, despite Albemarle, that the boys at whom youth work should primarily be aimed simply are not willing to conform to success criteria based on 'activity participation'. Also, the machinery set up by Albemarle for the dispensation of funds to 'experiments' (two-thirds to follow if one-third is found) succeed only in diverting funds to already-established, or respectably-backed, ventures. This is not to attack provision for 'respectable' boys, simply to attack provision for them *exclusively*.

But in the absence of work- and school-satisfactions, in the absence of incentives to legitimate autonomy in the educational and occupational areas, it is doubtful if even the provision of full autonomy in leisure would be functionally equivalent.

[12] See G. Williams, in *Anarchy*, Vol. 30, August 1963, pp. 250–251, for a note on the provision made by Tenants Associations of a completely voluntary nature.

Only the radical restructuring of achievement means and goals in work and school will lessen the likelihood that the bulk of semi- and unskilled working-class male teenagers will attain their leisure goals in ways which are frequently delinquent. Hence, the implicit assumption of policy-making institutions that youth work with these boys is a waste of time is substantially correct: the source of their problem lies in the school and work systems, and leisure-time provision for them can be a palliative only.[13]

In conclusion, a paradox must be resolved. It has been proposed that status-frustration (in Cohen's sense) is not the source of the vast bulk of teenage male delinquency: but the very measures proposed to cut down on delinquency might seem to aim at promoting status-consciousness and—by inference—status frustration, thus providing the necessary base for the emergence of delinquent motivations on 'American' lines. By breaking down working-class conservatism, the main force for aspiration-control would be removed. In defence, it is suggested that an attack on working-class conservatism is not—despite the data of Jackson and Marsden—*necessarily* an attack on working-class solidarity, in so far as it impinges on the working-class teenager. Rather, it is thought that the tendency is for skilled workers to be more politically-oriented in a non-extremist way than for semi- and unskilled workers, whose political awareness and involvement is either low-level or extremist.[14] Alterations in the present school-work *status quo* would, far from merely invigorating delinquency from status-frustration sources, make for political awareness—which is ultimately the only alternative to delinquency for the stifled working-class adolescent, in the phase of non-attachment preceding home-centredness and the channelling of his aspirations into family life.

It could be argued that, even if no re-structuring takes place, delinquency in the late teens will still be curbed by the further juvenilisation of marriage, in itself the main check to the spread-over of delinquency into early adulthood. But even granted this association, delinquency in the early and mid-teens will continue to intensify and, but for early marriages, would hoist the rates of

---

[13] This assertion naturally excludes work with disturbed and handicapped youngsters.

[14] See R. Dahrendorff, *Unskilled Labour in British Industry* (1956), unpublished Ph.D. thesis, L.S.E.

adult criminality. Foreseeably, delinquency rates in late adolescence will increase exponentially only, *provided* the socioeconomic conditions for fruitful early marriage are maintained: but slump, unemployment or redundancy in this sector would have its effect on marriage-orientation and, unless resultant discontents were politically focused, would result in postponement of the transition from quasi-delinquent to conforming behaviour. In an a-political context, the automatic solution would be an increase in delinquent activity, feasibly of a nihilistic, contracultural type, the more so since an increasingly affluent society has endorsed rising expectations and aspirations among male, working-class adolescents who—unlike older members of the community—have had no experience of real adversities in the labour market.

BIBLIOGRAPHY

ABRAMS, M., *The Teenage Consumer* (1959).
Teenage Consumer Spending in 1959: Middle Class and Working Class Boys and Girls (1961).
ALLERTON, R. and PARKER, T., *The Courage of his Convictions* (1962).
BAITTLE, B., 'Psychiatric Aspects of the Development of a Street Corner Group', *Amer. J. Orthopsych.*, Vol. 31, No. 4, Oct. 1961, pp. 703–12.
BALDAMUS, W., 'Types of Work and Motivation', *Brit. J. Sociol.*, March 1951.
BANTON, M., *The Coloured Quarter* (1955).
BELL, D., *The End of Ideology* (1961).
BERNSTEIN, B., 'Social Class and Linguistic Development: A Theory of Social Learning'. Ch. 24 in Floud, J., Halsey, A. H., and Anderson, A. C., *Education, Economy and Society* (1961), pp. 288–314.
BLOCH, H. and NIEDERHOFFER, A., *The Gang: A Study in Adolescent Behavior* (1958).
BORDUA, D., *Sociological Theories and Their Implications for Juvenile Delinquency*, Children's Bureau Conference Report, No. 2, 1960.
'A Critique of Sociological Interpretations of Gang Delinquency' in Wolfgang, M. E., Savitz, L. and Johnston, L., *The Sociology of Crime and Delinquency* (1962), pp. 289–301.
BRASHER, C., 'Turning 'em over in Finchley' in the *Observer*, 15 July, 1962.
CARTER, M. P., *Home, School and Work* (1962).
CENSUS 1961, County Report—London.
CHEIN, I. and ROSENFELD, E., 'Juvenile Narcotics Use', *Law Contemp. Problems*, Vol. 22, pp. 52–68.
CLARK, J. P. and WENNINGER, E. P., 'Socio-Economic Class and Area as Correlates of Illegal Behaviour among Juveniles', *Amer. Sociol. Rev.*, Vol. 27, No. 6, Dec. 1962, pp. 826–34; and

Bibliography

'Goal Orientations and Illegal Behaviour Among Juveniles', *Soc. Forces*, Vol. 42, No. 1, Oct. 1963, pp. 49–59.

CLOWARD, R. A., 'Illegitimate Means, Anomie and Deviant Behaviour', *Amer. Sociol. Rev.*, Vol. 24, April 1959, pp. 164–76.

'Social Problems, Social Definitions and Social Opportunities', unpublished paper (1963).

(and OHLIN, L. E.) *Delinquency and Opportunity—A Theory of Delinquent Gangs* (1961).

COHEN, A. K., *Delinquent Boys: The Culture of the Gang* (1955).

'Sociological Research in Delinquent Subcultures', *Amer. J. Orthopsych.*, Vol. 27, No. 4, Oct. 1957, pp. 781–8.

(and SHORT, J. F., JR.) 'Research in Delinquent Subcultures', *J. Soc. Issues*, Vol. 14, No. 3, 1958, pp. 20–37.

COTGROVE, S. and PARKER, S., 'Work and Non-Work', *New Soc.*, Vol. 41, 11 July, 1963.

CRESSEY, D. R., 'The State of Criminal Statistics', *N.P.P.A. Journal*, Vol. 57, No. 3, pp. 230–241.

'The Theory of D.A.: An Introduction', *Soc. Problems*, Vol. 8, No. 1, Summer 1960, pp. 2–6.

CROSLAND, C. A. R., 'Industrial Democracy and Workers' Control', Ch. 14 in *The Conservative Enemy* (1962).

DAHRENDORFF, R., 'Unskilled Labour in British Industry' (1956), unpublished Ph.D. (L.S.E.).

DENNIS, N., HENRIQUES, F. and SLAUGHTER, C., *Coal is Our Life* (1956).

DENTLER, R. A. AND MONROE, L. J., 'Early Adolescent Theft', *Amer. Sociol. Rev.*, Vol. 26, Oct. 1961, pp. 733–43.

DOUGLAS, J. W. B., *The Home and The School* (1964).

EPPEL, E. M. and E., 'Adolescent Values', *New Soc.*, Vol. 26, 28 March, 1963.

FERGUSSON, R., *The Young Delinquent in His Social Setting* (1951).

FINESTONE, H., 'Cats, Kicks and Color', *Soc. Problems*, Vol. 5, 1957, pp. 3–13.

FIRTH, R., *Elements of Social Organisation* (1951).

FYVEL, T. R., *The Insecure Offenders* (1961).

GIBBENS, T. C. N., *Psychiatric Studies of Borstal Lads* (1963).

GLASER, D., 'Differential Association and Criminological Prediction', *Soc. Problems*, Vol. 8, No. 1, Summer 1960, pp. 6–14.

GORDON, R. A., SHORT, J. F., JR., CARTWRIGHT, D. I. and STRODTBECK, F. L., 'Values and Gang Delinquency: A Study of Street Corner Groups', *Amer. J. Sociol.*, Vol. 69, No. 2, Sept. 1963, pp. 109–28.

GOSLING, R., *Lady Albemarle's Boys*, Young Fabian Pamphlet, No. 1, 1961;

'Dream Boy', *New Left Rev.*, Vol. 3, May–June 1960, pp. 30–4.

Bibliography

HENRY, A. F. and SHORT, J. F., JR., *Suicide and Homicide* (1954).

HOIJER, H., 'The Relation of Language to Culture', pp. 554-73 in KROEBER, L. (ed.) *Anthropology Today* (1953).

HOOD, R., *Sentencing in Magistrates' Courts* (1962).

HYMAN, H. H., 'The Value-Systems of Different Classes: A Social-Psychological Contribution to the Analysis of Stratification' in R. Bendix and S. M. Lipset (eds.) *Class, Status and Power* (1953).

JANSYN, L., 'Solidarity and Delinquency in a Street Corner Group' (1960), unpublished.

JEPHCOTT, P. and CARTER, M. P., 'The Social Background of Delinquency' (1954), unpublished.

KERR, M., *The People of Ship Street* (1958).

KITSUSE, J. I. and DIETRICK, D. C., 'Delinquent Boys: A Critique', *Amer. Sociol. Rev.*, Vol. 24, No. 2, April 1959.

KLUCKHORN, C. and KELLEY, W. H., 'The Concept of Culture' in LINTON, R. (ed.) *The Science of Man in the World Crisis* (1945), pp. 76-106; repr. in KLUCKHOHN, C., *Culture and Behavior* (1962), p. 19-73.

KOBRIN, S., 'Sociological Aspects of the Development of a Street Corner Group', *Amer. J. Orthopsych.*, Vol. 31, No. 4, Oct. 1961, pp. 685-702.
'The Impact of Cultural Factors on Selected Problems of Adolescent Development in the Middle and Lower Class', *Amer. J. Orthopsych.*, Vol. 32, No. 3, April 1962, pp. 387-90.
'The Conflict of Values in Delinquency Areas', *Amer. Sociol. Rev.*, Vol. 16, 1951, pp. 653-61.

LAWRIE, J., *The Marriage of Gor* (1960).

LITTLE, W. R. and NTSEKHE, V. R., 'Social Class Background of Young Offenders from London', *Brit. J. Delinq.*, Vol. 16, No. 2, Oct. 1959, pp. 130-5.

LOCKWOOD, D., *The Blackcoated Worker* (1958).

LONDON, JACK, *The People of the Abyss* (1900).

LOWSON, D., 'Delinquency in Industrial Areas', *Brit. J. Crim.*, Vol. 1, No. 1, July 1960, pp. 50-5.

MALINOWSKI, R., 'Culture' in *Encyclopedia of the Social Sciences* (1933).

MARSHALL, T. H., *Sociology at the Crossroads* (1963).

MATZA, D. and SYKES, G. M., 'Delinquency and Subterranean Values', *Amer. Sociol. Rev.*, Vol. 26, No. 5, Oct. 1961, pp. 712-19.

MAYS, J. B., *Growing Up in the City* (1954).
On the Threshold of Delinquency (1959).
Education and the Urban Child (1962).

MERTON, R. K., *Social Theory and Social Structure* (1957 rev. ed.).

METROPOLITAN POLICE DISTRICT, *Analysis of Crime* (1960).

MILLER, S. M. and RIESSMAN, F., 'The Working Class Subculture: A New View', *Soc. Problems*, Vol. 9, No. 1, Summer 1961, pp. 86–97.

MILLER, W. B., 'Lower-Class Culture as a Generating Milieu of Gang Delinquency', *J. Soc. Issues*, Vol. 14, No. 3, 1958, pp. 5–19.

(with GEERTZ, H. and CUTTER, H. S. G.) 'Aggression in a Boys' Street-Corner Group', *Psychiatry: Journal for the Study of Interpersonal Processes*, Vol. 24, No. 4, Nov. 1961, pp. 283–98.

MORISON, A., *Child of the Jago*.

MORRIS, T. P., 'The Teenage Criminal', *New Soc.*, April 1963.

The Criminal Area: A Study in Social Ecology (1957).

NYE, F. I., SHORT, J. F., JR., and OLSON, V. J., 'Socio-economic Status and Delinquent Behavior', *Amer. J. Sociol.*, Vol. 63, Jan. 1958, pp. 381–9.

PARSONS, T., *Essays in Sociological Theory* (rev. ed. 1954).

PFAUTZ, H. W., 'Near-Group Theory and Collective Behavior', *Soc. Problems*, Vol. 9, No. 2, Fall 1961, pp. 167–74.

POLSKY, H., 'Changing Delinquent Subcultures: A Social-Psychological Approach', *Soc. Work*, Vol. 4, No. 4, Oct. 1959, pp. 3–15.

POWER, M., 'Trends in Juvenile Delinquency', *The Times*, 9 Aug., 1962.

REISS, A. J., JR., and RHODES, A. L., 'The Distribution of Juvenile Delinquency in the Social Structure', *Amer. Sociol. Rev.*, Vol. 26, No. 5, Oct. 1961, pp. 720–32.

ROLPH, C. H. (ed.), *Women of the Streets* (1955).

SALISBURY, H. E., *The Shook-Up Generation* (1958).

SCHUR, E. M., *Narcotic Addiction in Great Britain: The Impact of Public Policy* (1963).

SCOTT, P., 'Gangs and Delinquent Groups in London', *Brit. J. Delinq.*, Vol. 7, July 1956, pp. 8–21.

SELLIN, T., *Culture Conflict and Crime* (1938).

SHORT, J. F., JR., (and NYE, F. I.) 'Extent of unrecorded Juvenile Delinquency', *J. Crim. Law Criminol. Police Sci.*, Vol. 49, No. 4, Nov.–Dec. 1958, pp. 296–302. 'The Sociocultural Context of Delinquency', *Crime and Delinq.*, Vol. 6, No. 4, Oct. 1960, pp. 365–75.

'Differential Association as a Hypothesis: Problems of Empirical Testing', *Soc. Problems*, Vol. 8, No. 1, Summer 1960, pp. 14–25. 'Street-Corner Groups and Patterns of Delinquency' (1961), unpublished.

(with TENNYSON, R. A. and HOWARD, K. I.) 'Behavior Dimensions of Gang Delinquency,' *Amer. Sociol. Rev.*, Vol. 28, No. 3, June 1963, pp. 411–28.

(and F. L. STRODTBECK) 'The Response of Gang Leaders to Status Threats', *Amer. J. Sociol*, Vol. 68, No. 5, March 1963, pp. 571–9.

Bibliography

SIGAL, C., *Weekend in Dinlock* (1960).

SILLITOE, A., *Saturday Night and Sunday Morning* (1959).

SIMMEL, G., *Conflict*, translated by WOLFF, K. H. (1955).

SPENCER, J. L., *et al.*: Preliminary Report of the Bristol Social Project (1961), unpublished.

SPERGEL, I., 'An Exploratory Research in Delinquent Subcultures', *Soc. Serv. Rev.*, Vol. 35, No. 1, March 1961, pp. 33–47.

SPINLEY, B., *The Deprived and the Privileged* (1954).

SUTHERLAND, E. H. (ed. CRESSEY, D. R.), *Principles of Criminology* (1955 and 1960 5th and 6th rev. eds.).

SYKES, G. M. and MATZA, D., 'Techniques of Neutralisation', *Amer. Sociol. Rev.*, Vol. 22, 1957, pp. 664–70.

THRASHER, F. M., *The Gang* (1936).

TOBY, J., 'Delinquency and Opportunity'. *Brit. J. Sociol.*, Vol. 12, No. 3, Sept. 1961, pp. 282–9.

TRASLER, G., *The Explanation of Criminality* (1962).

TUNSTALL, J., *The Fishermen* (1962).

TURNER, M. L., *Ship Without Sails* (1953).

(with SPENCER, J. C.), 'Spontaneous Youth Groups and Gangs', (in KUENSTLER, P. (ed.)) *Spontaneous Youth Groups* (1955).

TURNER, R. H., 'Modes of Ascent Through Education: "Sponsored" and "Contest" Mobility.' Ch. 12 in FLOUD *et al.*, *Education, Economy, and Society* (1961).

VEBLEN, T., *The Theory of the Leisure Class* (1899).

VENESS, T., *School-leavers: Their Aspirations and Expectations* (1962).

WEBB, J., 'The Sociology of a School', *Brit. J. Sociol.*, Vol. 13, No. 3, Sept. 1962, pp. 264–72.

WHYTE, W. F., *Street Corner Society* (1943, rev. ed. 1957).

WILKINS, L. T., 'The Measurement of Crime', *Brit. J. Crim.*, Vol. 3, No. 4, pp. 321–41.

WILLIAMS, R. M., JR., *American Society* (1951).

WILLMOTT, P. and YOUNG, M., *Family and Kinship in East London* (1957).

WILSON, H., *Delinquency and Child Neglect* (1962).

WILSON, M. D., 'The Vocational Preferences of Secondary Modern School Children', *Brit. J. Ed. Psych.*, Vol. 23, 1953, pp. 97–113.

YABLONSKY, L., 'The Delinquent Gang as a Near-Group', *Soc. Problems*, Vol. 7, No. 2, Fall 1959, pp. 108–17.

The Violent Gang (1962).

YINGER, J. M., 'Contraculture and Subculture', *Amer. Sociol. Rev.*, Vol. 25, No. 5, Oct. 1960, pp. 625–35.

MAP

Stepney and Poplar: 'Natural' Areas

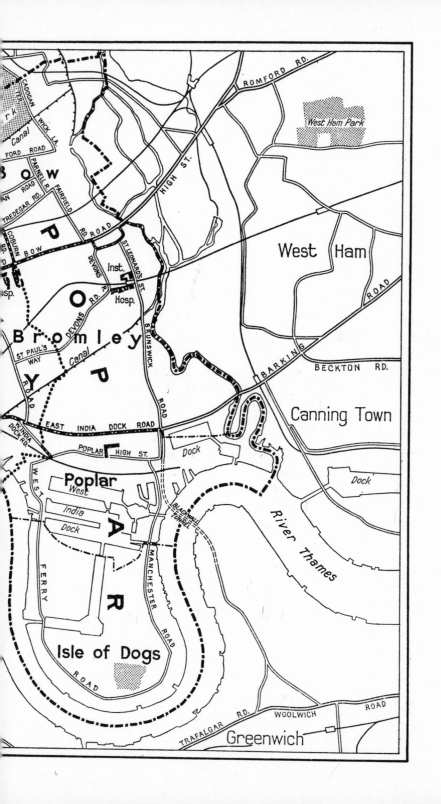

INDEX

Index

Finchley, 120
Finestone, H., 27n, 49
Firth, R., 2f
Fletcher, Ron, 121
Ford, C. S., 3
Fyvel, T. R., 119f, 123f, 128f

gangs, absence in England, 116f, 198f
  delinquent, 12ff
  survey area attitude to, 200f
  unstructured, 16
  values of members, 90f
Gibbens, T. C. N., 251n
Glaser, D., 97
goal orientations, 93f
Gordon, R. A., et al., 90n
Gosling, R., 130n, 132n
Green, Vic, 120f
group therapy, 7n
groups, adolescent, in London, 116ff
  delinquent, in survey area, nature of, 199
  diffuse, 117
  individual relation to, 7
  loyalty to, 106
guilt, elimination of, 42ff

Harvard, J. D., 155
Harvey, Audrey, 225n
hedonism, short-run, 26, 206f
hegemony, neighbourhood, 214
Henry, A. F., and Short, J. F., jnr., 45
heredity, social, 3
'hipster' cult, 30
Hoijer, H., 5
Hood, R., 114
housing problems, description of in survey area, 224-7
humour, 81
Hyman, H. H., 41, 59
hypocrisy, 46

immigrants, in survey area, 211f, 216ff
injury, denial of, 76

Institute of Community Studies, 197
integrated/unintegrated areas, 51, 223
integration, age-level, 227ff
interviews, technique of, 196
isolation, effects of, 65

Jackson, B., and Marsden, D., 47n
Jansyn, L., 88
Jephcott, A. P., and Carter, M. P., 107ff
'Junior Outlaws' (group), 17f

Kerr, M., 105, 113
'kicks', 30, 78
Kitsuse, J. I., and Dietrick, D. C., 63f
Kluckhohn, C., and Kelley, W. H., 2, 4, 5
Kobrin, S., 49, 51, 53, 85f, 190, 192n

Lander, B., 99
Language, and culture, 5
Lawrie, J., 218n
leisure, differential access to, 247
  goals, 243ff
  proposals concerning, 267ff
  relation to work, 239f
  values, 78ff, 133
Levi-Strauss, C., 5
Lipset, S. M., 74
Little, A. N., 192n
Little, W. R., and Ntsekhe, V. R., 114
Liverpool, 101ff, 125
location of delinquency, 32ff
  of offences, in survey area, 174f
Lockwood, D., 239
London, Jack, 217n
London, groups in, 116ff
London Hospital Survey, 139
lower-class culture, focal concerns, 69f
Lowson, D., 123, 132f
loyalties, higher, appeal to, 77

Mafia, 16
male–female ratio, 252

281

The International Library of
Sociology
and Social Reconstruction

Edited by W. J. H. SPROTT
Founded by KARL MANNHEIM

ROUTLEDGE & KEGAN PAUL
BROADWAY HOUSE, CARTER LANE, LONDON, E.C.4

CONTENTS

PRINTED IN GREAT BRITAIN BY HEADLEY BROTHERS LTD
109 KINGSWAY LONDON WC2 AND ASHFORD KENT

GENERAL SOCIOLOGY

Brown, Robert. Explanation in Social Science. *208 pp. 1963. (2nd Impression 1964.) 25s.*

Gibson, Quentin. The Logic of Social Enquiry. *240 pp. 1960. (3rd Impression 1968.) 24s.*

Homans, George C. Sentiments and Activities: Essays in Social Science. *336 pp. 1962. 32s.*

Isajiw, Wsevelod W. Causation and Functionalism in Sociology. *165 pp. 1968. 25s.*

Johnson, Harry M. Sociology: a Systematic Introduction. *Foreword by Robert K. Merton. 710 pp. 1961. (5th Impression 1968.) 42s.*

Mannheim, Karl. Essays on Sociology and Social Psychology. *Edited by Paul Keckskemeti. With Editorial Note by Adolph Lowe. 344 pp. 1953. (2nd Impression 1966.) 32s.*

Systematic Sociology: An Introduction to the Study of Society. *Edited by J. S. Erös and Professor W. A. C. Stewart. 220 pp. 1957. (3rd Impression 1967.) 24s.*

Martindale, Don. The Nature and Types of Sociological Theory. *292 pp. 1961. (3rd Impression 1967.) 35s.*

Maus, Heinz. A Short History of Sociology. *234 pp. 1962. (2nd Impression 1965.) 28s.*

Myrdal, Gunnar. Value in Social Theory: A Collection of Essays on Methodology. *Edited by Paul Streeten. 332 pp. 1958. (3rd Impression 1968.) 35s.*

Ogburn, William F., and **Nimkoff, Meyer F.** A Handbook of Sociology. *Preface by Karl Mannheim. 656 pp. 46 figures. 35 tables. 5th edition (revised) 1964. 45s.*

Parsons, Talcott, and **Smelser, Neil J.** Economy and Society: A Study in the Integration of Economic and Social Theory. *362 pp. 1956. (4th Impression 1967.) 35s.*

Rex, John. Key Problems of Sociological Theory. *220 pp. 1961. (4th Impression 1968.) 25s.*

Stark, Werner. The Fundamental Forms of Social Thought. *280 pp. 1962. 32s.*

FOREIGN CLASSICS OF SOCIOLOGY

Durkheim, Emile. Suicide. A Study in Sociology. *Edited and with an Introduction by George Simpson. 404 pp. 1952. (4th Impression 1968.) 35s.*

Professional Ethics and Civic Morals. *Translated by Cornelia Brookfield. 288 pp. 1957. 30s.*

Gerth, H. H., and **Mills, C. Wright.** From Max Weber: Essays in Sociology. *502 pp. 1948. (6th Impression 1967.) 35s.*

Tönnies, Ferdinand. Community and Association. *(Gemeinschaft und Gesellschaft.) Translated and Supplemented by Charles P. Loomis. Foreword by Pitirim A. Sorokin. 334 pp. 1955. 28s.*

SOCIAL STRUCTURE

Andreski, Stanislav. Military Organization and Society. *Foreword by Professor A. R. Radcliffe-Brown. 226 pp. 1 folder. 1954. Revised Edition 1968. 35s.*

Cole, G. D. H. Studies in Class Structure. *220 pp. 1955. (3rd Impression 1964.) 21s. Paper 10s. 6d.*

Coontz, Sydney H. Population Theories and the Economic Interpretation. *202 pp. 1957. (3rd Impression 1968.) 28s.*

Coser, Lewis. The Functions of Social Conflict. *204 pp. 1956. (3rd Impression 1968.) 25s.*

Dickie-Clark, H. F. Marginal Situation: A Sociological Study of a Coloured Group. *240 pp. 11 tables. 1966. 40s.*

Glass, D. V. (Ed.). Social Mobility in Britain. *Contributions by J. Berent, T. Bottomore, R. C. Chambers, J. Floud, D. V. Glass, J. R. Hall, H. T. Himmelweit, R. K. Kelsall, F. M. Martin, C. A. Moser, R. Mukherjee, and W. Ziegel. 420 pp. 1954. (4th Impression 1967.) 45s.*

Jones, Garth N. Planned Organizational Change: An Exploratory Study Using an Empirical Approach. *About 268 pp. 1969. 40s.*

Kelsall, R. K. Higher Civil Servants in Britain: From 1870 to the Present Day. *268 pp. 31 tables. 1955. (2nd Impression 1966.) 25s.*

König, René. The Community. *232 pp. Illustrated. 1968. 35s.*

Lawton, Denis. Social Class, Language and Education. *192 pp. 1968. (2nd Impression 1968.) 25s.*

McLeish, John. The Theory of Social Change: Four Views Considered. *About 128 pp. 1969. 21s.*

Marsh, David C. The Changing Social Structure in England and Wales, 1871-1961. *1958. 272 pp. 2nd edition (revised) 1966. (2nd Impression 1967.) 35s.*

Mouzelis, Nicos. Organization and Bureaucracy. An Analysis of Modern Theories. *240 pp. 1967. (2nd Impression 1968.) 28s.*

Ossowski, Stanislaw. Class Structure in the Social Consciousness. *210 pp. 1963. (2nd Impression 1967.) 25s.*

SOCIOLOGY AND POLITICS

Barbu, Zevedei. Democracy and Dictatorship: Their Psychology and Patterns of Life. *300 pp. 1956. 28s.*

Crick, Bernard. The American Science of Politics: Its Origins and Conditions. *284 pp. 1959. 32s.*

Hertz, Frederick. Nationality in History and Politics: A Psychology and Sociology of National Sentiment and Nationalism. *432 pp. 1944. (5th Impression 1966.) 42s.*

Kornhauser, William. The Politics of Mass Society. *272 pp. 20 tables. 1960. (3rd Impression 1968.) 28s.*

4

Laidler, Harry W. History of Socialism. Social-Economic Movements: An Historical and Comparative Survey of Socialism, Communism, Co-operation, Utopianism; and other Systems of Reform and Reconstruction. *New edition. 992 pp. 1968. 90s.*

Lasswell, Harold D. Analysis of Political Behaviour. An Empirical Approach. *324 pp. 1947. (4th Impression 1966.) 35s.*

Mannheim, Karl. Freedom, Power and Democratic Planning. *Edited by Hans Gerth and Ernest K. Bramstedt. 424 pp. 1951. (3rd Impression 1968.) 42s.*

Mansur, Fatma. Process of Independence. *Foreword by A. H. Hanson. 208 pp. 1962. 25s.*

Martin, David A. Pacificism: an Historical and Sociological Study. *262 pp. 1965. 30s.*

Myrdal, Gunnar. The Political Element in the Development of Economic Theory. *Translated from the German by Paul Streeten. 282 pp. 1953. (4th Impression 1965.) 25s.*

Polanyi, Michael. F.R.S. The Logic of Liberty: Reflections and Rejoinders. *228 pp. 1951. 18s.*

Verney, Douglas V. The Analysis of Political Systems. *264 pp. 1959. (3rd Impression 1966.) 28s.*

Wootton, Graham. The Politics of Influence: British Ex-Servicemen, Cabinet Decisions and Cultural Changes, 1917 to 1957. *316 pp. 1963. 30s.*
Workers, Unions and the State. *188 pp. 1966. (2nd Impression 1967.) 25s.*

FOREIGN AFFAIRS: THEIR SOCIAL, POLITICAL AND ECONOMIC FOUNDATIONS

Baer, Gabriel. Population and Society in the Arab East. *Translated by Hanna Szöke. 288 pp. 10 maps. 1964. 40s.*

Bonné, Alfred. State and Economics in the Middle East: A Society in Transition. *482 pp. 2nd (revised) edition 1955. (2nd Impression 1960.) 40s.*
Studies in Economic Development: with special reference to Conditions in the Under-developed Areas of Western Asia and India. *322 pp. 84 tables. 2nd edition 1960. 32s.*

Mayer, J. P. Political Thought in France from the Revolution to the Fifth Republic. *164 pp. 3rd edition (revised) 1961. 16s.*

CRIMINOLOGY

Ancel, Marc. Social Defence: A Modern Approach to Criminal Problems. *Foreword by Leon Radzinowicz. 240 pp. 1965. 32s.*

Cloward, Richard A., and **Ohlin, Lloyd E.** Delinquency and Opportunity: A Theory of Delinquent Gangs. *248 pp. 1961. 25s.*

Downes, David M. The Delinquent Solution. A Study in Subcultural Theory. *296 pp. 1966. 42s.*

Dunlop, A. B., and **McCabe, S.** Young Men in Detention Centres. *192 pp. 1965. 28s.*

Friedländer, Kate. The Psycho-Analytical Approach to Juvenile Delinquency: Theory, Case Studies, Treatment. *320 pp. 1947. (6th Impression 1967). 40s.*

Glueck, Sheldon and **Eleanor.** Family Environment and Delinquency. *With the statistical assistance of Rose W. Kneznek. 340 pp. 1962. (2nd Impression 1966.) 40s.*

Mannheim, Hermann. Comparative Criminology: a Text Book. *Two volumes. 442 pp. and 380 pp. 1965. (2nd Impression with corrections 1966.) 42s. a volume.*

Morris, Terence. The Criminal Area: A Study in Social Ecology. *Foreword by Hermann Mannheim. 232 pp. 25 tables. 4 maps. 1957. (2nd Impression 1966.) 28s.*

Morris, Terence and **Pauline,** assisted by **Barbara Barer.** Pentonville: A Sociological Study of an English Prison. *416 pp. 16 plates. 1963. 50s.*

Spencer, John C. Crime and the Services. *Foreword by Hermann Mannheim. 336 pp. 1954. 28s.*

Trasler, Gordon. The Explanation of Criminality. *144 pp. 1962. (2nd Impression 1967.) 20s.*

SOCIAL PSYCHOLOGY

Barbu, Zevedei. Problems of Historical Psychology. *248 pp. 1960. 25s.*

Blackburn, Julian. Psychology and the Social Pattern. *184 pp. 1945. (7th Impression 1964.) 16s.*

Fleming, C. M. Adolescence: Its Social Psychology: With an Introduction to recent findings from the fields of Anthropology, Physiology, Medicine, Psychometrics and Sociometry. *288 pp. 2nd edition (revised) 1963. (3rd Impression 1967.) 25s. Paper 12s. 6d.*
The Social Psychology of Education: An Introduction and Guide to Its Study. *136 pp. 2nd edition (revised) 1959. (4th Impression 1967.) 14s. Paper 7s. 6d.*

Homans, George C. The Human Group. *Foreword by Bernard DeVoto. Introduction by Robert K. Merton. 526 pp. 1951. (7th Impression 1968.) 35s.*
Social Behaviour: its Elementary Forms. *416 pp. 1961. (3rd Impression 1968.) 35s.*

Klein, Josephine. The Study of Groups. *226 pp. 31 figures. 5 tables. 1956. (5th Impression 1967.) 21s. Paper 9s. 6d.*

Linton, Ralph. The Cultural Background of Personality. *132 pp. 1947. (7th Impression 1968.) 18s.*

Mayo, Elton. The Social Problems of an Industrial Civilization. With an appendix on the Political Problem. *180 pp. 1949. (5th Impression 1966.) 25s.*

Ottaway, A. K. C. Learning Through Group Experience. *176 pp. 1966. (2nd Impression 1968.) 25s.*

Ridder, J. C. de. The Personality of the Urban African in South Africa. A Thematic Apperception Test Study. *196 pp. 12 plates. 1961. 25s.*

Rose, Arnold M. (Ed.). Human Behaviour and Social Processes: an Interactionist Approach. *Contributions by Arnold M. Rose, Ralph H. Turner, Anselm Strauss, Everett C. Hughes, E. Franklin Frazier, Howard S. Becker, et al. 696 pp. 1962. (2nd Impression 1968.) 70s.*

Smelser, Neil J. Theory of Collective Behaviour. *448 pp. 1962. (2nd Impression 1967.) 45s.*

Stephenson, Geoffrey M. The Development of Conscience. *128 pp. 1966. 25s.*

Young, Kimball. Handbook of Social Psychology. *658 pp. 16 figures. 10 tables. 2nd edition (revised) 1957. (3rd Impression 1963.) 40s.*

SOCIOLOGY OF THE FAMILY

Banks, J. A. Prosperity and Parenthood: A study of Family Planning among The Victorian Middle Classes. *262 pp. 1954. (3rd Impression 1968.) 28s.*

Bell, Colin R. Middle Class Families: Social and Geographical Mobility. *224 pp. 1969. 35s.*

Burton, Lindy. Vulnerable Children. *272 pp. 1968. 35s.*

Gavron, Hannah. The Captive Wife: Conflicts of Housebound Mothers. *190 pp. 1966. (2nd Impression 1966.) 25s.*

Klein, Josephine. Samples from English Cultures. *1965. (2nd Impression 1967.)*
1. Three Preliminary Studies and Aspects of Adult Life in England. *447 pp. 50s.*
2. Child-Rearing Practices and Index. *247 pp. 35s.*

Klein, Viola. Britain's Married Women Workers. *180 pp. 1965. (2nd Impression 1968.) 28s.*

McWhinnie, Alexina M. Adopted Children. How They Grow Up. *304 pp. 1967. (2nd Impression 1968.) 42s.*

Myrdal, Alva and **Klein, Viola.** Women's Two Roles: Home and Work. *238 pp. 27 tables. 1956. Revised Edition 1967. 30s. Paper 15s.*

Parsons, Talcott and **Bales, Robert F.** Family: Socialization and Interaction Process. *In collaboration with James Olds, Morris Zelditch and Philip E. Slater. 456 pp. 50 figures and tables. 1956. (3rd Impression 1968.) 45s.*

Schücking, L. L. The Puritan Family. *Translated from the German by Brian Battershaw. 212 pp. 1969. About 42s.*

THE SOCIAL SERVICES

Forder, R. A. (Ed.). Penelope Hall's Social Services of Modern England. *288 pp. 1969. 35s.*

George, Victor. Social Security: Beveridge and After. *258 pp. 1968. 35s.*

Goetschius, George W. Working with Community Groups. *256 pp. 1969. 35s.*

Goetschius, George W. and **Tash, Joan.** Working with Unattached Youth. *416 pp. 1967. (2nd Impression 1968.) 40s.*

Hall, M. P., and **Howes, I. V.** The Church in Social Work. A Study of Moral Welfare Work undertaken by the Church of England. *320 pp. 1965. 35s.*

Heywood, Jean S. Children in Care: the Development of the Service for the Deprived Child. *264 pp. 2nd edition (revised) 1965. (2nd Impression 1966.) 32s.*

An Introduction to Teaching Casework Skills. *190 pp. 1964. 28s.*

Jones, Kathleen. Lunacy, Law and Conscience, 1744-1845: the Social History of the Care of the Insane. *268 pp. 1955. 25s.*

Mental Health and Social Policy, 1845-1959. *264 pp. 1960. (2nd Impression 1967.) 32s.*

Jones, Kathleen and **Sidebotham, Roy.** Mental Hospitals at Work. *220 pp. 1962. 30s.*

Kastell, Jean. Casework in Child Care. *Foreword by M. Brooke Willis. 320 pp. 1962. 35s.*

Morris, Pauline. Put Away: A Sociological Study of Institutions for the Mentally Retarded. *Approx. 288 pp. 1969. About 50s.*

Nokes, P. L. The Professional Task in Welfare Practice. *152 pp. 1967. 28s.*

Rooff, Madeline. Voluntary Societies and Social Policy. *350 pp. 15 tables. 1957. 35s.*

Timms, Noel. Psychiatric Social Work in Great Britain (1939-1962). *280 pp. 1964. 32s.*

Social Casework: Principles and Practice. *256 pp. 1964. (2nd Impression 1966.) 25s. Paper 15s.*

Trasler, Gordon. In Place of Parents: A Study in Foster Care. *272 pp. 1960. (2nd Impression 1966.) 30s.*

Young, A. F., and **Ashton, E. T.** British Social Work in the Nineteenth Century. *288 pp. 1956. (2nd Impression 1963.) 28s.*

Young, A. F. Social Services in British Industry. *272 pp. 1968. 40s.*

SOCIOLOGY OF EDUCATION

Banks, Olive. Parity and Prestige in English Secondary Education: a Study in Educational Sociology. *272 pp. 1955. (2nd Impression 1963.) 32s.*

Bentwich, Joseph. Education in Israel. *224 pp. 8 pp. plates. 1965. 24s.*

Blyth, W. A. L. English Primary Education. A Sociological Description. *1965. Revised edition 1967.*

1. Schools. *232 pp. 30s. Paper 12s. 6d.*
2. Background. *168 pp. 25s. Paper 10s. 6d.*

Collier, K. G. The Social Purposes of Education: Personal and Social Values in Education. *268 pp. 1959. (3rd Impression 1965.) 21s.*

Dale, R. R., and **Griffith, S.** Down Stream: Failure in the Grammar School. *108 pp. 1965. 20s.*

Dore, R. P. Education in Tokugawa Japan. *356 pp. 9 pp. plates. 1965. 35s.*

Edmonds, E. L. The School Inspector. *Foreword by Sir William Alexander. 214 pp. 1962. 28s.*

Evans, K. M. Sociometry and Education. *158 pp. 1962. (2nd Impression 1966.) 18s.*

Foster, P. J. Education and Social Change in Ghana. *336 pp. 3 maps. 1965. (2nd Impression 1967.) 36s.*

Fraser, W. R. Education and Society in Modern France. *150 pp. 1963. (2nd Impression 1968.) 25s.*

Hans, Nicholas. New Trends in Education in the Eighteenth Century. *278 pp. 19 tables. 1951. (2nd Impression 1966.) 30s.*

Comparative Education: A Study of Educational Factors and Traditions. *360 pp. 3rd (revised) edition 1958. (4th Impression 1967.) 25s. Paper 12s. 6d.*

Hargreaves, David. Social Relations in a Secondary School. *240 pp. 1967. (2nd Impression 1968.) 32s.*

Holmes, Brian. Problems in Education. A Comparative Approach. *336 pp. 1965. (2nd Impression 1967.) 32s.*

Mannheim, Karl and **Stewart, W. A. C.** An Introduction to the Sociology of Education. *206 pp. 1962. (2nd Impression 1965.) 21s.*

Morris, Raymond N. The Sixth Form and College Entrance. *231 pp. 1969. 40s.*

Musgrove, F. Youth and the Social Order. *176 pp. 1964. (2nd Impression 1968.) 25s. Paper 12s.*

Ortega y Gasset, José. Mission of the University. *Translated with an Introduction by Howard Lee Nostrand. 86 pp. 1946. (3rd Impression 1963.) 15s.*

Ottaway, A. K. C. Education and Society: An Introduction to the Sociology of Education. *With an Introduction by W. O. Lester Smith. 212 pp. Second edition (revised). 1962. (5th Impression 1968.) 18s. Paper 10s. 6d.*

Peers, Robert. Adult Education: A Comparative Study. *398 pp. 2nd edition 1959. (2nd Impression 1966.) 42s.*

Pritchard, D. G. Education and the Handicapped: 1760 to 1960. *258 pp. 1963. (2nd Impression 1966.) 35s.*

Richardson, Helen. Adolescent Girls in Approved Schools. *Approx. 360 pp. 1969. About 42s.*

Simon, Brian and **Joan** (Eds.). Educational Psychology in the U.S.S.R. *Introduction by Brian and Joan Simon. Translation by Joan Simon. Papers by D. N. Bogoiavlenski and N. A. Menchinskaia, D. B. Elkonin, E. A. Fleshner, Z. I. Kalmykova, G. S. Kostiuk, V. A. Krutetski, A. N. Leontiev, A. R. Luria, E. A. Milerian, R. G. Natadze, B. M. Teplov, L. S. Vygotski, L. V. Zankov. 296 pp. 1963. 40s.*

9

SOCIOLOGY OF CULTURE

Eppel, E. M., and M. Adolescents and Morality: A Study of some Moral Values and Dilemmas of Working Adolescents in the Context of a changing Climate of Opinion. *Foreword by W. J. H. Sprott. 268 pp. 39 tables. 1966. 30s.*

Fromm, Erich. The Fear of Freedom. *286 pp. 1942. (8th Impression 1960.) 25s. Paper 10s.*
The Sane Society. *400 pp. 1956. (4th Impression 1968.) 28s. Paper 14s.*

Mannheim, Karl. Diagnosis of Our Time: Wartime Essays of a Sociologist. *208 pp. 1943. (8th Impression 1966.) 21s.*
Essays on the Sociology of Culture. *Edited by Ernst Mannheim in co-operation with Paul Kecskemeti. Editorial Note by Adolph Lowe. 280 pp. 1956. (3rd Impression 1967.) 28s.*

Weber, Alfred. Farewell to European History: or The Conquest of Nihilism. *Translated from the German by R. F. C. Hull. 224 pp. 1947. 18s.*

SOCIOLOGY OF RELIGION

Argyle, Michael. Religious Behaviour. *224 pp. 8 figures. 41 tables. 1958. (4th Impression 1968.) 25s.*

Nelson, G. K. Spiritualism and Society. *313 pp. 1969. 42s.*

Stark, Werner. The Sociology of Religion. A Study of Christendom.
Volume I. Established Religion. *248 pp. 1966. 35s.*
Volume II. Sectarian Religion. *368 pp. 1967. 40s.*
Volume III. The Universal Church. *464 pp. 1967. 45s.*

Watt, W. Montgomery. Islam and the Integration of Society. *320 pp. 1961. (3rd Impression 1966.) 35s.*

SOCIOLOGY OF ART AND LITERATURE

Beljame, Alexandre. Men of Letters and the English Public in the Eighteenth Century: 1660-1744, Dryden, Addison, Pope. *Edited with an Introduction and Notes by Bonamy Dobrée. Translated by E. O. Lorimer. 532 pp. 1948. 32s.*

Misch, Georg. A History of Autobiography in Antiquity. *Translated by E. W. Dickes. 2 Volumes. Vol. 1, 364 pp., Vol. 2, 372 pp. 1950. 45s. the set.*

Schücking, L. L. The Sociology of Literary Taste. *112 pp. 2nd (revised) edition 1966. 18s.*

Silbermann, Alphons. The Sociology of Music. *Translated from the German by Corbet Stewart. 222 pp. 1963. 32s.*

SOCIOLOGY OF KNOWLEDGE

Mannheim, Karl. Essays on the Sociology of Knowledge. *Edited by Paul Kecskemeti. Editorial note by Adolph Lowe. 352 pp. 1952. (4th Impression 1967.) 35s.*

Stark, W. America: Ideal and Reality. The United States of 1776 in Contemporary Philosophy. *136 pp. 1947. 12s.*

The Sociology of Knowledge: An Essay in Aid of a Deeper Understanding of the History of Ideas. *384 pp. 1958. (3rd Impression 1967.) 36s.*

Montesquieu: Pioneer of the Sociology of Knowledge. *244 pp. 1960. 25s.*

URBAN SOCIOLOGY

Anderson, Nels. The Urban Community: A World Perspective. *532 pp. 1960. 35s.*

Ashworth, William. The Genesis of Modern British Town Planning: A Study in Economic and Social History of the Nineteenth and Twentieth Centuries. *288 pp. 1954. (3rd Impression 1968.) 32s.*

Bracey, Howard. Neighbours: On New Estates and Subdivisions in England and U.S.A. *220 pp. 1964. 28s.*

Cullingworth, J. B. Housing Needs and Planning Policy: A Restatement of the Problems of Housing Need and "Overspill" in England and Wales. *232 pp. 44 tables. 8 maps. 1960. (2nd Impression 1966.) 28s.*

Dickinson, Robert E. City and Region: A Geographical Interpretation. *608 pp. 125 figures. 1964. (5th Impression 1967.) 60s.*

The West European City: A Geographical Interpretation. *600 pp. 129 maps. 29 plates. 2nd edition 1962. (3rd Impression 1968.) 55s.*

The City Region in Western Europe. *320 pp. Maps. 1967. 30s. Paper 14s.*

Jackson, Brian. Working Class Community: Some General Notions raised by a Series of Studies in Northern England. *192 pp. 1968. (2nd Impression 1968.) 25s.*

Jennings, Hilda. Societies in the Making: a Study of Development and Re-development within a County Borough. *Foreword by D. A. Clark. 286 pp. 1962. (2nd Impression 1967.) 32s.*

Kerr, Madeline. The People of Ship Street. *240 pp. 1958. 28s.*

Mann, P. H. An Approach to Urban Sociology. *240 pp. 1965. (2nd Impression 1968.) 30s.*

Morris, R. N., and **Mogey, J.** The Sociology of Housing. Studies at Berins-field. *232 pp. 4 pp. plates. 1965. 42s.*

Rosser, C., and **Harris, C.** The Family and Social Change. A Study of Family and Kinship in a South Wales Town. *352 pp. 8 maps. 1965. (2nd Impression 1968.) 45s.*

RURAL SOCIOLOGY

Chambers, R. J. H. Settlement Schemes in Africa: A Selective Study. *Approx. 268 pp. 1969. About 50s.*

Haswell, M. R. The Economics of Development in Village India. *120 pp. 1967. 21s.*

Littlejohn, James. Westrigg: the Sociology of a Cheviot Parish. *172 pp. 5 figures. 1963. 25s.*

Williams, W. M. The Country Craftsman: A Study of Some Rural Crafts and the Rural Industries Organization in England. *248 pp. 9 figures. 1958. 25s. (Dartington Hall Studies in Rural Sociology.)*
The Sociology of an English Village: Gosforth. *272 pp. 12 figures. 13 tables. 1956. (3rd Impression 1964.) 25s.*

SOCIOLOGY OF MIGRATION

Humphreys, Alexander J. New Dubliners: Urbanization and the Irish Family. *Foreword by George C. Homans. 304 pp. 1966. 40s.*

SOCIOLOGY OF INDUSTRY AND DISTRIBUTION

Anderson, Nels. Work and Leisure. *280 pp. 1961. 28s.*

Blau, Peter M., and **Scott, W. Richard.** Formal Organizations: a Comparative approach. *Introduction and Additional Bibliography by J. H. Smith. 326 pp. 1963. (4th Impression 1969.) 35s. Paper 15s.*

Eldridge, J. E. T. Industrial Disputes. Essays in the Sociology of Industrial Relations. *288 pp. 1968. 40s.*

Hollowell, Peter G. The Lorry Driver. *272 pp. 1968. 42s.*

Jefferys, Margot, with the assistance of Winifred Moss. Mobility in the Labour Market: Employment Changes in Battersea and Dagenham. *Preface by Barbara Wootton. 186 pp. 51 tables. 1954. 15s.*

Levy, A. B. Private Corporations and Their Control. *Two Volumes. Vol. 1, 464 pp., Vol. 2, 432 pp. 1950. 80s. the set.*

Liepmann, Kate. Apprenticeship: An Enquiry into its Adequacy under Modern Conditions. *Foreword by H. D. Dickinson. 232 pp. 6 tables. 1960. (2nd Impression 1960.) 23s.*

Millerson, Geoffrey. The Qualifying Associations: a Study in Professionalization. *320 pp. 1964. 42s.*

Smelser, Neil J. Social Change in the Industrial Revolution: An Application of Theory to the Lancashire Cotton Industry, 1770-1840. *468 pp. 12 figures. 14 tables. 1959. (2nd Impression 1960.) 50s.*

Williams, Gertrude. Recruitment to Skilled Trades. *240 pp. 1957. 23s.*

Young, A. F. Industrial Injuries Insurance: an Examination of British Policy. *192 pp. 1964. 30s.*

ANTHROPOLOGY

Ammar, Hamed. Growing up in an Egyptian Village: Silwa, Province of Aswan. *336 pp. 1954. (2nd Impression 1966.) 35s.*

Crook, David and **Isabel.** Revolution in a Chinese Village: Ten Mile Inn. *230 pp. 8 plates. 1 map. 1959. (2nd Impression 1968.) 21s.*
The First Years of Yangyi Commune. *302 pp. 12 plates. 1966. 42s.*

Dickie-Clark, H. F. The Marginal Situation. A Sociological Study of a Coloured Group. *236 pp. 1966. 40s.*

Dube, S. C. Indian Village. *Foreword by Morris Edward Opler. 276 pp. 4 plates. 1955. (5th Impression 1965.) 25s.*
India's Changing Villages: Human Factors in Community Development. *260 pp. 8 plates. 1 map. 1958. (3rd Impression 1963.) 25s.*

Firth, Raymond. Malay Fishermen. Their Peasant Economy. *420 pp. 17 pp. plates. 2nd edition revised and enlarged 1966. (2nd Impression 1968.) 55s.*

Gulliver, P. H. The Family Herds. A Study of two Pastoral Tribes in East Africa, The Jie and Turkana. *304 pp. 4 plates. 19 figures. 1955. (2nd Impression with new preface and bibliography 1966.) 35s.*
Social Control in an African Society: a Study of the Arusha, Agricultural Masai of Northern Tanganyika. *320 pp. 8 plates. 10 figures. 1963. (2nd Impression 1968.) 42s.*

Ishwaran, K. Shivapur. A South Indian Village. *216 pp. 1968. 35s.*
Tradition and Economy in Village India: An Interactionist Approach. *Foreword by Conrad Arensburg. 176 pp. 1966. (2nd Impression 1968.) 25s.*

Jarvie, Ian C. The Revolution in Anthropology. *268 pp. 1964. (2nd Impression 1967.) 40s.*

Jarvie, Ian C. and Agassi, Joseph. Hong Kong. A Society in Transition. *396 pp. Illustrated with plates and maps. 1968. 56s.*

Little, Kenneth L. Mende of Sierra Leone. *308 pp. and folder. 1951. Revised edition 1967. 63s.*

Lowie, Professor Robert H. Social Organization. *494 pp. 1950. (4th Impression 1966.) 50s.*

Mayer, Adrian C. Caste and Kinship in Central India: A Village and its Region. *328 pp. 16 plates. 15 figures. 16 tables. 1960. (2nd Impression 1965.) 35s.*
Peasants in the Pacific: A Study of Fiji Indian Rural Society. *232 pp. 16 plates. 10 figures. 14 tables. 1961. 35s.*

Smith, Raymond T. The Negro Family in British Guiana: Family Structure and Social Status in the Villages. *With a Foreword by Meyer Fortes. 314 pp. 8 plates. 1 figure. 4 maps. 1956. (2nd Impression 1965.) 35s.*

DOCUMENTARY

Meek, Dorothea L. (Ed.). Soviet Youth: Some Achievements and Problems. *Excerpts from the Soviet Press, translated by the editor. 280 pp. 1957. 28s.*

Schlesinger, Rudolf (Ed.). Changing Attitudes in Soviet Russia.
2. The Nationalities Problem and Soviet Administration. Selected Readings on the Development of Soviet Nationalities Policies. *Introduced by the editor. Translated by W. W. Gottlieb. 324 pp. 1956. 30s.*

Reports of the Institute
of Community Studies

(*Demy 8vo.*)

Cartwright, Ann. Human Relations and Hospital Care. *272 pp. 1964. 30s.*

Patients and their Doctors. A Study of General Practice. *304 pp. 1967. 40s.*

Jackson, Brian. Streaming: an Education System in Miniature. *168 pp. 1964. (2nd Impression 1966.) 21s. Paper 10s.*

Jackson, Brian and **Marsden, Dennis.** Education and the Working Class: Some General Themes raised by a Study of 88 Working-class Children in a Northern Industrial City. *268 pp. 2 folders. 1962. (4th Impression 1968.) 32s.*

Marris, Peter. Widows and their Families. *Foreword by Dr. John Bowlby. 184 pp. 18 tables. Statistical Summary. 1958. 18s.*
Family and Social Change in an African City. A Study of Rehousing in Lagos. *196 pp. 1 map. 4 plates. 53 tables. 1961. (2nd Impression 1966.) 30s.*
The Experience of Higher Education. *232 pp. 27 tables. 1964. 25s.*

Marris, Peter and **Rein, Martin.** Dilemmas of Social Reform. Poverty and Community Action in the United States. *256 pp. 1967. 35s.*

Mills, Enid. Living with Mental Illness: a Study in East London. *Foreword by Morris Carstairs. 196 pp. 1962. 28s.*

Runciman, W. G. Relative Deprivation and Social Justice. A Study of Attitudes to Social Inequality in Twentieth Century England. *352 pp. 1966. (2nd Impression 1967.) 40s.*

Townsend, Peter. The Family Life of Old People: An Inquiry in East London. *Foreword by J. H. Sheldon. 300 pp. 3 figures. 63 tables. 1957. (3rd Impression 1967.) 30s.*

Willmott, Peter. Adolescent Boys in East London. *230 pp. 1966. 30s.*
The Evolution of a Community: a study of Dagenham after forty years. *168 pp. 2 maps. 1963. 21s.*

Willmott, Peter and **Young, Michael.** Family and Class in a London Suburb. *202 pp. 47 tables. 1960. (4th Impression 1968.) 25s.*

Young, Michael. Innovation and Research in Education. *192 pp. 1965. 25s. Paper 12s. 6d.*

Young, Michael and **McGeeney, Patrick.** Learning Begins at Home. A Study of a Junior School and its Parents. *About 128 pp. 1968. 21s. Paper 14s.*

Young, Michael and **Willmott, Peter.** Family and Kinship in East London. *Foreword by Richard M. Titmuss. 252 pp. 39 tables. 1957. (3rd Impression 1965.) 28s.*

The British Journal of Sociology. *Edited by Terence P. Morris. Vol. 1, No. 1, March 1950 and Quarterly. Roy. 8vo., £3 annually, 15s. a number, post free. (Vols. 1-18, £8 each. Individual parts £2 10s.*

All prices are net and subject to alteration without notice

1268 H.B.